THAT UNTRAVELLED WORLD

• • • • • •

THAT UNTRAVELLED WORLD

· · · · · ·

AN AUTOBIOGRAPHY

ERIC SHIPTON

Foreword by
KATIE IVES

Line illustrations by
BIRO

LEGENDS AND LORE SERIES

MOUNTAINEERS
BOOKS

Mountaineers Books is the publishing division of The Mountaineers, an organization founded in 1906 and dedicated to the exploration, preservation, and enjoyment of outdoor and wilderness areas.

MOUNTAINEERS BOOKS

1001 SW Klickitat Way, Suite 201 • Seattle, WA 98134
800.553.4453 • www.mountaineersbooks.org

Printed in the United States of America
18 17 16 15   1 2 3 4 5

Layout: Emily Ford
Series design: Karen Schober
Cover photograph: *Eric Shipton at the top of Peak 21120 during 1935 Everest Reconnaissance Expedition* © Royal Geographic Society (with IBG)
Frontispiece: *Portrait of Eric Shipton* © Royal Geographic Society (with IBG)
Illustrations: © The Estate of Val Biro
All photographs by Eric Shipton unless otherwise credited.

Library of Congress Cataloging-in-Publication Data

Shipton, Eric, 1907-1977.
  The untravelled world : an autobiography / by Eric Shipton ; foreword by Katie Ives ; Line Illustrations by Biro.
    pages cm
  Includes index.
  ISBN 978-1-59485-897-0 (trade paper)—ISBN 978-1-59485-898-7 (ebook)
  1. Shipton, Eric, 1907-1977. 2. Mountaineers—Biography. I. Title.
  GV199.92.S53A35 2015
  796.522092—dc23
  [B]
                    2014032091

 Printed on recycled paper

ISBN (paperback): 978-1-59485-914-4
ISBN (ebook): 978-1-59485-915-1

CONTENTS

THE REENCHANTED WORLD

IN OCTOBER 1928, A YOUNG British man stepped out of a bungalow at sunrise. Beyond the vast and shadowed plains, the twin summits of Mount Kenya rose through layers of lilac haze, sharpening into a crystalline tower. Sunlight glittered across jewel-like patches of ice. It was the first morning of his apprenticeship on a coffee farm in Nyeri, Kenya, then part of the British Empire. Already, he felt enchanted. In the evening, he waited for the mist to fade and the peaks to reemerge in fragments of ice gullies and gilded arêtes. "In the brief tropical twilight," Eric Shipton recalls in his autobiography, *That Untravelled World*, "the revelation was always fleeting."

After the death of his father, who had been a tea planter in Ceylon, Shipton had spent his early years travelling in Europe and British India with his restless mother and older sister. When the family settled in London, he found the routines of urban life to be grey and dull. Taking refuge in adventure books, he conjured up "vague dream worlds of strange lands" that glowed and shifted like the images of a magic lantern: the pale expanses of the Arctic, the green rings of Pacific atolls, and the chaotic sweep of glaciers. During adolescence, he learned to climb in the Alps, and he realized that mountaineering might become a "focus for [his] vague longing for contact with wild country."

Not long after his first glimpse of Mount Kenya, Shipton and his climbing partner Percy Wyn-Harris reached the mountain's dual summits, making a first ascent of the rocky spire of Nelion. In 1930 Shipton returned to complete a traverse of the peaks, accompanied by another British coffee

planter, Bill Tilman. It was the start of one of the most famous friend-
ships in mountaineering history. The two men went on to explore numerous unclimbed peaks in the Himalaya together, roaming through unmapped
regions during an era when few mountaineers had ventured above 25,000
feet. Over time, their names became synonymous with a particular way of
climbing and wandering: moving as lightly and as simply as possible through
isolated ranges; planning minimalist expeditions "on the back of an envelope"; and concentrating, not on the conquest of summits or the publicizing
of achievements, but on finding a means—as Shipton called it—"of identi-
fying [oneself] with this enchanting world."

Bob A. Schelfhout-Aubertijn, a Dutch collector of mountaineering books,
once declared: "Of course new and fascinating tales and heroic or tragic stories are being written, even as we speak. Recent adventures that will become
classics. But with the older ones, it is as if time has added some kind of
patina, a mystique that takes a number of decades and adds a certain charm."
For many readers of alpine literature, the mere thought of Shipton's work
can summon up vast worlds of lost time: the sighting of purported Yeti
footprints near the glacial basin of Snow Lake; the discovery of the hidden
passage along the cliffs and ledges of the narrow Rishi Gorge to the Nanda
Devi Sanctuary; the crossing of Patagonia's immense, windswept continental icecap; or the vision of ice blocks crashing soundless down the north
face of K2, long before the mountain was climbed, in an epoch when only a
handful of mountaineers had even seen it from that side.

It is one of Shipton's quieter moments that I imagine most. On a 1937
Karakoram expedition, while he lay on the sandbanks of a clear stream in
the Shaksgam Valley, far from any inhabited place, he watched as the dusk
turned the desert summits into ghostly shadows and the stars seemed to flow
across the darkening heavens. "How satisfying it was to be travelling with
such simplicity," he writes in *Blank on the Map*. "Did I sleep that night—or
was I caught up for a moment into the ceaseless rhythm of space?" On late
evenings, wandering alone in other lands and ranges, I have felt a similar
blurring of snow, ice and sky. Walking across a barren steppe before dawn

or climbing frozen waterfalls by starlight, I have imagined myself following the arc of the Milky Way.

In a sense, the history of mountaineering is a narrative of classic tales giving rise to new adventures. Since Shipton's death in 1977, generations of climbers have been caught up in the rhythm of his prose until it echoes through adventures of their own. Throughout his long career, the Indian explorer Harish Kapadia has read and reread Shipton's and Tilman's books, adapting their back-of-the-envelope approach to his own quests for uncharted peaks and quiet valleys, seeking an intimate connection with wild lands and local myths. As a young man, the Japanese mountaineer Tamotsu Nakamura discovered a copy of Shipton's *Upon That Mountain* at his university alpine club. The old stories of "the remote borderlands of the world" helped stir Nakamura's dreams of mapping unclimbed mountains in western Sichuan and eastern Tibet. For decades now, Nakamura's photos of silvery rock walls and sharp snow crests have reminded climbers of the vast and radiant unknowns that still remain.

When the American alpinist Conrad Anker was first starting to climb, he also encountered Shipton's books in a library. After Anker travelled to Everest in the 1990s and saw the crowds along the mountain's fixed lines, he wondered what might have happened had Shipton's small team reached the top in 1935, without oxygen or large amounts of equipment. Perhaps an early precedent might have been set for a philosophy of minimalist high-altitude climbing—in contrast to the grand militaristic sieges of the 1950s, such as the one that supported Edmund Hillary and Tenzing Norgay's first ascent in 1953. Anker felt closer to Shipton's spirit on lesser-known peaks, establishing new routes alone in Antarctica, leaving his base camp with little more than a down sweater, a sun hat, mittens and light gear, surrounded by a huge, shining emptiness of ice; or climbing an 8000-foot ridge on Spansar Brakk in Pakistan with just two friends, wearing sneakers and carrying only one rope, a water bottle and some food, "not knowing where we'd go and happy with what we found."

Since the new millennium, New Zealand alpinist Pat Deavoll has ventured up remote and untouched mountains in Pakistan, India and China.

She, too, describes Shipton as her hero. Her 2011 autobiography, *Wind from a Distant Summit*, resonates with similar dreams of fleeting, magic worlds in labyrinths of icefalls and intricate bands of rock, of mountaineering as a means to an aesthetic, deeply imaginative life. "Sometimes I have to pinch myself," she writes, "when I think, was it *me* who reached the summit of the unclimbed peak in India in a gathering storm on dusk, with lightning flashing on the horizon?"

During the mid-twentieth century, while a series of massive national expeditions placed the first men atop some of the Himalaya's giant peaks, Shipton's love of simplicity and spontaneity made him part of a small group of non-conformists. Much of his current reputation grew in later decades—as more climbers turned away from ponderous siege tactics in favor of increased uncertainty, freedom and adventure. The American mountaineer and author David Roberts recalls, "You can't separate the fast-and-light aesthetic from the wry, ironic, understated brilliance of Shipton and Tilman's narratives. . . . No glory for the Fatherland bullshit, no 'first British ascent'—just good days in the mountains with friends."

In 1978 the South Tyrolean Reinhold Messner and the Austrian Peter Habeler became the first to summit Everest without supplemental oxygen. Two years later, again breathing only natural air, Messner climbed the north face alone, moving delicately across tilted panes of snow without fixed ropes or high-altitude porters. And with that alpine-style ascent, he finally proved Shipton's assertion that the earth's highest mountain could be climbed by "a small party lightly equipped and shorn of supernumeraries and superfluous baggage." During the following years, growing numbers of elite mountaineers adopted this style throughout the Himalaya. By 2013, Kyle Dempster would write in an article for *Alpinist*, "Minimalism is no longer seen only through the eyes of the rebel and the mystic." Instead, for leading climbers from around the world, this ethos has become the accepted ideal.

Reading Shipton's stories today, we see a man who was both of—and against—his own time. As the climber and historian Steve Swenson points out, "Shipton and Tilman may have felt like they were out to do pure exploration, but they were funded by those who believed that their activities contributed to building or protecting the empire." Shipton's adventures took place within the context of the struggles between Britain and Russia to dominate Central Asia. Although he often strove to minimize the environmental and cultural impact of his expeditions, Shipton (like other explorers of his day) brought back geographic information that could facilitate the movement of armies and the dominance of trade. In *That Untravelled World*, Shipton notes how easily he received a permit to survey peaks and valleys along the undemarcated, sensitive border area between Kashmir and Sinkiang in 1937 after he persuaded the British colonial authorities of the "benefit to be derived from better knowledge of the frontier region."

In his East Africa chapter, Shipton insists that he believed in the benevolence of British rule—at times ignoring the realities of colonial violence and using language that today's readers might find imperialist. Nonetheless, he struggled against some of the prejudice he witnessed. During World War II, Shipton jeopardized his military career by protesting when he believed an Anglo-Indian cadet had been kicked out of officer training school because of his race. Moreover, Shipton's opposition to siege-style mountaineering stemmed partly from its resemblance to conquest. Of the 1933 British attempt on Everest, he writes, "The sight of our monstrous army invading the peaceful Tibetan valleys . . . gave me a feeling of being chained to a juggernaut."

Unlike many Western mountaineers of his era, Shipton described the Sherpa climbers on his expeditions "as friends, rather than as hired porters and servants," attributing his success to their determination and occasionally to their co-leadership. After the 1951 Everest reconnaissance, Shipton warned that a climb through the Khumbu Icefall could prove unconscionable, "not because the way to it was beyond our powers, but because on a small section of the approach the party, and particularly the Sherpas, must repeatedly be exposed to the risk, however slight at each individual exposure, of extermination." By the 1990s, this same maze-like stretch of ice pinnacles and crevasses would become part of one of the most common commercial routes on the mountain. In April 2014, sixteen Sherpa and Nepali expedition workers would die there in a single catastrophic avalanche.

Despite the ongoing resonance of Shipton's words, modern readers may find it challenging to imagine how different his world was—and how much it was already changing during his lifetime. The span of Shipton's later career encompassed the chaos of World War II, the fall of the British Empire, the Partition of India and Pakistan, and the rise of Communist China. The terrain marked "unexplored" on the maps that first lured Shipton to the Karakoram now glows with elaborate detail in Internet satellite photos. While many independent alpinists still follow Shipton's lightweight path, commercial and quasi-commercial teams have launched ever more numerous heavyweight expeditions. Some of the 8000-meter peaks, unclimbed during his prewar journeys, are now draped with hundreds of meters of fixed ropes. Even the steep K2, the "mountaineer's mountain," that gleamed with such daunting brilliance above Shipton in 1937, has been sieged (at times disastrously) by crowds. With the spread of social media, a quality of inner solitude recedes. The endless streaming of information on computer and phone screens can seem to glare brightly enough to obscure even the floodwaters of the Shaksgam and the golden spires of the Baltoro. Only a few current alpinists (the Spanish big-wall expert Sílvia Vidal, for example) leave behind all forms of communication technology when they climb in isolated places. The traditional narrative continuity of remote adventures has been interrupted by trends that Shipton could not foresee, such as the practice of posting blog updates from the faces and summits of mountains themselves. As the editor in chief of *Climb* magazine, David Pickford, wrote in 2014, it is possible that for such "wilderness-mystics" as Shipton, our "digitally determined world . . . would be an alienating, unreal place."

What, indeed, would a modern Shipton think of the changes rippling across the places and pursuits he once knew? In the last few years, the oft-repeated word *precariousness* has been applied to so much of contemporary life, amid worldwide uncertainties of political upheavals, globalization, economic meltdowns and climate change. These forces reverberate through the Himalaya as well, where the legacies of colonialism and the Cold War now blend with the instabilities of a post-9/11 world. In June 2013, terrorists murdered eleven climbers at the Diamir Base Camp of Nanga Parbat, and the presence of militant groups continues to threaten the safety and livelihoods of local communities in northern Pakistan and Kashmir. At the same time, Himalayan landscapes have shown some of the most visible effects of climate change: the shrinking of icefields, the calving of seracs, the devastations of glacier-outburst floods, the shifting of ecosystems and the endangerment of future water sources and crops.

But there are other transformations that Shipton might have come to welcome, a steady movement away from some of the lingering hierarchies and assumptions of the past. In the aftermath of the disastrous 2014 Everest season, many Sherpa expedition workers have called for greater equality between themselves and Western guides, better life insurance and more recognition of the risks they face. A few of the remaining ghostly structures of past empires may be collapsing. Future stories about Himalayan alpinism will not only depict the significant roles of indigenous climbers, as Shipton's books did; these tales will also increasingly be written by them.

Today, as Conrad Anker points out, the old praise once accorded to the "first Westerners" to explore certain places no longer seems so meaningful, given the modern awareness that local people have travelled through many of those landscapes for thousands of years. More pertinent to current readers (and possibly to Shipton himself) are the discoveries that Shipton made about his imagination as he climbed. The deliberation of his writing—the slow unfolding of untamed nature to the pace of solitary, undistracted thought—recalls what lies beyond the slogans, logos, sound bites and film crews of made-for-media extreme adventure. "Shipton speaks to our better natures," the historian Maurice Isserman explains. "He is the high-altitude Thoreau, the Muir of the Garhwal." Immersed in Shipton's lyricism, we remember that mountains can be places of communion with the wild, rather than mere arenas for athletic competition. Through his quests for "enchantment," Shipton strove to undo the effects of banality and consumerism in the industrial civilization of his time, the dulling of the ability to marvel at the earth, the decline of mystery that the sociologist Max Weber famously termed "the disenchantment of the world."

During the twenty-first century, as the consequences of environmental destruction become more serious and as children in urban areas spend less and less time outdoors, Shipton's message is more relevant than ever. In a

2009 essay in *The Re-Enchantment of the World*, literature professor Andrea Nightingale describes a growing awareness that "if we cannot develop the capacity to wonder at the nonhuman world, then we will have no motivation to save it. . . . We will end up 'solving' every ecological problem with technology rather than exercising restraint and setting limits to our desires." In many ways, the preservation of our innate natural wonder was the true goal of Shipton's adventures. "There are many ways of finding those moments of delight which come from a sense of complete harmony with wild surroundings," he declares. "The springs of enchantment lie within ourselves: they arise from our sense of wonder, that most precious of gifts, the birthright of every child. Lose it and life becomes flat and colorless; keep it and—*all experience is an arch wherethro' / Gleams that untravell'd world, whose margin fades / For ever and for ever when I move.*"

Those lines may well contain the heart of Shipton's books, prompting his readers to ask: What is, in fact, that "untravelled world" that he describes, quoting Tennyson's poem about Ulysses's last, imaginary voyage across a dusky sea? Perhaps, amid the succession of new vistas that flow through Shipton's writing, it is the unattainable "vague dream" that matters most, the endless deferral of mystery beyond the next land, the next ocean, the next hill. One of Shipton's biographers, Jim Perrin, defines this elusive place as "a lost landscape of early experience," an almost mythic geography evoking the imaginative richness of childhood. Although Shipton rarely writes directly of his emotions, some of his most expansive—and perhaps self-revelatory—prose dwells on images of mist and half-light. Again and again, he returns to visions of faraway mountains, to that magic time at dawn or dusk when the light strikes the top of a distant summit and for an instant, the ordinary forms and colors of the world turn to gold, blaze and then vanish. The distance, the anticipation and the dreaming appear to matter more than any fulfillment.

Climbing has long served as a metaphor, a means of organizing the chaos of experience into structure and narrative, of focusing inchoate longings into clear and elegant lines. Shipton's writings reveal one pattern of existence devoted to the wonder of the earth and to the obligations that this passionate love entails. But as his stories now draw a new audience to wander

through the landscapes in their pages, to marvel at high snows and glaciers that extend in undiminished splendor, these readers might find fresh
visions of their own emerging and fading like the twilit summits the author
glimpsed so many years before. In the gaps between Shipton's era and theirs,
they might discover ways to understand what has been lost, what might be
preserved, what must be changed and what should be let go. Beyond the
last sentences of *That Untravelled World*, they might gaze past the contour
lines of one man's cartography of dreams, deeper into the inner wild that he
believed was boundless—and then outward, once more, at the innumerable
and still-untravelled worlds of humanity's many possible futures.

Katie Ives
Cambridge, Vermont, July 2014

|I|

Early Influences

CHILDHOOD EXPERIENCES WE ARE TOLD play an important, indeed a decisive, part in the shaping of our individual characters. This can hardly be denied; but I find it less easy to believe that their effect can be confidently predicted in terms of good or bad, success or failure, happiness or misery. Children are remarkably resilient and readily accept as normal the most preposterous situations to which they are accustomed; but, as with adults, one child may benefit by a traumatic ordeal, which would warp the development of another. Churchill's parents, for example, seem to have broken every rule in the book, and it is evident that the young Winston was bitterly resentful of their neglect. Is it not probable that this provided the stimulus for the fanatical determination to make good which characterised his early career, and that had he been pampered as a child we might well have been deprived of our wartime leader? The early struggles of David Livingstone, which resulted in the development not only of a tenacious explorer but also of a great humanitarian, might have broken a less robust spirit. The course of our lives is steered by a complex interaction of influences, and it is often from our setbacks, even our weaknesses, that we derive some of our greatest blessings.

I was born in 1907 in Ceylon, where my father was a tea planter. He died before I was three, so that I have no recollection of him; nor have I the slightest idea what he was like. That I did not attempt to discover something about him was due mainly to the fact that my mother was extremely reserved and never encouraged intimate discussion. She never mentioned him, and as I had no reason to suppose that a father was in any way essential to my existence, his absence and with it his character had no particular significance. That my lack of curiosity about him persisted throughout adolescence and early manhood is less easy to explain; but early habits of thought become securely lodged. My sister, two years older, believes that my mother was afraid that she would be unable to cope adequately with my upbringing alone, and her reticence may well have been due to her fear that by talking about my father I would come to miss him. I do not even know the cause of his death. Recently, however, I have learned two facts about him: one, that he was a devoted husband, the other, that he spent a great deal of his spare time in the jungle watching birds—a passionate interest of his—and that he had a remarkable ability to attract them to him. Presumably he, too, had been born in Ceylon, for his father, a doctor, had come to live there about 1870. His mother I vaguely remember as a sweet old lady.

For several years after my father's death we were constantly on the move, travelling between England and Southern India and Ceylon, where my mother retained close ties; and also in France, where she had many friends and where her mother had a house on the South Coast. We were never in one place for long and had no settled home, which is generally thought to be essential for the psychological welfare of children. So far as I remember, I found this nomadic existence wholly delightful; I revelled in the thrill of train and ship travel and in each change of scene. One of my earliest recollections is of arriving somewhere after a particularly exciting journey and asking eagerly how long it would be before we set off again; I was told that we would be staying a fortnight. Four nights seemed an awful long time to wait; and when I discovered that the word meant two weeks I wept bitterly. Of course my memories of this period are scattered and quite unrelated in time and place; nonetheless some of them remain vivid, exquisite gems of delight framed in mist: steep sun-drenched valleys around Sospel, inland from Menton; a path running between green cliffs to a little bay of coral sand shaded by coconut palms; a whale spouting and an island volcano belching smoke. (Later I thought this an unlikely combination until, a few years ago, I saw a whale at very close quarters near Stromboli, which I must have passed several times as a child.)

About 1914 we spent a year in the Nilgiri Hills in South India, the longest period we had hitherto stayed in one place. But it was a happy one, for we were allowed a great deal of freedom and there was plenty to stimulate the imagination in that lovely country. It was then that my mother remarried, an event that made little impact upon me. My step-father was not with us for long, as he joined the Army soon after the outbreak of war and was sent to France; so I suppose I regarded him as just another adult who came and went like the rest. He was killed in action in 1917.

A solitary child, I preferred doing things on my own to the company of other children. I hated parties, and competitive games made me feel miserably embarrassed. I had a persistent belief that I was generally disliked; this may well have been the case, for, though tolerant, my behaviour was sufficiently anti-social to make me unpopular with children and adults alike. But I was by no means unhappy, for I spent most of my time in a pleasant, often exciting daydream, concerned entirely with my natural environment: the jungles, the hills, the sea and the sky. I think I was unusually aware of scenery; sunset colours, for example, or morning mists rising out of a valley stirred me deeply. The moon had a powerful effect upon my imagination, and I remember several dreams in which I was chasing it over the hills behind our house. My travels had no doubt stimulated my concept of a boundless world. In matters of practical application I was, even at this age, decidedly inept.

The last of my journeys as a child left by far the most memorable impression; partly because I was old enough to co-ordinate the events connected with it and partly because of its contrast with the comparative flatness of the years that followed. It started by train from the jungle-clad gorges of the Nilgiris to the sandy tip of India; then across the Palk Strait to an enchanted dawn of intoxicating scents and vivid colours, travelling swiftly past coconut palms and paddy fields to the central highlands. We stayed several weeks in various parts of Ceylon waiting for a ship (no doubt the war had already disrupted normal sailings); each place seemed more exciting than the last. At length

Eric Shipton's father

we went to Colombo and embarked in S.S. *Kashgar* for what seemed then a lifetime of bliss. Because of the U-boat menace and other wartime exigencies, the voyage took nearly twice as long as usual. We called at many ports; at some we stopped for several days. Everything was wildly exciting. There were few children on board; the crew were very kind to us, and we were allowed to visit every part of the ship. One evening when I was supposed to be in bed I was found to be missing; some hours later, when the whole ship's company had been alerted, I was discovered in the wireless cabin. Considering the anxiety I had caused, my mother was remarkably tolerant. For many years that voyage represented a peak of happiness which seemed unlikely ever to be regained. The name *Kashgar* assumed a kind of mystic significance, which, oddly enough, was revived some decades later in quite another context.

It is hardly surprising that wartime England seemed drab, or that I found it hard to settle into a circumscribed life in a London flat; its main features were lessons with a governess and walks in the park. I began to live more and more in a dream world and to respond still less to the company of other children. My sister, on the other hand, was a gregarious little girl, and though she was kind and affectionate towards me, my feeling of being odd man out in any company increased. The following year I was sent to a preparatory school.

Much is said these days about the psychological evils likely to result from sending eight-year-old children to boarding school. Personally I am inclined to think that the danger has been exaggerated, at least so far as the great majority of boys is concerned. In my own case, though I was both physically and mentally backward and more than usually shy, I do not believe that I suffered any serious harm from the experience. On the other hand, though I always disliked school and seem to have learnt incredibly little in the nine years I spent there, I am prepared to admit that I acquired some important attributes, such as a moderate ability to deal with my fellows and some measure of stoicism, which would have been less likely to develop at home. Certainly during my first term or two I often suffered an aching loneliness, all the more bitter for the boisterous company surrounding me. But the instinct for self-preservation is strong, and I managed soon to adapt myself to the strange way of life, to the outlandish jargon of my schoolmates, to the use of surnames (at first I was scarcely aware of my own; my mother having a different one, I suppose I had hardly ever heard it) and to conformity with a series of meaningless rites.

One of the more colourful of these was concerned with the recording of our daily achievement in the lavatory. After breakfast we had to await our turn for the use of one of the half dozen latrines (an advanced place in the queue could be bought for a favour, so that the stronger and more influential boys never had to wait long). We then repaired to the headmaster's bedroom, where his wife awaited us in her double bed, propped against voluminous pillows, a lace night-cap on her head, a cosy-covered teapot and the remnants of toast and boiled eggs on a tray by her side (her breakfast diet never varied), and an open ledger resting against the mound formed by her knees. She called out the names, in order of scholastic seniority, of the sixty or so boarders, and as we drifted in at various times several repetitions were required. The normal response was, "Yes, Mrs. Gifford, and not again yesterday," and any variation on this theme caused a mild flutter. As, however, a negative reply was likely to evoke a dose of castor oil, it was not common. Meanwhile a few of the more weedy specimens among us were made to exercise ourselves on an elastic appliance attached to the bedroom wall in the hope of expanding our pigeon chests. Such was my acquiescence, my blind acceptance of authority, that never, in all the six years I was at the school, did this daily ritual of "reporting ourselves" with its bizarre setting strike me as faintly ludicrous.

On the whole we were not unkindly treated; but I am inclined to think that the frequency and severity with which we were flogged was a bit excessive. Certain crimes, such as breaking bounds, "impertinence" or "cheating" (dread words), carried automatically the supreme penalty, as did the second offence in a term of "ragging after lights out" (a mere whispered conversation was so regarded). But we were also beaten if an accumulation of petty offences—losing a pencil or being late—resulted in more than three hours imposition in any one week. The instrument generally used was a wide leather strap, and the culprit was required to remove his shorts, roll up his shirt and lie face downward across the headmaster's bed (that same confessional bed, but without its lace-capped occupant). I have reason to remember the routine, for according to contemporary (unofficial) statistics only one other boy had, by the time I left, received more beatings than I. These resulted more from an inordinate number of minor lapses or from failure to move from the bottom of my class than from occasional major escapades, in which I indulged largely from motives of ego-boosting bravado. During my first year or so some of my troubles stemmed from the fact that I suffered a great deal from the cold, presumably because much of my life had been spent in the tropics. When playing football we were not allowed to wear sweaters, even on the coldest days. Being small and physically incompetent, I was unable to take much part in the games, with the result that, after an hour of standing about in a bitter wind, I returned to the changing room with my hands so immobile that I could not do up my buttons, and therefore was usually late for the next period. Gradually I acquired a reputation for being quite unperturbed by flogging, a delusion I was careful to foster for reasons of pride. In fact, I was always terrified; I cared nothing for the humiliation and feared only the pain, which was always worse than I had expected. But the most unpleasant thing about those beatings was that they were never executed on the spot; we had to wait for several days, even as much as a week, for the dread summons. By then one was often in the company of other victims who formed a queue outside the bedroom, counting the strokes and listening to the wails of their fellows.

Much as I hated corporal punishment, it was a small matter compared with the anguish caused by my inability to read aloud. This was probably the most inhibiting influence of my youth. I believe I must have suffered from a condition now known to child psychologists as dislexia (word blindness), a visual defect that causes letters to appear transposed from their correct sequence. At any rate, I was quite exceptionally slow in learning to read, and even when I could do so to myself, the words continued to get hopelessly tangled when I tried to read aloud. At first it did not matter much, but of course it became increasingly conspicuous as I grew older, and I was bitterly ashamed. The chief occasion for my humiliation was after morning prayers when, before the whole school, we had to stand up and read a passage from a scripture book. As time allowed for only half a dozen boys to perform in any one session, my turn came about once a fortnight. Then, my knees trembling, my stomach dissolving, I would rise to my feet and stammer, misread or remain quite silent, to the accompaniment of derisive applause, which was never checked and often encouraged by the master in charge. Sometimes I managed to evade my turn by absenting myself from prayers, which of course was suitably punished; sometimes I feigned illness, but generally without success. Eventually, however, I contrived a means of escape. A musical neighbour gave piano lessons to one or two of the boys; and when I discovered that the time allocated for them was during the period of morning prayers I persuaded my mother to allow me to take this "extra." So for my remaining years at the school I plodded happily through my five-finger exercises, and though I displayed not the slightest aptitude, the expense was, from my point of view, amply justified. Nevertheless, the fear of being made to read aloud continued to haunt me, particularly in the last few days of the holidays, when I was terrified that I might be trapped by some change of routine. Two notable effects of this experience, covering as it did so many of my formative years, were a totally irrational prejudice against the Church and a firm conviction that I was abnormally stupid. The latter in turn, no doubt, was a significant cause of my abysmal failure to learn my lessons.

I imagine that the standard of tuition was low, partly owing to the difficulty in wartime of obtaining suitable staff, and certainly there was little attempt either to make the subjects interesting or to help the more backward boys over their difficulties; but I fancy that even more expert teachers would have found me a tough nut to crack. It was not that I was particularly lazy or that I did not care; in fact, I was pathetically eager to make the grade. Quite soon I developed a consuming ambition to pass the Common Entrance

(I was "down for" Harrow), and for years my nightly prayers included an urgent plea that I might do so. (The lack of response had no bearing upon my anti-Church bias, which did not manifest itself until much later.) When eventually I took the exam I did so with no more than one hour's notice: I was merely told one morning after breakfast that I was to go at 9:00 to a small classroom reserved for the purpose. One of the papers was Geometry, a subject which hitherto I had not touched. The first question began with an instruction to draw a triangle, which I did with great care. But the rest of the question was unintelligible to me, as were all the others; so my triangle remained the sole evidence of my aptitude. As I feared, it was not enough to satisfy the examiners. I was not permitted a second chance.

Most children, it seems, dislike being different from their fellows. This was not so in my case, possibly because I was so conspicuously unable to achieve normal standards that I instinctively repudiated all attempt to conform. There were only two matters in which I could claim distinction, and of these I was inclined to boast: one was that I had been born in Ceylon, the other that I had no father; but I was anxious to increase my repertoire. On Sunday afternoons the gods of the sixth-form room used to summon any junior reputed to have a trick which might amuse them. For a brief but glorious spell I achieved this role of court entertainer by the simple expedient of drinking the contents of ink-wells. (Some fifteen years later, while on my way to join my first Himalayan expedition, I saw one of my illustrious patrons in the Royal Bombay Yacht Club. I approached him with considerable diffidence and reminded him that we had been at school together. He regarded me coldly for a moment and then, warming with recognition, said, "Of course! You were the man who used to drink ink." I was deeply flattered.) In time, I managed to acquire a modicum of respect for less eccentric attributes, a reasonably well-developed physique, for example, and as a result became less introverted and better able to make friends. Chief among these was Jack Wilson, my only rival in the matter of beatings, which no doubt induced our initial bond of mutual esteem. One of his troubles was a vivid sense of humour which caused him to explode with mirth in the most inappropriate circumstances. He was a Londoner, and we used to meet frequently during the winter holidays to conduct exciting clandestine (though wholly innocent) adventures in such places as China-town. Since then I have always had a cosy affection for London. Most summer holidays my sister and I spent in the Isle of Wight together with a girl cousin who was the same age as me but much larger and more mature. The two girls were close companions, and they clearly found me tedious company. However, I was very happy to be left alone searching for secret coves and reviving my early daydreams of exotic lands.

For my age, I took an unusu-ally keen interest in the progress of the war, largely, I believe, because it added the spice of reality to the

Eric Shipton's mother

solitary games I used to play with toy soldiers to stage the capture of St. Quentin or the defence of Verdun. The realities of the ghastly con-flict scarcely impinged on my imagination; and when, on Armistice Day, a whole holiday was declared, my chief emotions were relief at escaping a lesson for which I had failed to prepare, and mild regret that my bat-tle games would lose much of their interest. In 1919 an assistant master named Mr. Singleton came to the school. He had recently been demobil-ised, having served on the Western Front throughout the war. One day, finding me looking at a map of France, he remarked, "Oh! that Godfor-saken country." He said it with a kind of nostalgic loathing which both shocked and thrilled me. I questioned him about one or two of the battles, and he started talking with simplicity and complete candour about the horrors and the appalling futility of trench warfare. I was entranced, partly by the substance of what he said, but mostly because no one had ever spoken to me like that before; for the first time I found myself treated like an intelligent human being, capable of understanding adult conversation, and I felt a warm glow of sympathetic intimacy. That I still remember it so clearly is perhaps a measure of its intensity. No doubt he was aware of my response, for from that day he treated me with special friendliness. He was in charge of our miniature rifle range, and finding that I had an aptitude for shooting (the only positive talent I had ever discovered), he appointed me his "Range Staff" with responsibility of looking after the rifles and ammunition. I was delighted, particularly as it provided the opportunity of many more talks with him. He had an amused slightly cynical attitude to life in general and to school activities in particular that I found vastly intriguing. All this provided a strong stimulus to my self-esteem which, hitherto, had been sadly lacking. Unfortunately he stayed for only two terms. It is significant that, although he had had no previous experience of teaching, he taught me more than I had learnt in all the preceding years.

When I was fourteen, after six years at my preparatory school (then far more than half the total compass of my memory), the time came for me to leave. My failure to pass Common Entrance faced my mother with the difficult problem of what to do with me. This was eventually resolved by sending me to Pyt House, in South Wiltshire, an establishment founded three years before by Dr. Crawford, an ex-Harrow master, to accommodate boys who, because of their disinclination to work or their refusal to conform, had been forced to leave their public schools: I was among the first of a fresh intake of boys too dense to get there at all. The headmaster had previously had only one assistant, Captain Upwood, a very military gentleman known to us as "the Bum Skipper"; but to help with the expanding numbers, a kindly old bachelor, Mr. Ashfield, was recruited, and came the same term as I did. He immediately became known as "The Mormon"; this must have puzzled him greatly, for I am sure he never discovered the reason, which was simply because his failure to appear at prayers on the first morning led us to conclude that he did not belong to the Established Church. He, poor chap, lasted only two terms; his successors were mostly more eccentric characters (much later, one of them was Evelyn Waugh; but by then the school had moved elsewhere).

After the restricted, dull routine of my prep-school I found life at Pyt House decidedly stimulating, though not always in ways intended by the worthy Doctor. In the first place most of the seniors (the ex-public-school boys) were staunch individualists who had little respect for authority. The Bum Skipper, despite his impressive appearance and soldierly bearing, was no match for them, and it seemed to us that they came and went and did more or less as they pleased. If they attended school functions it appeared that they did so more for the opportunity they provided for light-hearted foolery than from any sense of obligation. For example, morning P.T. was generally a riot of fun, with the Bum Skipper in front of us performing the usual exercises with impeccable precision while most of his class, feigning total incompetence, fell about in the most ludicrous postures. We played football and cricket in the appropriate seasons, but neither was taken seriously, least of all by the élite. Sometimes we played against local village teams; the results were always farcical. Luckily, for all their undisciplined conduct, the seniors were a pleasant lot, and treated us newcomers with the kindly patronage of established aristocrats. As some of them had cars, their range of activity could be wide, but I never heard that they became involved in serious trouble. It may seem odd that they bothered to attend school at all, but I suppose in fact most of them accepted the need to have sufficient knowledge crammed into their heads to enable them to pass University or Army entrance examinations. One of them was already twenty-one; he was a charming, amusing and highly sophisticated fop, and quite incredibly lazy. So far as I know, the only one to achieve any considerable distinction in later life was Arnold Haskell.

As for us, we regarded the seniors as a privileged class (as indeed they were); we neither resented their status nor made any attempt to emulate their behaviour, so it was not difficult for the masters to establish normal authority over us. We were not overburdened with work: six mornings and three evenings each week were so occupied; every afternoon and the remaining evenings were free, though we were sometimes required to play football or cricket in the light-hearted fashion I have mentioned. But I found the teaching far more intelligible than any I had received at prep-school, and for the first time (except for that brief spell of illumination with Mr. Singleton) I began to assimilate a modicum of knowledge of the subjects I was supposed to be studying. In our ample spare time we were free (within the limits imposed by common law) to do as we pleased and to go wherever we liked. As Pyt House was in the heart of one of the loveliest parts of rural England, surrounded by great stretches of woodland and with many lakes near by, this freedom was specially valuable and I was not slow to appreciate it. In my first two terms, spring and summer, I spent most of my time with Jim Horsfall, a boy of my age whose chief interest was wildlife, particularly birds. He had already pursued the hobby for many years, and in his collection of the eggs of British birds only four were missing. I was thoroughly happy scouring the countryside with him, climbing trees and sandstone cliffs or swimming in the lakes in search of rare nests, and I shared his excitement when we came upon one. The following season we found the nest and eggs of a hobby hawk, one of Jim's missing four: as the eggs were very like those of a kestrel, we had to wait at the top of a neighbouring tree for the bird to return so as to make sure of its identity.

In this way we became intimately acquainted with every corner of the country for many miles around, and that in itself was most satisfying. We had little regard for private property, beyond taking simple precautions not to be seen on it. Among our many enchanting discoveries was a lake on the estate of Fonthill Abbey, set in a steep-sided valley and surrounded by rhododendrons, giant sequoias and a remarkable variety of other trees. In those days the vegetation was so rank that the lake itself was invisible until one reached the water's edge; and approaching it through the forest to avoid detection, we frequently had difficulty in locating it. We often went there to swim, diving into the still, green water from branches of trees; but we kept it secret between ourselves. Another favourite haunt was the ruins of Old Wardour Castle, which had been largely destroyed in the Civil War. It has since been taken over by the National Trust and partially restored, but then its surrounds were completely overgrown and its ancient walls untouched. We began to scale them in search of nests, but later the climbing became an end in itself. I have probably never been in more perilous situations than when balancing high upon its crumbling masonry.

A neighbouring farmer told us of a local belief that there was a secret tunnel running from the old castle to somewhere near Pyt House, by which the Lady Arundel of Cromwell's day was thought to have escaped shortly before the castle was destroyed. For a time we became obsessed with a desire to find it. We discovered what we thought was the start of an underground passage among the ruins, but after a very short distance it was blocked by a wall which we could not penetrate. For weeks we searched assiduously in the cellars and among the foundations of Pyt House, in the crypt of a ruined chapel, among the rambling stable buildings, anywhere where there was the suggestion of a hole in the ground. We found some promising leads, but none of them took us far. Eventually, the only cavity that remained unexplored was below a gardeners' latrine in the woods: a small hut with a stoutly built wooden seat. The hole was too small to allow me to squeeze through, so in a moment of thoughtless zeal, I hacked the seat to pieces with a hatchet, and lowered myself on a rope into the dark, evil-smelling chasm below. Needless to say, this was not the exit to the tunnel by which Lady Arundel had emerged. Sobered by this disappointment, I began at once to appreciate my folly. It was the last day of the term (a fact that had probably stimulated my recklessness), and throughout the holidays I was haunted by the seemingly inevitable consequences of my deed. The gardeners would certainly complain that their latrine had been destroyed, and I would be compelled, probably after prayers on the first morning of the new term, to confess my guilt. The more I thought about it, the more ludicrous appeared the true explanation of my action, and I could think of no other plausible reason to offer. Still inordinately sensitive to ridicule, it was not the punishment I feared, but being made a laughing-stock. In fact, to my profound relief, nothing whatever happened. Shortly after my return, like a murderer drawn to the scene of his crime, I visited the latrine. A new seat had replaced the old.

Later I found myself in another embarrassing position. For a while Jim and I made a practice of creeping downstairs late at night to raid the kitchen to supplement our diet, which we considered inadequate. On one such an occasion, after a successful sortie, we returned together to my room to share out and consume our loot. As it was a cold night and we were clad only in pyjamas, we both got into my bed to keep warm. The other three occupants of my room were asleep. We had finished our feast, and Jim was about to depart for his own room, when we heard approaching footsteps in the corridor. The door opened, the Bum Skipper entered and flashed his

Eric Shipton's sister

torch around the room. Though Jim had ducked his head under the bed-clothes, this was hardly sufficient concealment.

Presently the blankets were whipped away, and the Bum Skipper enquired pleasantly, "Having a good time?" To which we replied in unison, "Yes, sir." What else was there to say? We were told to report ourselves after prayers the next morning, and I was left alone to my reflections. I remember being mildly surprised that no explanation had been demanded of us, and hoping that we might think of some way to conceal the fact that we had stolen food from the kitchen. Jim's thoughts, I gathered later, were running along similar lines. It was not until after breakfast, by which time the whole school had heard about the incident and we had been exposed to the ribald comments of the more sophisticated seniors, that the ugly reality of our situation dawned upon us. We were aghast, and when we went to keep our appointment with the Bum Skipper we were only too eager to establish the true explanation of the night's adventure. Luckily this was accepted, and we escaped with five hundred lines each. It is perhaps worth recording that in the nine years I spent at school I was never aware of any homosexual activity.

At neither school was there any form of sex instruction, and as the subject was never mentioned by my mother, what little knowledge I gleaned came mostly from the usual schoolboy anecdotes. I somehow acquired the belief, which persisted throughout adolescence, that extra-marital sex was the number one sin in the sight of God, for which the penalty was eternal damnation, and that masturbation resulted in insanity; so it was as well to refrain from both. My belief in God still remained unquestioned; but I found it hard to reconcile the notion of His boundless mercy and love with that of a jealous God who, we were told with monotonous regularity every Sunday, visits the sins of the fathers upon the children unto the third and fourth generation. Of the two contrasting ideas, that of a malignant deity was strongly dominant, mainly because of my dread, harboured since early childhood, of eternal torture in a red-hot incinerator. I had been told, I forget when or by whom, that at the moment of dying one saw, like the green flash in a tropical sunset, the instantaneous image either of God or the Devil according to whether one was destined for Heaven or Hell. It did not occur to me to question the source of this piece of intelligence; and one night I dreamed that I died and saw the unmistakable figure of Beelzebub with his horned head and arrow-shaped tail. I awoke in a state of sweating, heart-pounding terror. From an early age I used to ponder the staggering concept of eternity; my acquaintance with punitive pain had given me an awareness of the horrible potentialities of torture; the combination of the two lent ample point to the weekly exhortations I received to "fear God." The fact that I did so, coupled with my private nightmare that by going to church I might one day be made to read the lesson, made me the more willing to listen to suggestions that He might not in fact exist. Thus I became a willing convert from Christianity to agnosticism.

On the whole, for all its eccentricities, Pyt House was a beneficial influence: the freedom to enjoy the lovely countryside fostered a taste, already latent, for outdoor pursuits; the comparative laxity of routine encouraged individual thought; the company of boys as, or even more, stupid than I, did something to dispel my deep-rooted sense of inferiority; we were persuaded to read books; I became fairly expert at climbing trees; above all, I enjoyed myself. Unfortunately, when I had been at the school little more than two years it moved from Wiltshire to Aston Clinton, between Tring and Aylesbury. With the gradual departure of all the old gang of seniors, which deprived us of much delightful entertainment, the place had already begun to assume a more conventional form (we were even required to wear top hats and tails on Sundays and straw hats bound with school colours on weekdays); and this process flourished in the new, relatively suburban environment. I thought it entirely retrograde. By then, however, the holidays had begun to play an increasingly important part in my life.

After the First World War the currencies of most Continental countries collapsed, and the rates of exchange in terms of sterling soared, in many cases to astronomical figures (the German Mark, for example, stood at more than 300,000 to the pound). Although prices increased considerably, they lagged far behind the inflated exchange rates. Fantastic stories were told: one, of an Englishman who, finding himself in a Polish city and needing accommodation, bought the best hotel in town, stayed there a fortnight and then gave it to the head waiter as a tip. Though no doubt this tale was somewhat exaggerated, it was certainly true that for nearly a decade the British could travel on the Continent very cheaply indeed; in fact, relatively few did so. My mother, however, was not slow to take advantage of this delectable state of affairs, and soon we began to spend most of our holidays abroad. I had lost none of my old delight in travel; the cross-Channel steamer with the gulls crying in her wake; the sight of those huge Continental locomotives; lying in my bunk listening to the rhythmic clatter of the train hurtling through the night or the sigh of the steam brakes as it came to rest at some unseen station; the dawn lighting some new land; all these essentials of a European journey filled me with joyous excitement, however familiar they became, and indeed even now they have much the same effect. Certainly some of our objectives were not to my taste: a tour of the chateaux of the Loire, visits to Versailles and the art treasures of the Louvre, the inspection of countless cathedrals; alas, they all left me quite unmoved. Luckily, the majority of the holidays abroad were spent in places such as Austria, Provence, the Italian Lakes, the coast of Brittany, the Pyrenees; these, with their amazing scenic variety, evoked a very different response, and revived a sense of wonder, that priceless gift so often dulled, even extinguished, in the process of formal education. More and more I delighted to read of strange places, the Matto Grosso, the measureless gorge of the Blue Nile, of volcanoes and glaciers, of subterranean rivers and coral atolls. The men who explored them were my heroes—Humboldt, Nansen, Darwin, their names were magic.

...

Greece Public Library
(585) 225-8951
www.greecelibrary.org

11/25/2019   4:14:28 PM

Customer Number: 2907702064XXXX

Items Borrowed:

1: The wolf of Wall Street /
Item #: 39077073338744
Due Date: 12/16/2019

2: Liar's poker : rising through the wre
Item #: 39077077322686
Due Date: 12/16/2019

3: The untravelled world : an autobiogr
Item #: 39077080095279
Due Date: 12/16/2019

Cost of buying these items:
$62.00
Cost of using the library:
Priceless!

--Please retain this slip as your receipt--

...

It is interesting to trace the factors which have shaped the course of our lives. For most of us, I suppose, it is not so much isolated events or decisions that bear the most far-reaching results, but rather our psychological response to long-term influences, the subtle interaction between our individual characteristics and our physical and emotional environment. I often wonder what would have become of me if, for example, I had been taught to read more readily and had thus acquired the knack of book-learning. I would certainly have gained a measure of self-confidence and with it a belief in my ability to succeed in some normal pursuit. I would have gone to Harrow, and there, no doubt, would have been content to allow my average ability to be channelled towards the goal of an ordinary professional career. Most probably I would have abandoned my vague dream world of strange lands for a pleasant if uninspiring reality. Later, the prospect of security and comfortable affluence would have encouraged conformity: indeed, it was many years before I ceased to regret that I had not pursued this primrose path with more tenacity. As a reasonably successful stockbroker, advertising agent or civil servant I might have achieved these seductive ends, but I very much doubt if I would have led such an agreeable life.

| 2 |

MOUNTAINS

SHORTLY BEFORE THE SCHOOL MIGRATED from Pyt House, a Norwegian boy named Gustav Sommerfelt came there for two terms. He spoke little English, which provided the other boys with an irresistible opportunity for sport at his expense. Largely because of my interest in foreign lands, and perhaps partly because I had a fellow feeling for oddities, I took him under my protective wing, and we became close friends. Not that he needed my patronage, for though a year younger than I, he was an ebullient character, well able to look after himself. Early in the summer term he suggested that I should go with him when he returned to Norway, and spend part of the holidays walking across the Jotunheimen, the highest range in the country, and the rest at a chalet belonging to his family in the forest of Hallingdal. I had already been drawn to mountains, and my imagination deeply stirred by the vast precipices of the Cirque de Gavarnie and by books of mountain travel, particularly Whymper's *Travels Among the Great Andes of the Equator*, with its wealth of strange experiences and its evocative illustrations. The prospect of wandering for several weeks among the wild mountains of Norway was unbelievably wonderful.

Gustav's father arranged for us to travel free on a cargo ship from Blyth to Fredrikstad, and after two days in Christiania (as the capital was then called) collecting equipment we travelled by train and bus to Bygdin, at the southern edge of the Jotunheimen, where our adventure began. The first few days provided some spells of painful disillusionment. We humped enormous rucksacks, quite absurdly heavy considering that we carried neither food nor camping gear; Gustav had a kettle attached to his, which clanked monotonously and was never used. The straps of my pack bit cruelly into my shoulders, my new boots chafed my blistered feet, cold rain drenched my clothes and trickled down my spine, my whole body ached as I plodded miserably behind my companion, hating his unfeeling nonchalance. Worst of all was the bitter realisation that I was not, after all, of the stuff that made explorers. But these moods of blank despair were dispelled by food and warmth at the next hostel and by the sheer wonder at having survived long enough to reach it. In time, of course, my aches and pains eased and eventually vanished, and I began to experience the sensual pleasure of rhythmic movement over rough ground. My attention no longer concentrated upon my woes, I became aware of the scenes about me, and of the fascination of finding the way. Gradually the mountains regained their lost enchantment. They were very different from those I had seen in the Alps and Pyrenees, rounder, smaller, less aloof and mysterious, but there was a rugged desolation about the country, a breadth of horizon which was exciting. Crossing a pass and seeing a new range of peaks ahead, I was enthralled to learn that it would take us several days to reach it. Gustav, having often done this kind of trip before, was very much in charge; he instructed me in the use of map and compass and decided all the details of our journey. Mostly we were by ourselves, but once we joined with others to cross a difficult pass which required the use of a rope. Perhaps the most memorable day was one I spent alone. Gustav having decided to take a rest, I walked to the head of the valley, which was filled by a large glacier. It was the first I had seen at close quarters, and the impression made by the vast mass flowing down from the silence of a mysterious ice world was all the stronger for my solitude. In fear and exultation I climbed up it until I came to a line of gaping crevasses.

After our strenuous weeks in the Jotunheimen the chalet in Hallingdal, a day's march from the railway, provided a delicious contrast; we spent most of our time there pulling pink-fleshed trout out of the lake and eating them.

When at length I set out on my return journey to England it was with a feeling of great contentment. This, however, was marred when I reached Bergen and found that, due to some slight miscalculation, I had only just enough money for my ticket to London and none to spare for food. In those days I had a healthy appetite, and the prospect of a two-day fast was not pleasant. I grew more and more ravenous as the voyage progressed. Finally, I could stand it no more and, as the other passengers were entering the saloon for the last meal, I accosted a kindly looking old gentleman and asked him if he would bring me some bread when he had finished. He looked at me in astonishment, and said, "But why don't you come in and eat?" I explained my plight, to which he replied pityingly, "But you don't have to pay; meals are included in your ticket."

That holiday in Norway was the best thing that had happened to me since the voyage in *Kashgar*. Moreover, it opened up a vista of wonderful possibilities. It is curious how few of my contemporaries went abroad in those days, particularly as it was so inexpensive. Apart from Gustav, not one of the boys I met at school showed any desire to do so, though some had, like myself, been born in the Colonies; certainly no one displayed more than a cursory interest in my own travels, and I soon learnt not to expect it. It would have been fun to have found someone with whom to share the seductive but highly speculative plans which now raced through my mind; but as I did not, I kept them to myself, assuming, not for the first time, that I must be a little odd. As yet my ambitions were not focused upon any one aspect of travel, and I would have been equally enchanted by a desert, a polar ice-cap or a tropical forest. I was very intrigued by volcanic phenomena and had collected a number of books on the subject; the only classical writing which stirred my interest was the younger Pliny's account of the eruption of Vesuvius, and that, naturally, in an English translation and not in the course of my Latin studies. Lately, of course, mountains had begun to assume a special importance because of my personal acquaintance with them, though hitherto I had not thought of them much in terms of climbing. Now, however, I acquired books by some of the early Alpine mountaineers and was thrilled to read in these the expression of so much of my own inarticulate feelings. I was reassured to notice that even these illustrious men found it necessary to justify their exploits, Tyndall on scientific, Leslie Stephen on aesthetic grounds, to a public who obviously regarded them as highly eccentric. Once again it was Whymper, with his simple approach and exciting narrative, his lively observation and power of description, who most captivated me. Significantly, I was more fascinated by his early explorations in the Dauphiné than by his much more dramatic and competitive adventures on the Matterhorn. I do not claim that my dislike of competition was a virtue, since it stemmed largely from my failure to compete successfully; but it is certainly true that part of the attraction that I later found in mountaineering was that it could be practised without any sense of rivalry.

For the Christmas holidays my sister and I were taken to Adelboden for winter sports. That year, 1924, there was no snow in the lower valleys, and as ski-lifts did not then exist, at least in that part of Switzerland, there was no skiing to be had. While the rest of my party lamented the fact, I was secretly delighted, for it provided both the excuse and the opportunity to climb. The village was dominated by a mountain called the Gross Lohner, 10,023 feet high, which I had noticed on the map before leaving England. Mid-winter, I realised, was not the time for mountaineering, nor did I suppose that I could tackle it alone; nevertheless, I had nursed a forlorn but passionate hope that I might find a way of climbing it. Now, the general air of frustration enabled me to persuade five people in our hotel to join me in the venture and share the expense of two guides. We set out one afternoon, spent the night in a snow-bound hut in a silent coombe below the Wildstrubel and started again several hours before dawn. In summer one could probably scramble up the Lohner without any difficulty, but in winter conditions, with the rocks sheathed in ice, steps had to be cut and a good deal of care was needed to avoid a slip which, but for the protection of the rope, would in many places have sent the victim hurtling down a precipitous slope. I was greatly impressed, and tried hard to emulate the balanced movements and nonchalance of the guides. I was gratified to notice that several of my companions, some of whom had been on a mountain before, were scared. From the summit we saw some of the giants of the Oberland and, far away to the south, the Matterhorn, the Weisshorn, Monte Rosa, names that now held magic. Then came the descent: the slow, cautious movements down the steep upper face; the sudden release of tension when the difficulties were passed; the wild plunge down long snow slopes to the forest; lastly the exultation and utter content as I plodded, tired, along the path through the resin-scented trees.

One of the guides offered to take me, for a greatly reduced fee, up a rock spire with the impressive name of Tschingelochtighorn. I had been very apprehensive at the prospect of rock-climbing, for, despite my fondness for scaling trees, I had often been terrified standing at the edge of a tall building (in fact, I still dislike it intensely), and so assumed that I had a bad head for heights. But by then nothing would have induced me to miss the chance of climbing another mountain. In fact, I found that looking down a vertical drop from a narrow ledge was not nearly so bad as I had feared. (It is difficult to explain the difference; it may be due to one's absorption in climbing or to the fact that on mountains one approaches the vertical more gradually than is usually the case on buildings.) Later I joined two experienced French amateurs on a third climb. Thus, by the time the holiday ended I had found a focus for my vague longing for contact with wild country, and the seeds had been sown of a passion which was to have such a decisive effect upon the course of my life that it is difficult now to imagine what would have become of me without it.

In the Easter holidays I went to Italy to join my mother and sister at Menaggio, on Lake Como. The surrounding hills were still covered with snow, and on my first morning I set out to climb one which stood about 5000 feet above the town. Lacking any route-finding finesse, I went straight at it, aiming at a gully which split a line of high cliffs. This looked easy from below, but when I got into it I found that it was far steeper than I had supposed. I was wearing ordinary walking shoes which gave little purchase on the snow-covered shale ledges. After a series of desperate struggles I became much too scared to think of going down. Eventually, however, I emerged, with trembling limbs and pounding heart, on a snow slope above the cliffs. This, too, was much steeper than it had appeared. I had climbed two or three hundred feet up it when my foot slipped and I found myself somersaulting down the slope. So far as I know, it was nothing that I did which stopped my fall a short way above the brink of the cliffs. I felt curiously light-hearted (I may well have been light-headed) as I struggled back up the slope and on to the top. I descended by an easy route on the other side of the hill, and arrived back at the hotel with a cut forehead and a black eye. I forget how I accounted for these, but whatever explanation I gave, it was not the truth.

My mother's attitude to my climbing was wholly admirable. Despite her reserve, I sensed that she was worried about it, which indeed was hardly surprising, for she knew no mountaineers and nothing of climbing, and no doubt she shared the popular belief that it was a highly dangerous pastime. Yet she did nothing to dissuade and much to encourage me. Aware of her concern, I was reticent about my new-found enthusiasm, but she was well aware of its intensity, and it was her firm principle never to stand in the way of either of us in the fulfilment of any reputable ambition. For this and a great deal besides, I am deeply grateful. I was very fond of my mother; but though we had a great deal in common, we were never very close. This was largely due to her reticence which prevented intimate discussion, an indulgence to which I have always been addicted.

My little contretemps above Menaggio did nothing to quench my determination to see something of the high peaks during that holiday, though the season was now even less suitable for climbing. The most accessible big mountain seemed to be Monte Disgrazia, more than 12,000 feet high, some thirty miles to the north-east of Lake Como. A week or so after my arrival I set out by train for Ardenno, the hotel manager having wired a few days previously to a colleague there asking him to engage a guide. I was met at the station by a stocky little man named Jaquomo Fierelli, a guide from the village of San Martino. He had brought a horse and cart, and in this we set off along a narrow road into the mountains. Soon this became so steep that, although only eight miles away, it took us more than three hours to reach the village, which was situated at the junction of three gorges and surrounded by magnificent precipices. Jaquomo, who provided me with hospitality for the night, spoke only Italian, of which I knew only a few words; this, however, did not seem to inhibit conversation so far as he was concerned. I managed to convey to him that I wanted to climb Monte Disgrazia; he seemed agreeable and lent me a pair of ill-fitting boots and an ice-axe; but he insisted that we must engage a porter to come with us. Soon after 2:00 the following morning we set off by the light of a candle lantern down the road and presently diverged on to a path which zigzagged steeply up through the forest. Though still half asleep, I was delighted with this evidence that we were bound for the summit of Monte Disgrazia; at the same time I was a little uneasy. I did not see how we could possibly climb a 12,000-foot mountain in a single day from San Martino, little more than 3000 feet above sea level; and if we were not intending to do so, why this early start? When dawn broke we were in a snowy valley far above the tree line. The snow was firm, the morning cloudless and there before us stood our mountain, looking very big and deceptively close. At 7:30 a.m. we reached a hut, the Capana Cecilia, belonging to the Italian Alpine Club. It was largely buried in snow and we had some difficulty in forcing our way in. I assumed that we had merely stopped for breakfast; but when, after eating some bread and some evil-smelling cheese, my companions stretched themselves out on a wide, communal bunk and went to sleep it dawned on me that they had no intention of going farther that day. When, later, I went for a walk and immediately plunged into a morass of snow, now melted by the sun, I was forced to admit the wisdom of their decision. But the perfect weather made it hard to curb my impatience.

We had nothing to eat but bread and cheese. For supper this was boiled into soup, which improved the taste of the cheese, but gave it the consistency of chewing gum. We went early to sleep. I was woken at 12:30 a.m. and given some more bread-and-cheese soup. Outside it was snowing hard and there was a fairly strong wind. The guides were curiously unperturbed by this sudden change in the weather; indeed, they seemed delighted. At 2:00 we left the hut and started trudging through deep, unfrozen snow in the general direction of the mountain. At first the ground was fairly level, but soon it steepened to a moderate slope and our slow progress became still slower. Even when the dawn came there was nothing to be seen through the mist and swirling snow. At about 6:30 we reached the crest of a ridge. To my astonishment, the guides let out triumphant shouts, beat me on the back and shook my hand. I understood enough of what they said to realise that they were congratulating me on having reached the summit of Monte Disgrazia. Much as I wished to believe them, I had the gravest doubts, for I could not reconcile the ground we had covered with what I had seen of the mountain. But my slender command of Italian made it impossible for me to argue the point; and in any case I was not given time, for a moment later we were plunging down the other side of the ridge. Here the guides' equanimity seemed to desert them, for they dragged me along in frenzied haste, shouting "*Multo pericoloso*" and gesticulating in a manner which made it plain that we were in imminent danger of annihilation by an avalanche. At length we reached a path which led us down the eastern of the three gorges back to San Martino, which we reached at 10:30 a.m., in time for a second, more substantial breakfast. After this a priest was summoned, presumably to help resolve the question of the guides' fees; but he spoke neither English nor French. We tried to communicate in Latin, but eight years' intensive study of that language had left me strangely ill equipped for practical discussion. I tried to express my doubts about our having reached the summit, but it was useless. Eventually the matter of the fees was settled to the guides' satisfaction if not to mine, and Jaquomo, now mellowed by much wine, drove me in his horse and cart at a terrifying speed down the twisting road to Ardenno, where I caught a train back to Lake Como.

I had taken an excellent photograph of Monte Disgrazia from the Capana Cecilia, and for the next few months I used frequently to pore over this, trying desperately to convince myself that we had really reached the top; but I never succeeded. In fact, I very much doubt if Jaquomo had any intention of climbing the mountain in April conditions, in which case he must have been wondering when he was going to disillusion me; the sudden change in the weather had provided a neat solution to his problem. Forty years and four months later I climbed Disgrazia with my son, John, and I think I was able to identify the spot we had reached, some 2000 feet below the summit.

Now, more than anything, I longed for a reasonably long spell in the summer Alps. The main difficulty, which seemed insuperable, was the cost of hiring guides. I had a little book called *Swiss Mountain Climbs,* by A. D. Abraham, which listed the guides' tariffs for all the Swiss mountains. These seemed prohibitive, and it was obvious that I could not possibly afford more than a couple of climbs in a holiday; particularly since my book made it clear that a guide would not usually venture on a difficult climb alone with an inexperienced amateur, and that it would be necessary also to hire a porter (an unqualified guide, employed not so much to carry loads as to assist his senior). Obviously I could not climb alone, and even if I had been able to find someone to go with, it had been repeatedly impressed upon me that to climb in the Alps without guides was the height of folly. In those days there were no youth organisations to help youngsters to learn the techniques of mountaineering; and even if there had been, my highly developed dislike of communal activities might well have prevented my joining it.

I had already decided to spend part of the next summer holidays (1925) walking through the Auvergne, mainly with the object of looking at the extinct volcanoes and crater lakes of that region (for volcanoes still intrigued me). This plan had my mother's approval, partly because it would help me to learn French, and partly because she had an old friend living in Clermont-Ferrand who, she supposed, would be able to keep a fatherly eye on me. But I intended to spend the second half of the holidays visiting the scenes of Whymper's early exploits in the Dauphiné. Though the very name made me dizzy with excitement, I thought it better to keep this part of my programme to myself until I actually got there.

The old-fashioned walking tour seems to be a thing of the past. Perhaps, in a way, this is a good thing, for even in the overcrowded holiday Europe of today there is still a lot of country which can hardly be reached except on foot, and thus remains untouched by the ravages of tourism. In 1925 tourists were a great deal easier to avoid. There is no better way of becoming intimately acquainted with country than by walking over it, as I had already discovered in Norway, and soon I was so absorbed in exploring the Massif Central that I almost forgot my eagerness to reach the Dauphiné. I found that there were advantages in being on my own: not only the freedom to do just as I pleased but also a heightened impact of scenes and situations induced by solitude. Certainly I felt a bit lonely at first, particularly as, being stupidly diffident about airing my school French, I kept my human contacts to the minimum necessary for my survival.

One day, having started very early to cross a wild, unpopulated region, I reached a little *auberge* at 2:00, hot, parched and ravenous. There I ordered an omelette; the girl serving me asked, "Two eggs?" to which I replied, "No, six, please." She looked a little surprised, but went off to prepare it. In those days it was the custom in France for even the poorest inns to supply their customers with free wine. There was a large carafe on the table, and as my thirst was even more pressing than my hunger, I drank most of the contents while I waited. The acid *vin ordinaire* acted rapidly on my empty stomach, and by the time my monster omelette appeared I was feeling horribly sick. I paid at once and departed as casually as I dared, leaving the dish untasted and the girl to reflect upon the eccentricities of foreigners. I just managed to get out of sight in time; then, too embarrassed to return for my abandoned meal, I walked sadly on. Gradually, however, the universal kindness I met from the country people dissolved my shyness, and I began to delight in my daily encounters. Once I met a young Greek at an inn, and together we hired a punt which took us down the rapids of the Gorges du Tarn. Apart from this one extravagance (and the six-egged omelette), I managed, eating frugally but adequately, to live on little more than a shilling a day. This was well below my budget, so that by the end of my three weeks' trek through the Auvergne and Cevennes I had saved a fair sum of money.

I went by train to Grenoble, where I stayed for a day to buy maps and plan the next part of my programme. I had intended to walk from there into the high mountains (in those days I had never heard of hitch-hiking), but in the windows of the tourist bureaux I saw pictures of the great ice peaks of the Dauphiné, whose names, Mont Pelvoux, Les Ecrins, La Meije, were already enchantingly familiar from Whymper. Swept by a fever of impatience, I booked a seat on a bus which left early the following day for La Bérarde. It was a dismal morning; rain was falling when the bus started, and when, after a couple of hours, it turned into a narrow valley leading into the heart of the range there was nothing to be seen but mist. I listened to the despondent talk of my fellow passengers, who were all, it seemed, making a day trip. Never, they said, had there been such a summer; the sun had not appeared for weeks; it wasn't really worth visiting the high valleys, as there was nothing to be seen. I was rash enough to admit that I proposed to stop in La Bérarde to climb. This evoked an outburst of cynical witticism which made me feel foolish and profoundly depressed. Then, as we approached St. Christophe, a miracle happened. The rain stopped; the clouds retreated up the mountainsides; a window opened to frame a sharp white peak which seemed to be hanging almost over our heads, glistening like a huge diamond; another appeared and another, and soon the valley was filled with sunlight.

We stopped at Les Etages, a small hamlet a few miles below La Bérarde, and while the driver refreshed himself and the other passengers photographed each other I enquired at the inn for a guide. I was promptly introduced to a bandy-legged little man, barely more than five feet tall, a beret cocked over one eye, who was sitting at a table drinking wine. His name was Elie Richard. Yes, he was free to act as my guide; it had been a terrible summer, very little climbing had been possible in August, and the peaks were deeply laden with fresh snow; but now, I would see, the weather would change and we would climb. Several weeks of unemployment during his short professional season (in those days one did not ski in the Dauphiné) had made Elie as eager as I to start. The very next day, he said, we would climb Pic Coolidge, which for all its 12,000 feet was easy enough to be possible in the worst of snow conditions; after that we would go for bigger game. His enthusiasm took my breath away; but how much would it cost? I told him I had very little money. He brushed this aside as lightly as he had dealt with the weather and the snow; he would charge me sixty francs (seven shillings) a day, or less if I couldn't afford it; we would climb every day if I wished, as we would live in huts which were free, and the cost of our food, which we would carry with us, would be small. It was settled; Elie would meet me in La Bérarde at 1:00 the following morning; the whole transaction had taken barely ten minutes. I climbed back into the bus in a daze of happiness, scarcely able to believe my good fortune.

At La Bérarde there were few people staying at the inn, and nearly all were climbers. For supper we sat together at one table. From their talk it was clear that the others were mostly experts, and I sat in awed silence listening to a discussion of their lofty ambitions, which could not be attempted until several days of fine weather had removed or settled the new snow. One of them was Nea Barnard, a girl of nineteen, already in her third Alpine season and soon to become one of the most distinguished women climbers of her generation. A warm-hearted extrovert, she was not slow to notice my shyness and to draw me gently into the company of the gods. Later, it was through her that I first made the acquaintance of other British climbers.

The ten days that followed were beyond my wildest dreams. Hitherto I had regarded the climbing of mountains as isolated experiences and had not conceived the idea of linking them together in a continuous mountaineering journey by travelling from place to place over the ranges and even by crossing the peaks themselves. Elie was as good as his word, and his optimism regarding the weather was justified; every day we climbed a peak or crossed a high pass; each night was spent in fresh surroundings. At that time he was a *Guide de Deuxième Classe*, and anxious to attain first-class status, which partly accounted for his willingness to do as much as possible in the time, and to climb on peaks that were new to him; but I believe this was also due to his sympathetic awareness of my delighted response. Luckily, my trek in the Auvergne had left me very fit, or I would not have been able to stand the pace; even so, I was often more tired than I had ever been before, and the prospect of yet another 2:00 a.m. start seemed intolerable. In the valleys Elie was the mildest of men; often on a mountain, particularly when descending a difficult passage of rock or snow-covered ice, his placid, retiring demeanour would undergo a violent change. He would curse and bawl at me in a mighty voice, while his small stature seemed to grow by several cubits: *"Enfoncez vos talons—Bon Dieu, regardez la corde— Ah, nom de nom de nom!"* At first I thought that these outbursts were due to his fear that my clumsiness would result in our destruction; later I began to suspect that they were an expression of joy at his own mastery. In moments of relaxation he was not grudging in his praise, which helped to restore my shattered self-esteem.

I rediscovered, with greater poignancy than before, the harsh truth that a strenuous pursuit cannot be undertaken without some suffering, and there were many times that I wished myself in softer circumstances: being woken at 1:00 a.m. from a deep sleep of physical fatigue to face a bleak world of stale bread, hard boots, stiff joints and cracked lips; the endless trudge up a slope of soft snow under a broiling sun with nothing to divert my attention from aching thighs and a raging thirst. There were moments, too, of clumsy fear which made me feel abysmally helpless and foolish. But these things were a minor part of the symphony of varied emotions that composed the experience of a mountaineering day, the sombre background to the contrasting highlights: the quickening of life at dawn after the dead weariness of the night approach; the sheer joy of controlled, rhythmic movement on steep rock and ice; the moment of attainment on the summit; the bliss of relaxation after tensed effort; in whole, the profound satisfaction of achieving a small measure of mastery, and with it a sense of belonging, in a majestic and enthralling environment.

I was surprised and a little shocked to find that I was not greatly impressed by the views from the tops, particularly of the highest peaks. I had supposed that one of the chief delights of climbing was to be found in such views; in fact, I found that the surrounding mountains seemed sadly dwarfed and, by their very profusion, tended to lose their splendid individuality and become shapeless masses in an untidy jumble of snow and rock. Since every climbing book that I had read continually stressed the magnificence of summit views, I assumed that there must be something wrong with me. It took me some time to realise that, for me at least, the aesthetic appreciation of scenery cannot be turned on like a tap; that it comes unbidden, usually at unexpected moments, when the mind happens to be attuned to the realisation of the subtle interplay of form and colour, light and shadow. Views from summits are usually seen in the harsh glare of the noonday sun when this component is notably lacking.

Our last mountain was Les Ecrins, the highest in the Dauphiné and the scene of one of Whymper's more dramatic, if less credible, adventures. My financial resources were now almost at an end, and as in any case I had arranged to spend the last part of the holidays with my mother and sister in Paris, it was time to go. So I set off on the long trek back to Grenoble, too thrilled with the fabulous success of my first real Alpine season to have any regrets. Moreover, Elie and I had agreed to climb together the following summer, and for a far longer time.

In Paris I fell ill with a high fever. When, after a week, this subsided the doctor advised my mother to take me home. I spent the last weeks of the holidays feeling like death but determined to make the most of my remaining days of freedom. It was not until the final day, when my sister became ill and a doctor was summoned, that her complaint, and mine, was diagnosed as scarlet fever. As I had been peeling profusely when still in Paris, the doctor there must have been well aware that I had the disease, and had no doubt extracted a substantial bribe from the hotel manager to suppress the fact. As a result, I later developed serious complications and a dangerous illness, from which I did not recover for several months. After that, to aid convalescence, I went in a banana ship to Teneriffe, where I spent a splendid week climbing the Peak and exploring the site of the 1909 eruption.

Meanwhile I had persuaded my mother that, as I was now eighteen, it was high time that I left school. She was anxious that I should go to Cambridge. I was not keen on the idea, but the realisation that three years at the University would furnish me with the chance of three long Alpine seasons before becoming tied to a job was sufficient inducement, and I settled down in London to "cram" for the entrance examination. In those days, for boys of normal ability, this was a mere formality; for me it was not the case. My chief difficulty was with Latin; this had formed a solid mental block, and in nine years of study I had hardly advanced beyond the most elementary stage. The only alternatives allowed were Greek or Sanskrit, but neither appeared to offer a promising by-pass. The Latin exam consisted of two papers: one on a set book which required prior study; the other, called for some reason the "unseen," demanded the translation from Latin of two short passages, one prose and one verse, with the use of a dictionary. In my case the set book was *The Odes of Horace*, Vols. 2 and 3. I acquired a crib, which supplied the meaning of each small phrase, together with an explanation of any abstruse allusion, and began by paraphrasing it as completely as possible; then I set myself to learn the whole lot by heart. In this I was so successful that, when I took the exam in December 1926 I scored more than 90 per cent in the set-book paper. But, alas, as I could decipher no meaning from either passage in the "unseen," I failed in that to achieve the minimum requirement of 20 per cent and was ploughed. The following year the set book was Cicero's defence in the trial of Milo, and I began the tedious process all over again. It involved the most prodigious mental effort I have ever made—and the most useless. By an odd coincidence, when I took the exam again in June 1927 I occupied the rooms of an undergraduate named L. R. Wager, and was enchanted to find, from books on the shelves and pictures on the walls, that he, too, was a mountaineer. My second attempt was successful.

In the end I never went to Cambridge at all. This was very largely because at my interview with the Master of my prospective college (a kindly man, but presumably a classicist) he poured such scorn on my proposal that I should read Geology that I became thoroughly discouraged. I have often regretted my cowardly decision, but unless my teachers had been quite exceptionally lucid and inspiring, I would probably have achieved as little learning at the University as I had at school. In any case, not long afterwards my mother was so hit financially by the Slump that it would have been difficult for her to keep me there. Instead, I spent some time at a college of estate management in London, where I learnt a modicum of accountancy, the difference between the English and the French methods of laying bricks, and the elements of cadastral survey, when I made my first acquaintance with a theodolite. (Incidentally, I attended several lectures on this instrument without realising that its function was to measure angles.) The reason for this exercise was that it had been decided that I should seek my livelihood in Kenya, where, it was hoped, I might one day manage an estate. Tea planting in Ceylon was the obvious choice of a career, because, apart from the fact that it required no knowledge of Latin, my mother still had interests and connections there. But I found East Africa a more attractive alternative, simply because it contained some high mountains.

Meanwhile, my (to me more important) Alpine career prospered. In the summer of 1926, now the proud possessor of an ice-axe and a length of rope, I spent six weeks climbing in the Dauphiné with Elie. The value of the franc had slipped to 240 to the pound, which meant that Elie's fee was now only 5s. a day; and as we continued to sleep in huts (with an occasional bivouac for a remote peak) and to live with stern frugality, my total expenditure was less than the cost of a normal holiday at home. Even then I realised how lucky I had been to have found Elie Richard, for apart from being a most pleasant companion, his attitude to our activities exactly suited my needs: he always seemed to be enjoying himself and never gave the impression that he was climbing because he had to make a living; he certainly never had to be urged to work for his meagre wage. He was by no means a great guide, but very sound, and anyway, the climbs we tackled were not of a high standard. He took great pains to instruct me in various points of technique. As before, we were very energetic; more than once we climbed four peaks on successive days, and we rested only when bad weather compelled us to do so. On a few of the more difficult climbs, such as the traverse of La Meije, Elie made me hire a second guide, but usually we were alone together. He was always keen to climb in areas unknown to him; this I particularly enjoyed, for it emphasised the exploratory aspect of mountaineering and enabled me to take a modest part in finding the way. In this I was again fortunate, for in those days a large part of the high Dauphiné was still wild, and rarely visited even by mountaineers. Only on three of the twenty peaks we climbed that year did we meet another party.

Climbing in the Alps without guides used to be a rare indulgence, and even in my day it was frowned upon in some circles. But the practice had already become common, even for beginners, particularly among Continental people. This was the main reason for the great increase after the First World War in the popularity of mountaineering, which had hitherto been regarded as a rich man's sport, but was now found to be one of the least expensive. At that time most Britons began their climbing in Wales, Cumberland or Scotland; indeed, many, perhaps most, of the ablest performers became so attached to pure rock-climbing that they did not bother to go to the Alps. Since the Second World War there has been a remarkable reversal of this tendency. I began to climb with guides because I knew no one else to climb with; I was able to do so only because of the fortunate coincidence of a freak economic situation. I began in the Alps because I was attracted by the environment rather than by the actual process of climbing, and became interested in this as a means to an end rather than an end in itself. It was not until Easter 1927 that I climbed on British rock; this was on the crags around Wasdale Head, where Nea had invited me to join her party. I found the climbs a great deal harder than any rock I had tackled before, and I was very scared. When, however, I had grasped two salient facts—that on all the standard routes the rock was absolutely sound, quite unlike the treacherous cliffs to which I was accustomed in the Dauphiné, and that the climbs were so short that the time factor was of little consequence—I became adjusted to what amounted to a different technique, and began to enjoy myself. But the most important event of that short holiday was my meeting with Gilbert Peaker, with whom I climbed.

Gilbert, some eight years my senior, was a lecturer in mathematics and a marathon runner. Though he had done little in the Alps, he was an experienced rock-climber. He seemed to be quite imperturbable, and I was fascinated by his precise way of speaking and his unusual choice of phrase. He was anxious to extend his knowledge of the Alps, and as he shared my preference for covering as much ground as possible rather than climbing from a centre, we agreed to go there together the following summer. It was wonderful at last to have someone to share my plans, the excitement of anticipation and the outward journey; and I realised that, before, I had been lonely without knowing it. We began in the Graian Alps, and by traversing a series of peaks we worked our way eastward across the Italian frontier to the Gran Paradiso Group. The climbs we did were not difficult, but the new responsibility of being without a professional made them quite interesting enough. The weather was fine, and in three weeks we never took a day off. At the end of that time we crossed the Col du Géant to Chamonix, where we hoped to climb on the famous Aiguilles.

At the Montenvers we met Nea, surrounded as always by many friends. This was her second season in the Chamonix area, and she had already made the acquaintance of several of the most distinguished French climbers of the day, including Jean Morin, whom, not long afterwards, she married. For the past few weeks she and Jean and Joe Marples had been trying to make the first ascent of the Aiguille du Roc, but continuous bad weather had prevented a serious attempt, and it was not until the following year that they achieved it. The atmosphere in the Montenvers was vibrant with expertise, and I became aware, for the first time, of the revolution in Alpine climbing, then well under way, and which escalated throughout the next decade. It was primarily due to the great increase in the popularity of the sport, which led to far greater competition for the dwindling number of feasible new routes, and to the development of bold new techniques designed to break through the old barriers of impossibility. This resulted in an enormously higher standard of performance (and often, alas, in the acceptance of narrower margins of safety). For a while French climbers were in the forefront of this new era of achievement, which was then largely concerned with rock-climbing; thus Chamonix, with its unique opportunities in this field, became its focal centre. It was clear that, among the élite at least, my type of mountaineering was quite out of date, but I was still enjoying myself far too much to mind, or to have any great ambition to join their ranks.

The weather around Mont Blanc showed no promise of improving, so after one or two climbs in the smaller aiguilles Gilbert and I went by bus to the Dauphiné, where the climate is usually, and was then, very much better. There I celebrated my twentieth birthday, which came, literally, within an inch of being my last. That afternoon I was leading down one of the ridges on the north face of Les Bans when a boulder weighing (according to Gilbert) about five hundredweight became dislodged by the rope above, and came bounding down towards me. I ducked as low as the small ledge I was standing on would allow, and the huge missile flew over my head, missing my skull but brushing my hair. When Gilbert had to return home at the end of his holiday I went to Zermatt, where I finished the season with three guided climbs: a traverse of the Zinal Rothorn, the north ridge of the Obergablehorn and the Z'mutt ridge of the Matterhorn. Conditions on all three were bad, and the last took the unusually long time of twenty-four hours. But I was satisfied that I was now competent to tackle climbs of this order unguided.

Gilbert and I spent the following Easter holiday together at Helyg in North Wales. At first we had the hut to ourselves, but later it was taken over by the Cambridge University Mountaineering Club, and we with it. A few years before, this Club had been revived from its post-war doldrums by the inspiration of Van Noorden and Wyn Harris, and it was now so active that it was producing a very large proportion of the new generation of British Alpine Climbers. I have kept up my acquaintance ever since with many of those who were at that Easter meet. Jack Longland and L. R. Wager, who, having left University and having formed a distinguished Alpine partnership, were then doyens of the Club. At the time they were attending one of Winthrop Young's famous Easter parties at Pen-y-Pass, and they used to visit us occasionally in the evenings. I don't think we actually stood up when they entered, but I remember thinking that perhaps we should.

In 1928 came one of those rare Alpine summers when the weather is predominantly fine; and as it was my last season, I had reason to be specially thankful. Gilbert had persuaded H. M. Kelly to join us. He was probably the finest British rock-climber of that period, and the Lakeland guide-books were full of his pioneer ascents; he had, however, made only one brief visit to the Alps. We went out early in July and spent three weeks in the Zermatt valley. For the whole of this time the sky remained almost cloudless, and we managed to climb nearly all the major peaks and some of the classic routes. All too aware that it might be a very long time before I saw the Alps again, I was perhaps more anxious than my companions not to waste any of this incredible weather, so on two occasions while one rested I climbed with the other. The next part of our programme was to traverse the high-level route from Zermatt to Chamonix, stopping to climb various peaks on the way. But by then Kelly had had enough and decided to return home. This was disappointing, as we had looked forward to watching him perform on Chamonix granite, much more his métier than the ice and unsound rock of the great peaks, which he did not really enjoy.

Our first climb after his departure was the west ridge of the Dent Blanche from Bricola. We left at 2:00 a.m. and got back to the hotel shortly before supper. Except for a tin of strawberries consumed on the summit, we had eaten nothing and drunk little. We ordered a bottle of wine, a rare indulgence, and drank a couple of glasses while waiting impatiently for the first course. I should, of course, have known better. When the soup arrived the room and the other diners were already revolving around me. I got to my feet and announced that I was going to bed. I remember Gilbert's startled face and then a loud explosion, presumably my head hitting the floor. When

I came to I was lying on my bunk, a priest sitting at my side pouring some peppermint liquid down my throat. The next morning we made a late start on our westward journey.

In 1928 Chamonix was already gross with tourism, an unlovely conglomeration of luxury hotels, motor coaches and cheap jack exploiters of the mountain scenery. Had its noisy crowds been confined to the valley, it would not have been so bad, but they spread far up to the high mountain huts, which were often so filled with tourists that there was no accommodation for the climbers for whom they were built. But no mountaineer can miss the opportunity of experiencing at least once the superb granite of the Aiguilles. When Gilbert and I got there we were very fit after more than a month of hard exercise, and as the weather was still fine, we were able to enjoy it to the full. Later we joined forces with Jack Longland and George Trevelyan to attempt one of the southern ridges of Mont Blanc (this was foiled by a storm) and other climbs. As I was not due to sail to Kenya until October, I was in no hurry to return to England, so when the others departed, I spent another week climbing with Graham Macphee from the Couvercle Hut.

On the way there I had a most unusual accident. In the late afternoon we were carrying heavy packs up the Mer de Glace, unroped because we were still on "dry" ice. Two days before, a storm had deposited hail on the glacier, which had collected in drifts like patches of old snow. I was a couple of paces ahead of Graham, who was telling me some involved tale, when I stepped in one of these patches. In fact, it was a small *moulin* (a hole in the surface of the glacier drilled by the action of a surface stream), filled with hailstones, into which I fell, landing in an upright position eight feet down the hole. Graham fell on top of me but extricated himself immediately. When, however, I tried to get out I found that my weight had packed the hail so that my legs were encased in a tightly fitting mould of solid ice; and as the hole was too narrow for me to lean forward I could do nothing to free them. Graham lowered a rope which I tied to my waist, but he was quite unable to move me. There were several parties of climbers coming down the glacier. The first to arrive was composed of six Italians, who joined in the tug-of-war; but their combined strength, apart from nearly cutting me in two, achieved nothing. Meanwhile I had become painfully aware that rivulets of icy water were pouring over the lip of the hole on to me. Apart from the discomfort this caused, the ugly thought occurred to me that the packing of the hail below might well have blocked the outlet to this stream, and that the hole might now fill with water. In time, however, these fears were proved unfounded. Other parties arrived; each in turn needed to be convinced by practical demonstration that I could not be pulled out, and I began to feel like a "Try Your Strength" machine at a fair. I explained repeatedly, mostly in French, that unless my feet were pulled off this method of extracting me was impracticable. Eventually I owed my salvation to a young Frenchman with a red beard, who arrived on the scene some two hours after I had fallen into the trap. He lowered himself head first into the hole and, hanging more or less upside down on the rope, proceeded with a saucepan lid to scrape at the block of ice which imprisoned my legs. It was a long and tedious job, for each lidful had to be passed laboriously up to the surface; but at length he succeeded in freeing my limbs, which by then had lost all feeling, and I was hauled out like a cork, amid rousing cheers from the onlookers. These now numbered about thirty. As some of them were women, I was discreetly screened by a ring of men, while my breeches were ripped off and my legs massaged; I was then plied with brandy and the assembled company sang "It's a Long Way to Tipperary," which, presumably, was thought to be the best method of comforting an Englishman in distress. I was deeply touched. I did not contract frost-bite, though for several weeks my legs felt curiously numb and lacked strength in the shin muscles. However, after a short rest in the valley, Graham and I went to the Couvercle, from which we did three excellent climbs, which proved to be my last in the Alps for thirty-seven years.

| 3 |

EAST AFRICA

ANYONE ACQUAINTED WITH EAST AFRICA and knowing something of its history can hardly fail to be amazed by the rapid transformation of this huge territory from barbarism to its present state of development. Less than one hundred years ago a handful of explorers were still groping their way about the Dark Continent, discovering its main geographical features and bringing back tales of horrible cruelty; of fair and fertile lands largely depopulated by famine and disease, by pitiless tribal warfare and by massive deportations by Arab slave-traders. It has so long been the fashion to decry both the conduct and achievements of British Colonial rule, to scorn and revile its founders, that now we tend to hang our heads in shame for the misdeeds of our forbears, their colossal arrogance in seeking to impose their codes of ethics and justice and their religious beliefs upon the native people. We are inclined, perhaps, to forget that this was done by Greeks and Romans, by Norsemen and Mongols and countless others before us, to say nothing of Chinese Communists since. Moreover, in the situation which faced them in East and Central Africa, it is difficult to see how our Victorian grandfathers should have acted to ensure our approval and save our tender consciences. In this vast and savage region they could hardly have hoped to abolish slavery, alleviate disease and reconcile the warring tribes without first taking over its administration; yet that, it seems, was their cardinal sin. Should they, perhaps, have ignored the reports of the explorers and the appeals of the missionaries, and refused to become involved? Certainly many of their statesmen advocated this policy. Those of us who delight in wild, unpeopled lands may regret that they did not adopt it; but it is at least doubtful if the cause of humanity would have been better served. Any suggestion that British rule brought immense benefits to the subject people invariably evokes the retort that it was established in the first place for selfish ends. Even if this were wholly true, which in many instances it was not, it does not invalidate the work of generations of able administrators, dedicated to the welfare of those they governed.

Kenya was one of the few British African Colonies whose climate attracted White settlement. With the completion, in 1901, of the Uganda Railway linking Lake Victoria with the coast, the Government of the East African Protectorate, as Kenya was then called, began to encourage European settlement. Their main reason was the urgent need to establish an economy to defray the expense involved in governing and developing the primitive, sparsely populated territory. The usual allegation that the land for this purpose was wrested from the African population is false. In fact, the only areas to be allocated for European settlement were those which at that time were either completely uninhabited or sporadically occupied by nomadic tribes. Never, during the whole period of British rule, did they amount to as much as 6 per cent of the total land area of the Colony.* From the outset the chief concern of both the Colonial and British Governments was the welfare of the African people. In 1923, when a great increase in European immigration was beginning, the policy was reaffirmed in the declaration that "Primarily, Kenya is an African territory and His Majesty's Government think it necessary definitely to record their considered opinion that the interest of the African natives must be paramount, and that if, and when, their interests and the interests of immigrant races should conflict, the former should prevail." One can imagine the howl of indignation which would follow such a statement by the present Government in regard to a possible conflict of interest between the natives and the immigrants in Britain today.

*For a concise account of European settlement in the Colony see "The 'White Highlands' of Kenya," by Professor W. T. W. Morgan, *The Geographical Journal*, June 1963.

When I arrived in Kenya in October 1928, with every intention of settling there for the rest of my life, I certainly had no feeling of guilt. My first job was an apprenticeship on a large coffee farm at Nyeri, which lay at the end of a branch line, one hundred miles north of Nairobi. The farm was owned by two partners, one working, the other non-working; the latter was a rich, conventionally eccentric Irish peer, who lost no opportunity of expressing his intense dislike of the British. The property was bounded on one side by a small river, across which was a native reserve. Shortly before, the partners had entered into an agreement with the local chief whereby they would develop part of his adjacent land in return for a percentage of its produce; but this plan was firmly vetoed by the Government, who refused to countenance any attempt by Europeans to encroach, however obliquely, upon native reserves.

My work was interesting and my surroundings agreeable; but what delighted me most was my proximity to Mount Kenya; its base was only twenty miles away. I had not seen it on my journey from Nairobi, so the vision which greeted me as I came out of my bungalow at dawn the following day seemed all the more fantastic. I was standing on a ridge looking across a wide plain, still dim in the early light. The northern horizon was filled by a gigantic cone of misty purple, capped by a band of cloud. Over this, apparently floating high above a still sleeping world of tropical colour, was a graceful spire of rock and ice, hard and clear against the light blue sky. The sun, not yet risen to my view, had already touched the peak, throwing ridge and corrie into sharp relief, sparkling here and there on a gem of ice.

Mount Kenya is an ancient volcano rising from a plateau some 5000 feet above sea-level, on a base seventy miles in circumference. On its upper part is a wide ring of crags, the shattered remnants of the crater. In the centre of these is a granite peak draped by fifteen glaciers and crowned by twin summits. It was originally a plug blocking the throat of the volcano, and as the soft, friable rocks of the crater weathered away it was left standing high above the ruins. Ludwig Kraph was the first European to see the mountain, from a great distance, in 1849, but it was not until forty years later that explorers succeeded in getting close to the peak. In 1899 it was climbed by Halford Mackinder with two Alpine guides César Oilier and Joseph Brocherel. Considering the circumstances, this was a remarkable achievement: from Nairobi it took the party many weeks to reach the foot of the mountain through country still wild and little known; they had several critical encounters with hostile tribes; their stores were looted and they had to send back for more; the penetration of the great forests which cover the lower slopes was a long and laborious task. After several attempts Mackinder and the guides reached a very steep glacier descending from a gap between the twin peaks. The ice was so hard that they named it the Diamond Glacier, and they had a severe struggle to reach the gap, which they called the Gate of the Mist. From there they climbed the higher of the two peaks, which Mackinder named Batian and Nelion after two Masai chiefs. Batian (17,040 feet) is the taller by some thirty feet.

In 1928, nearly thirty years later, in spite of many attempts, no one had succeeded in climbing Batian again, while the summit of Nelion still remained untrodden. Small wonder, then, that I was enchanted by this lovely mountain, and consumed by an aching desire to reach it. This was not easy to conceal, and as no one locally had the slightest interest in the mountain except as a scenic oddity, my obsession soon became something of a joke. For my first few weeks, until the short rains came, the mountain was generally clear in the early morning. Usually, too, the clouds would dissolve in the evening to reveal the peaks. The unveiling varied daily: sometimes the twin summits would appear above the cloud mass, looking incredibly high and remote; sometimes the glacier skirts would come first into view, grey and cold under the dark pall; sometimes a window would open to show a section of flying buttress and deep ice-filled couloir, steep and forbidding; sometimes the clouds would drift away from the west to reveal the peaks already golden in the sunset glow, shreds of rose-tinted mist clinging to their sides. In the brief tropical twilight the revelation was always fleeting. I never failed to watch it, entranced and exquisitely tantalised. Happily, by a wonderful stroke of fortune, I did not have to wait long for a chance to realise my dream.

On leaving Cambridge, Wyn Harris had joined the Colonial Service in Kenya; he was then nearing the end of his first tour as Assistant

District Commissioner in Kakamega, and was due for home leave soon after Christmas. He had already made one attempt to climb Mount Kenya the previous year. In reply to a letter introducing myself, he suggested that if I could join him for another attempt at the end of December he would postpone his sailing date for three weeks. It was an opportunity not likely to occur again, perhaps for years and, though I had so recently arrived, my boss was understanding and allowed me to seize it. But for a while it seemed that Fate was not inclined to be so co-operative. One Sunday, early in December, I fell from a cliff into the fork of a tree and damaged my ankle. Terrified lest this should ruin everything, I made as light of the injury as possible, though at first I could only hobble with a stick. (Some months later an X-ray showed that the ankle was in fact broken.) Then, shortly afterwards, I received a much more shattering blow: a telegram arrived from Wyn saying that he was unable to join me owing to some disturbance in his district. I was desolated.

It so happened that my old friend Gustav Sommerfelt had also come to live in Kenya and was working on a farm near Eldoret. He had no climbing experience, but I thought that together we would at least be able to make a reconnaissance of the peak; so I wrote to him explaining the situation and imploring him to fill the breach. His response was swift and enthusiastic; and, though now I scarcely hoped to make a serious attempt on the peak, my spirits revived a little. Finally, on Christmas Eve, another telegram from Wyn saying that all was well sent them soaring as high as the peak.

The three of us met in Nairobi on New Year's Eve and, that same afternoon, having bought supplies for sixteen days and hired a lorry, we set out on the 150-mile drive to Chogoria, a small Meru village at the eastern foot of the mountain. In those days all Kenya roads were bad, and as the lorry, which had been chosen for its cheapness rather than its mobility, was not really roadworthy, it was past midnight before we reached our destination. At dawn, a large number of Meru tribesmen assembled to inspect us, and when they were told of our need for porters there was such an eager rush that we had no trouble in recruiting the fifteen we required. They were an impressive group: their lithe, long-muscled bodies, naked except for a loin cloth, brass arm bangles and a rolled blanket over one shoulder, their feet bare, their long hair dyed red and thatched into a bun; each carried a spear. Our lorry driver was paid off (we had made no arrangement for the return journey), the porters hoisted their loads on to their heads and before the sun had reached the clearing, our little safari disappeared into the forest.

It was cool in the deep shade of the giant trees, and silent save for the occasional cry of a bird or the chatter of colobus monkeys which swung high above our heads, their long white hair glinting against the dark canopy of foliage. The trail was good, but slippery in some places where elephants had slid down the steep inclines. My ankle was still painful, and as I had to hold my foot flat and rigid, I found it hard to keep up with the others; but this did nothing to mar my happiness. That day's march was delightfully varied: at 8000 feet the forest gave place abruptly to dense bamboo; at 10,000 feet this in turn changed to giant heath, bearded with moss and lichen and, finally, late in the afternoon we emerged into open parkland, with tall, lush grass interspersed with thickets of bamboo and massive trees, exiles from the forest, growing singly or in groups. In these delectable surroundings we spent the night.

The following day our way led us up a wide ridge, like the segment of a vast orange, covered with tussocky grass and those strange plants, giant lobelia and giant groundsel, which are peculiar to the high mountains of East and Central Africa. To our left was a deep ravine cupping the dark waters of Lake Murcheson and dominated by a wild array of cliffs and pinnacles. Our view expanded as we climbed, and before long we saw before us the north-east aspect of the twin peaks. We spent the second night near the head of the gorge, at a height of 14,000 feet. There we discharged most of the porters, and as it was near the upper limit of giant groundsel, the only fuel available apart from our one Primus stove, the men that remained used the place as a base camp while we were on the peak.

Mackinder's ascent of Batian and all the subsequent attempts had been made from the south-east, and this was the line of attack we had intended to follow. But our distant views of the north-east face of the peaks encouraged the hope that it might offer a practicable route. So, next morning, we carried a camp to the crest of a saddle, part of the rim of the ancient crater, from which, only a mile away across the head of the Mackinder Valley, we could see the whole of the 3000-foot north-east wall. It was divided by a dark gully which plunged in one perpendicular sweep from the Gate of the Mist. Nelion appeared smooth, vertical and quite unclimbable from that side; but the face of Batian, though very steep, was broken by a network of ledges and gullies. We examined it carefully with binoculars, and though an ugly-looking bulge in the upper part of the face seemed likely to be very difficult, we thought it could be negotiated by one of several vertical cracks. As, however, much depended upon the type of rock on the face, Wyn and I set off that afternoon to make a closer inspection, while Gustav pitched camp. After sliding rapidly down a thousand feet of scree, we skirted below two small glaciers to reach the foot of the face. We were delighted to find that the rock was as firm and clean-cut as Chamonix granite, and though we climbed several hundred feet up it, we found nothing to chasten our confidence. Night was falling as we scrambled back to our camp up the scree slope, our lungs bursting and our spirits high. The weather was fine, and neither of us doubted that, the very next day, the summit of Batian would be reached for the second time, after a lapse of thirty years.

Sheer excitement prevented me from sleeping much that night, and I was glad when it was time to prepare breakfast. As soon as it was light the three of us were running down the scree and across to the foot of the peak. Not far beyond the point we had reached before, the climbing became increasingly difficult, and our progress, already hindered by the presence of a third man on the rope, became slower and slower. Gradually we began to fear that the short equatorial day was not long enough for us to reach the summit and return. At length, at about 3:00, only 400 feet below the summit ridge, we reached a smooth, steep slab offering some tiny holds but no belay. Immediately above was the great bulge, which extended right across the face. We saw that the cracks by which we had hoped to climb it were in fact shallow, rounded grooves, offering little purchase and overhanging in their lower sections. The bulge has since been climbed by using pitons and "artificial" techniques. We had none of these means, and our defeat was decisive. Nevertheless, we were too slow to admit it, with the result that night had fallen before we regained the foot of the wall when, thoroughly dejected, we were faced with a long, stumbling, weary climb in the dark back to camp.

The next morning the porters came up and helped us to move our camp round to a frozen lake by the side of the Lewis Glacier, the largest of the Kenya ice-streams, which flows beneath the south-east face of Nelion. As, by then, the whole mountain was wrapped in cloud, we had some difficulty in finding the way; but we reached the frozen lake by noon. From Mackinder's account of his climb we knew that he and his guides had attempted several different lines on this side of the mountain, but it was not at all clear which of these they had followed successfully. It appeared, however, that they had reached the head of a sharp southerly ridge running up from the glacier to a point half-way up the face of Nelion; there they had spent the night before traversing under the upper wall of Nelion to reach the Diamond Glacier. We decided therefore to make our next attempt along the crest of this ridge.

Soon after we had pitched our tent, a short clearing of the mist showed us the way across the glacier to the foot of the ridge; so Wyn and I set off to reconnoitre it. We had no trouble in reaching its crest, from which we looked down a sheer precipice to the Darwin Glacier, visible only as a luminous whiteness far below. We climbed along the ridge, which was narrow and serrated, like the edge of a huge saw, until we came to a wide gap. Beyond this there was a smooth pinnacle, which we could neither climb nor pass on either side, and once more our hopes were shattered. It was nearly 6:00 and, as I had so often watched it from the farm, the mist shrouding the peaks began to dissolve. There was blue sky above us, and it seemed for a while as if we were standing on a rocky islet in the midst of a storm-tossed sea. Then the towering buttresses of Batian and Nelion appeared; the rays of the setting sun broke through and, in the east, sharply defined, a great circle of rainbow colours framed our own silhouettes. It was the only perfect Brocken Spectre I have ever seen.

Our morale was low when we emerged reluctantly from our tent the next morning to face the frozen dawn. Gustav remained behind while Wyn and I slouched across the glacier to the foot of the south-east face of Nelion. This now seemed to be our last hope, but in the cold, grey light it looked anything but promising. Wyn led up a gully slanting to the left; from the top of this we traversed along a horizontal terrace to the right, searching for a breach in the smooth wall above; but soon the terrace ended against a vertical rib, and it looked as though we had reached yet another impasse. Descending a little, Wyn disappeared below and around the obstructing rib while I belayed the rope and waited anxiously. Presently I heard a wild yell from around the corner, and braced myself to receive the jerk of Wyn's falling body. But instead came an excited shout: "All right, come on." When I reached him he was standing on a square platform below a steep cleft, perhaps fifty feet high, crowned by an overhanging rock. Down the cliff dangled a rope, white and threadbare with age. It could only have been left there by Mackinder's party, and it marked the breach in the lower part of the face. It was, of course, too frail to be used. I took over the lead, and after a brief struggle with the overhang succeeded in hoisting myself above it. After that, easy climbing took us to the point where the south ridge, which we had tried to climb the previous evening, abuts against the upper wall of Nelion. There, at 8:30 a.m., we stopped for a rest.

The sky was clear, the rock warming in the sun; gone was the despondency that had so lately oppressed us. We looked over a vast sea of cloud, a gently rising tide that would soon envelop us. To the south, a great dome of shining ice stood above the white billows. It looked so close that it was some moments before we realised that it was Kilimanjaro, nearly 250 miles away. We had reached the place where Mackinder's party had spent the night, before traversing across to the Diamond Glacier. It had been our intention to follow their route; but the steep slabs they had crossed below the bulging wall of Nelion were now plastered with ice and would have been extremely difficult to negotiate; so we decided to try for the summit of Nelion direct.

We climbed a chimney to a cleft behind a sharp pinnacle where Wyn wedged himself while I started up the wall. After climbing with difficulty for fifteen feet I found that the rock above was smooth and almost devoid of holds. A traverse to the left yielded no more success and I returned to the cleft. On my second attempt I edged my way along a narrow, sloping ledge which took me round a corner to the right. There, poised over a sheer drop, I came upon a shallow crack which split the wall above. It was not wide enough for me to wedge my foot, and the only holds were smooth and outward sloping, but it was clearly the only way. My movements were very slow, and at each upward step I expected to find further progress blocked. At last, sixty feet above the cleft, I reached a comfortable stance with a good belay. The pitch had taken more than an hour to accomplish. When I looked up my heart sank, for 200 feet above my stance, I saw a great overhang, which had been hidden from the ridge below but which now appeared to dominate the entire upper face of Nelion. I shouted the dismal news to Wyn, and suggested that I should return forthwith so as to waste no more of our precious time. But he insisted on coming up to join me, saying that it was now too late to try another route.

We climbed to a point directly beneath the overhang. From there, a wide gully ran steeply down to the right and plunged out of sight. We saw that, by climbing some way down it, we could cross to the buttress on the far side which formed our skyline in that direction. We knew that beyond it lay the vertical eastern face of Nelion, but there was no alternative. Wyn climbed 100 feet down the gully and then up the other side. The rope was stretched taut between us before he found a stance where I could join him. Then we mounted diagonally up to the crest of the buttress. As we reached it, I noticed that we were already above the lower part of the great overhang. Beyond the crest we had expected to be faced with a smooth, vertical cliff; to our astonishment we found ourselves on easy, broken rock. We could not see the summit, but it was obvious that we were already above the great eastern wall, and that there was now nothing to stop us. For the second time that day we experienced a dramatic reversal of fortune; this time, the certainty of success made it still more intoxicating. Only an easy scramble remained and we were there, on the hitherto untrodden summit of Nelion.

It was nearly noon. Though by then the peak was wrapped in cloud, we could just discern the rocky dome of Batian. After a short rest we started down the ridge towards the Gate of the Mist. Our first attempt to reach it failed, but by cutting steps down an icy slope above the north-east face, we turned an overhanging pinnacle and so gained the col. From there we climbed to the summit of Batian at 1:30 p.m. It was hard to believe that barely six days had elapsed since we had left Nairobi.

Climbing a peak for the first time or by an unknown route, particularly with no prior reconnaissance, the difficulties are greatly enhanced by the anxiety of finding the way, by not knowing where each step will lead or how far to press the attempt upon each doubtful section, and above all by the nagging time factor. Both Wyn and I were greatly impressed by the climb we had done and, standing on the summit of Batian with the cold, damp mist swirling about us, we were far from confident that we could find the way down before dark. But we need not have worried, for every step of the route had been so engraved on our memories that we were never at a loss. We avoided the crack by roping down the sixty-foot wall below the over-hang, and reached the foot of the peaks as the clouds were breaking in the evening light. Tired and utterly happy, we made our way across the glacier in the sunset glow.

Two days later Gustav persuaded us to repeat the ascent of the twin peaks with him. Neither of us wanted to do so, but we found it most rewarding. Free from all the anxieties which had previously beset us, we enjoyed the climb a great deal more; nor, with tension relaxed, did any of it seem particularly difficult. Afterwards we had one cloudless day, a rare occurrence on Mount Kenya, which we spent exploring the magnificent western side of Batian. Then the weather broke and we started down the mountain in a heavy snowstorm. The return march took us two days; it was sheer delight. We waited on the road below Chogoria for two days before a lorry belonging to a Dutch missionary came along and gave us a lift back to Nairobi.

Gustav and I were anxious to defray part of our expenses, which amounted to £15 each, by selling our story to the *East African Standard*. Wyn, who was drawing a princely salary of £30 a month, would have no part in this vulgar ostentation. Our modest, factual account was accepted by the editor, and we expected it to feature in a discreet column on an inside page, together, perhaps with one or two of our photographs. To our astonishment the newspaper appeared the next morning with almost its entire front page given over to the article under the banner headline, "New Conquest of the Twin Peaks of Mount Kenya," while the back page was filled with photographs we had taken. Though part of me was appalled by this gross inflation of our achievement, another less articulate part was flattered by its recognition. For our pains, Gustav and I received the sum of £2 10s. between us.

After the First World War, partly stimulated by such undertakings as the Ex-Soldier Settlement Scheme, there was a great influx of European settlers into Kenya. The development of motor transport now made proximity to the railway less important than before, and remote areas, such as Uasin Gishu and Trans-Nzoia, originally earmarked for immigrant settlement but hitherto largely unoccupied, became practicable for farming. Unhappily, but understandably, the "new" colony attracted a fair number of undesirable citizens, misfits, remittance men, alcoholics and the like, who took advantage of the freedom from normal restraints to indulge in wild excesses. One such group established the notorious community known as "The Happy Valley" near Gilgil; their chief preoccupation seems to have been a free interchange of spouses. Before long Kenya acquired such a tarnished reputation that it became a music-hall joke. In reality, these people formed a very small minority, and most of the settlers were decent, hard-working folk, bent upon building a home and livelihood in a country they had grown to love. They were by no means all British; people of many nationalities were there, and all, even our late enemies the Germans, had an equal chance to prosper—or become bankrupt. The most bigoted liberal can hardly deny that the settlers played a major part in the development of the country, in the alleviation of poverty and in laying the foundations of a prosperity such as the region had never known. By their efforts and their example, bush and savannah were transformed into productive fields, and worthless, disease-ridden herds replaced by grade beef and dairy cattle. They also provided employment not only for unskilled labour but also for masons, carpenters and mechanics, mostly trained in mission schools.

In April 1929, I left Nyeri and went to Uasin Gishu, near the borders of Uganda, to work with Gustav on a large farm. After the prosperity I had seen on the old-established farms down-country, my new environment presented a sorry spectacle. The post-war boom in flax had encouraged many farmers to grow it and to install the necessary machinery; the price had collapsed, leaving them burdened with mortgages often far in excess of the value of their land. Others had planted coffee which, with rare exceptions, failed to flourish in the district. In 1928 an invasion of locusts, the first within living memory, had caused widespread devastation among the crops and plantations. On top of all this came the Great World Slump, which rocked the economy of every country and reduced the price of most primary commodities to a level below the cost of production. As a result, much of the land was left uncultivated, and the farmers lived from hand to mouth hoping for better times. Some of them undertook road-building contracts, others obtained temporary employment as locust control officers.

Gustav and I, working for a company, each drew a salary of £15 a month. On this, sharing a barely furnished, one-roomed bungalow and living frugally (many of our needs were produced on the farm), we were able to run a decrepit old station waggon and to travel at week-ends over a range of fifty miles. The country within our compass was wild and varied, and included a magnificent section of the Rift Valley and the great forests of Mount Elgon, teeming with game. We soon had a widely scattered circle of friends, for people living in these remote places were generally glad to see strangers, and we always met with warm hospitality. I greatly enjoyed my dealings with the Africans, particularly the Nandi, a pastoral tribe like the Masai and sharing their virtues of courage and openhearted gaiety. Altogether it was an agreeable life, and though our prospects of reasonable prosperity seemed very remote, we shared the general hope that things might improve.

From time to time I took a fortnight's holiday. By driving hard I could reach Mount Kenya from Uasin Gishu in a day and a half; and I longed to return to the peak to explore some of the many ridges and faces which as yet had never been attempted. I now realise how lucky I was to have had this extraordinary peak virtually to myself; a situation which would be the dream of any modern climber. My problem was to find someone to climb with, since Wyn had been posted to a place on the shores of Lake Rudolf, so remote that it was impossible for him to take local leave. In December 1929 I visited the mountain with Pat Russell, a young lawyer practising in Eldoret. He had never climbed before, but was willing to try. This time we approached the peaks from the north-west. On reaching the head of the Mackinder Valley I had an attack of malaria. The disease was then prevalent in Uasin Gishu, and I often suffered from it. Luckily, mine was the least dangerous form known as *benign tertiary*, though when half delirious with a high fever I was unable to appreciate its benignity. When I had recovered little of our time was left, so, as Pat was very anxious to climb the peak, I abandoned my plan to reconnoitre the western side of Batian and took him up our old route.

A brief notice of this climb, furnished by a local reporter, appeared in the *East African Standard*. As a result, shortly afterwards I received a letter from a stranger who farmed in Sotik, saying that when he was last in England he had done some rock-climbing in the Lake District with a guide, and asking me to advise him how to set about climbing in Kenya. His name was H. W. Tilman. This was the start of a long and fruitful partnership in many mountain ranges. Our first undertaking together was the ascent of Kilimanjaro, which, despite the fact that the mountain is little short of 20,000 feet high, is nothing but a long and, in the conditions we encountered, somewhat gruelling walk. We also climbed Mawenzi, a smaller peak on the same mountain, which was rather more difficult. I soon realised that my new companion (it was many years before I called him "Bill"), though having virtually no mountaineering experience, was ideally suited to the game. I asked him to join me six months later in an attempt to make a complete traverse of the twin peaks of Mount Kenya by climbing the western ridge of Batian and descending by our old route, a project I had cherished ever since I had first seen that glorious ridge.

I decided again to approach the mountain from the north-west. This route had the advantage that pack-ponies could be hired from a white hunter, Raymond Hook, in Nanyuki, and as these could be sent back from our base camp, it was a great deal cheaper than employing porters. The forest was less spectacular than on the Chogoria side, but the journey through the various zones of vegetation was very beautiful, and in the comparatively open country on the lower slopes we saw many wild animals, including elephant and rhinoceros. The forest, too, was full of strange creatures. One of these was the honey-bird, which flitted from branch to branch, singing loudly, evidently trying to attract our attention. According to the Wanderobo, a tribe of forest dwellers who live by hunting, these birds make a practice of leading them to beehives, expecting to be left a share of the booty once the bees have been smoked out. Unfortunately we had no time to make the experiment.

Reaching the head of the Mackinder Valley on July 29, 1930, we found a comfortable cave which served admirably as a base camp. Though 14,000 feet above sea-level, there was some giant groundsel near by which provided us with the luxury of fires. We spent the following day climbing two sharp granite pinnacles, partly for training and acclimatisation, partly because they both afforded fine views of the northern aspect of the main peaks. Few mountains have such a superb array of ridges and faces. From the summit of Batian a sharp, serrated crest runs northward for some distance before dividing into two main ridges, one plunging steeply to the north-east, the other descending westward in a series of huge steps to a col dividing Batian from a massive peak known as Point Piggot. This was the ridge that we hoped to climb. The largest of the steps appeared to be some 500 feet high and vertical; I called it the Grand Gendarme, a name it still bears. Below was the Petit Gendarme, a pinnacle standing above the col at the foot of the ridge. The west ridge was obviously a formidable proposition; certainly not the place to take a novice for his first serious mountaineering exploit, and it was stupid of me even to think of doing so. I was aware of my responsibility, but for a while I fooled myself with the thought that we might at least "have a look at it." So early the next day we set out for the col at the foot of the ridge. Most of the morning was occupied cutting steps up a steep little glacier, across a bergschrund and on up a gully filled with ice. We would have been saved a great deal of trouble if we had had crampons, but as I had hardly ever used them, I did not regret the lack. Reaching the col, we sat with our legs dangling over the Tyndall Glacier, several hundred feet below. Across the chasm was the great west face of Batian, so close that we might have been suspended from a balloon before its ice-scarred ramparts and hanging glaciers. The upper part of the mountain was in cloud, and we could see little of the west ridge; but this was daunting enough. The Petit Gendarme, towering above us in the swirling mist, looked impregnable. The only way to out-flank it was by climbing diagonally up a very steep slope of snow or ice to the right. Snow or ice? It was a matter of considerable importance, for if it were ice the step-cutting involved would take the best part of a day and, with no protection, a slip would have been impossible to check. Again, no place to take a novice, even one of Bill's calibre. Above and beyond, we could see the vertical flanks of the Grand Gendarme thrusting up into the mist.

I returned to camp in a state of some mental conflict, in which prudence fought a losing battle. Happily for Bill, he had no such doubts; for him the issue was simple: we had come to climb the ridge and, if it were possible, climb it we would. As always, he started preparing breakfast long before the time we had planned to do so. At 3:00 we emerged from our warm cave into the frozen silence of a moonlit night. I was too numbed with sleep to heed its beauty. I remembered that it was August 1, my twenty-third birthday, and wondered vaguely what it would bring. When we reached the small glacier we kindled a candle lantern to supplement the light of the moon, roped up and, at last fully awake, began to climb rapidly. Our steps of the previous day were still large and comfortable, so hours of toil now sped beneath us with an effortless rhythm as we climbed towards the dawn. It was getting light when we crossed the bergschrund, and we reached the col with the whole day before us. And what a day! Crisp, sparkling, intoxicating. The western face of Batian caught the reflected light of the newly risen sun, and every detail of ice fretwork and powerful granite column showed hard and clear.

The west ridge, towering above us, looked no less formidable, but we paused barely a minute before traversing to the long slope below the Petit Gendarme. It turned out to be composed of ice covered by a layer, not more than an inch or two thick, of frozen snow. It was very steep and its lower edge hung over a sheer drop to the Tyndall Glacier. It was possible, by kicking toe-holds in the snow and by using the blade of the ice-axe for additional support, to climb diagonally up the slope without cutting steps. Moving one at a time, I felt reasonably confident that, should Bill slip, I could hold him; but since I was in the lead, he could not possibly have held me. The slope was in shadow and would remain so for several hours, but once the sun had reached it the thin layer of snow would melt and no longer afford any purchase. It would perhaps have been more prudent to cut steps into the ice beneath, particularly as we would most probably fail to reach the summit, and so be forced to retreat; but this would have taken far too long. In any case I was fairly sure that we could rope down from the Petit Gendarme to the col, thus avoiding the slope on our descent. So I decided to adopt the quicker method.

Even so, it was slow work, particularly as, in several places near small rock outcrops, the layer of snow was lacking and I was forced to cut steps in the blue ice; so it took us some hours to gain the crest of the ridge behind the Petit Gendarme, where we halted for five minutes to eat some chocolate. By then the mountain was wrapped in cloud, which reduced visibility to a hundred yards or so. For a short distance the ridge was broad and gently inclined, but this section ended abruptly under the Grand Gendarme, which towered above us, smooth and vertical for hundreds of feet, its top hidden by mist. It was clearly impossible for us to climb it direct, and our only chance was to find a way of turning it on the left. So we traversed out on to the north face and presently came to a deep gully which led directly upwards. Pitch by pitch we clambered up its dark recess, never able to see far above us, always expecting to be stopped by an impossible overhang. But after an hour and a half we suddenly emerged on the crest of the ridge above the Grand Gendarme. This was a wonderful surprise, and for the first time I began to believe that we might succeed.

When I looked at the next obstacle, however, my optimism dissolved. This was a step, reddish in colour, 130 feet high, extremely steep and under-cut at its base. This time there was no way of turning it: to the right was a giddy drop to the hanging glaciers of the west face; to the left the scoop at the base of the step continued as a groove, running obliquely downwards across the north face, overhung by a continuous line of ice-polished slabs. By standing on Bill's shoulders I could just reach two finger-holds; hanging on these, with a final kick off my companion's head, I managed to hoist myself up to grasp a hold higher up, and also to find some purchase with my feet to relieve the strain on my arms. The wall above the scoop was nearly vertical, and the holds were only just large enough for a boot nail; but, though few, they were well spaced and the rock was sound. Half-way up, however, there was a very awkward section, involving a long stride from one nail-hold to another, with only the roughness of the surface for my fingers to maintain my changing centre of balance. I contemplated the stride for a long time before cautiously swinging my right foot to the upper hold. But it felt so precarious that I hastily withdrew it. After repeating this faint-hearted manoeuvre several times, prompted by my increasing distaste for the position of my left foot, which was becoming painful, I gradually transferred my weight to my right foot which, to my relief, did not slip, and by clawing at the rock face, I managed to hoist myself up.

After this the holds, though small, became more plentiful. By now, however, there was a new source of anxiety: I realized that the rope was not long enough to allow me to reach the top of the step. It was no use Bill unroping, for he could not possibly climb the initial overhang without it. Luckily there was a little recess some fifteen feet below the top which I just managed to reach as the rope came taut. In this I could wedge myself firmly enough to support his full weight. I hauled up the ice-axes and our small rucksack and sent the end of the rope down again. For all my pulling, Bill had a tremendous struggle to surmount the scoop. When he had succeeded I climbed quickly to the top of the step, and the rest was easy.

After that I was infused with a pleasant sense of abandon. Our rope was not long enough for us to abseil down the red step, and the idea of climbing down it without support from above was not to be contemplated; therefore we just *had* to reach the summit. Time was my chief concern. The steps that followed were much easier than the first, and they became progressively smaller until we reached the junction of the north-east and the west ridges. Eagerly we turned towards the south to discover what was in store; but the mist had thickened, and all we could see was some fifty yards of the narrow arête. We clambered along it; sometimes we could balance on the top, sometimes we had to crawl astride it, sometimes we swung along with our hands on the ridge and our feet on ledges below. It was a thrilling situation: thrust up infinitely high, isolated by the mist from all save the slender granite crest along which we *must* find a way. Somewhere in the grey depths to the left was the great rock bulge which had foiled my first attempt to climb the peak. The white glow below our feet to the right was the upper hanging-glacier of the west face.

Presently we were confronted by a gap in the ridge, thirty feet deep; we roped down into it without hesitation, for, our boats having already been burnt, there was nothing to be lost by cutting off our retreat still further. One after another pinnacles loomed into view, greatly magnified by the mist; one after the other we set about the problem presented by each new obstacle, always hoping that it would be the last. I lost count of time; the ridge seemed to go on forever, but at least we were going with it; surely nothing could stop us now. At last, in place of the sharp spire we had come to expect, a huge, dark-grey mass appeared before us and my last doubts vanished. A few steps cut in an icy gully, a breathless scramble up easy rock and we were standing beside the little cairn which I had helped to build on the summit of Batian.

It was 4:30 p.m. There was no chance of getting down before dark, but I was much too happy to be bothered about that. Needless to say, much of my joy stemmed from sheer relief; for, since climbing the red step, failure to reach the summit would have placed us in an ugly situation, and the issue had remained in doubt till the last few minutes. Bill had been magnificent; he had shown no sign of anxiety throughout the climb, and his stoicism no less than his innate skill in climbing and handling the rope made a vital contribution to our success.

The rocks on the southern side of Batian were plastered with snow, which delayed us; but conditions improved between the Gate of the Mist and the top of Nelion, which we crossed without a pause and hurried down the gully beyond. There Bill slipped and came on the rope, dropping his ice-axe, which vanished out of sight in a single bound. This near-accident checked our haste. Dusk was falling when we reached the top of the sixty-foot wall above the head of the south ridge, and it was almost dark by the time we had completed the abseil down it. At this point I was sick, whether because of nervous excitement or something I had eaten during our hurried meal on the summit, I do not know.

The clouds had not cleared at dusk in their usual manner, and it looked as though we would have to remain where we were until morning. Later, however, breaks appeared in the mist and the moon came out, providing sufficient light for us to climb slowly down. I felt tired but pleasantly relaxed; the moonlight, the phantom shapes of ridge and pinnacle, interlaced with wisps of silvered mist, the radiant expanse of the Lewis Glacier plunging into the soundless depths below induced a sense of exquisite fantasy. I experienced that strange illusion, not uncommon in such circumstances, that there was an additional member of the party—three of us instead of two. Having been over the route, up or down, six times before, I remembered every step of the way, and dropping from ledge to ledge required little effort. We took a long time negotiating Mackinder's chimney; but that was the last of our troubles, except the long, weary plod across the saddle at the head of the Lewis Glacier, back to our cave.

The traverse of the twin peaks of Mount Kenya was probably the hardest climb I have ever done; though no doubt the cumulative difficulty was greatly exaggerated in my mind by the fact that the ascent of the west ridge was all over virgin ground. Certainly we were ill-equipped by modern standards; crampons, for example, and above all, a length of abseil line would have added greatly to our security.

We spent another six days based on the cave, and did several more climbs. The last of these provided an adventure which came unpleasantly near to disaster. It was up a beautifully symmetrical spire standing above the lower end of the Lewis Glacier, several hours' march from our base camp. Though we started early, the clouds had already enveloped the mountain when we reached it; but as this was almost a daily occurrence, we attached no significance to it and started to tackle the peak. The climbing was difficult, but the rock was sound and dry, and it was most enjoyable. Two-thirds of the way up we climbed into a sort of cave; its only exit was by way of a narrow, slightly sloping ledge jutting above a massive overhang. Though there was no handhold above, it was not unduly difficult to stand on the ledge and shuffle along it. It was only three yards long and led to a comfortable platform at the foot of a steep, narrow gully. From the top of this, easier climbing led to the summit of the peak.

We were sitting there, relaxed and content, when suddenly it started to snow heavily. This put an abrupt end to our complacency, for we realised that the difficult climbing we had enjoyed on the way up would be anything but pleasant on the way down, with the holds covered in fresh snow. We started down as fast as we could. The rock was still fairly dry when we reached the top of the narrow gully, though the snow was beginning to settle. There was a large rock bollard round which I hitched the rope while Bill climbed down the gully and disappeared. The rope went out for a while then stopped, and I guessed that he had reached the foot of the gully and was starting to cross the sloping ledge which would now be wet. Suddenly there was a violent jerk and the rope stretched down the gully, taut as a violin string. I waited for a moment, expecting to be told whether to hold fast or lower away, but there was silence. I shouted, but got no reply; so I assumed that Bill was dangling unconscious. I tried to haul him up, but the friction of the rope against the rock, added to his weight, made this impossible. Perhaps the best thing would have been to make the rope fast and climb down to investigate the situation; but it is not wise to leave an unconscious man dangling, as he could suffocate in a short time; so I began to lower away, hoping that he would come to rest on a ledge within the thirty feet of slack which still remained. Foot by foot I allowed the rope to slip round the bollard until there was none left, and still there was no easing of the weight below. I should, of course, have taken the strain from my shoulder in the first place; but I realised that too late; and now there was nothing for me to do but to remove the rope from around the bollard and start climbing down with it dragging from my waist. Now the friction of the rope against the rock helped me by acting as a brake on the downward movement. On the other hand, whenever I bent my hips or knees I could not straighten them again except by stepping down, and I had to plan each movement very carefully. Luckily the gully was narrow enough for me to brace my arms against the walls, which alone enabled me to retain my balance. By now the rocks were deep in snow.

I had not gone far when suddenly the strain lifted. Hurrying down to the platform below the gully, I fastened the rope to a spike of rock and looked over the edge. Bill was sitting on a ledge about fifty feet below looking up at me. He appeared dazed, but he answered my questions with his usual calm and seemed to be unhurt. I discovered later that he was still only half conscious and had no idea where he was. I asked if he could see a way down from where he was sitting, and he replied quite firmly that he could. So I abseiled down to join him. To my dismay I found that his ledge was, in fact, quite isolated, with no way of climbing from it in any direction, and that the next ledge below was beyond the range of our rope. There was nothing for it but to swarm back up the doubled rope by which I had abseiled. Luckily the wall was not deeply undercut and I found sufficient purchase for my feet to relieve the strain on my arms; even so, I had a desperate struggle to regain the platform. I then knotted the doubled rope round the rock spike, and hauled on the half which was tied to Bill's waist, while he swarmed up the other. In this way he managed to join me, a remarkable achievement in his condition.

We still had to cross the sloping ledge which was now covered by a thick layer of snow. I did not fancy shuffling along it as we had done when it was dry; instead, I placed one foot as far out as I could reach and with a combination of a spring and a dive I leapt forward and landed, sprawling, on the lip of the cave beyond. Bill followed in the same way, and the worst of our troubles were over. It was only then that I realised that he was suffering from concussion, for he was unable to remember the accident or any of the events which followed it. Only after we had reached the cave did his mind begin to clear.

By then the rocks were deeply covered with snow, and we could only proceed down by a series of abseils. For each we had to cut off a yard or two of rope to make a sling, so that by the time we reached the base of the peak, our original 120-foot length was reduced to some forty feet. It was still snowing steadily as we trudged slowly up the Lewis Glacier once more to cross the saddle at its head. It was dark when we reached our camp; I have seldom been so glad to arrive anywhere.

Our next expedition together, in January 1932, was to Ruwenzori, where we made the third ascent of the highest peaks. The range had been discovered by Stanley only forty-four years before. Though most of its secrets had since been revealed, notably by expeditions led by the Duke of the Abruzzi in 1906 and by Noel Humphreys in the late 1920s, it was still rarely visited. Due to heavy precipitation and almost perpetual cloud-cover, the upper valleys are filled with a mass of vegetation so dense that it is often difficult to penetrate. Though much of the flora is unique, the dominant species are giant groundsel and lobelia, which grow there in thick forests; their fallen trunks, soft and pulpy, form an exasperating barrier to progress. Moss grows everywhere, deep and emerald, massive curtains, tunnels of it; often the very air appears tinged with green. The streams are hushed and a strange silence prevails. It is a world of fantasy, where nothing seems quite real.

| 4 |

HIMALAYAN HEY-DAY

EARLY IN 1931 THREE OF my neighbours, returning from an unsuccessful prospecting trip in Tanganyika, found a rich deposit of gold in a stream-bed in Kakamega, not forty miles from where we lived. They told me in confidence of their discovery and asked me to join them as a working partner. To be in the very forefront of a gold rush is not an opportunity one would normally reject; but it happened that, a few weeks before, I had received an invitation from Frank Smythe to take part in an attempt to climb Kamet which he was planning to make that summer, and I was far too dazzled by the glitter of the Himalaya to be much tempted by the lure of gold. It was a shortsighted choice, no doubt, but not one that I have greatly regretted, despite the fact that my would-be partners made a good deal of money, not so much by the gold they extracted as by the judicious sale of their claims at the height of the ensuing scramble.

In common, I suppose, with most young climbers, I had nursed a passionate longing to visit the Himalaya, but with no real hope that it would ever be satisfied; so Smythe's invitation seemed like the realisation of an impossible daydream. But I was even more fortunate than I knew in the timing of my introduction, for Himalayan mountaineering was then barely beyond its infancy; it was in a state analogous to the early years of the Golden Age in the Alps, when the simple mountain explorer, with no special ability, was still free to pick the plums in a random harvest of delight.

The few pioneers of the late nineteenth and early twentieth centuries were mainly concerned with unravelling the secrets of the huge unexplored ranges, and their fine achievements in this fascinating task did much to smooth the path of their successors in the 1920s and 1930s. They also probed the defences of some of the giants and scaled a handful of smaller peaks. Until 1930, the highest summit to have been reached was Trisul (23,600 feet), climbed by Longstaff in 1907. Meanwhile the Survey of India had mapped most of the inhabited valleys of the Himalaya, and plotted and measured the principal peaks of each region; most of these were indentified only by numbers in triangulation pamphlets, and there were thousands more unmeasured. The second phase of Himalayan mountaineering began with the Everest Expeditions of the 1920s, which made the first thrusts into the unknown realms of extreme altitude. Conducted on a grand scale and quasi-military lines, they set a new fashion in mountaineering enterprise, and focused attention upon the "conquest" of the highest peaks. This led to a popular misconception of the problems and difficulties of Himalayan travel and did much to obscure its vast potential.

Kamet proved a gentle and wholly delightful initiation. By the standards of the day the expedition was considered small and modestly equipped; nevertheless, I doubt if de Saussure travelled in greater comfort. Eight Sherpas, brought from Darjeeling, saw to all our needs, acting as valets to look after our personal belongings, rousing us in the mornings with mugs of tea, pitching and striking our camps and even removing our boots. We had a cook, and meals were served in a mess-tent. We ate a certain amount of local produce, but for the most part we were provisioned from a large and varied stock of tinned delicacies. Apart from Bill Birnie, who had the job of organising our transport with the help of two Gurkah N.C.O.s, we had nothing to do but saunter along the well-made paths through the lovely foothills of Garhwal, enjoying the woods of oak and pine and the flower-starred valleys of that most Alpine of Himalayan districts.

The atmosphere in the party was pleasantly relaxed, as though we were engaged in a tranquil holiday trek, with no sense whatever of rivalry. At twenty-three I was far younger than my five companions, all in their thirties, and I have little doubt that they found me brash and naïve; but they were very tolerant. For my part, I revelled in their, as I thought, highly sophisticated conversation, and was greatly impressed by the width and variety of their acquaintance. I particularly enjoyed Raymond Greene's friendly irony and his gift as a raconteur, evidently a joint heritage with his brother Graham.

Frank Smythe was the most distinguished British climber of that period. He had climbed extensively in the Alps, both in summer and winter, and his two great routes on the Brenva Face of Mont Blanc were already regarded as classics. The previous year he had been a member of a mammoth international expedition to Kangchenjunga. He was by no means robust, and certainly not athletically built; indeed, to a casual observer he seemed physically inept. As a mountaineer he was sound rather than brilliant, and he owed his outstanding success to his remarkable endurance. In adverse conditions he seemed to have a fakir-like ability to shut himself in a mental cocoon, where he was impervious to fatigue or boredom, discomfort or psychological stress, and thus emerged with his resources quite unstrained. Later, on Everest, this extraordinary gift was most conspicuous. In ordinary life he was notably absent-minded. I remember an occasion, after a formal dinner-party, when he sauntered out of the dining-room with the ladies, and sat in the drawing-room for quarter of an hour, chatting to his embarrassed hostess, before noticing his gaffe. His air of vagueness belied his undoubted business acumen. He was an agreeable companion, even-tempered and tolerant, but not a stimulating one, for he lacked originality, and tended to talk and think in clichés. But, though his prolific writing also suffered from this defect, which caused some of his critics to accuse him of sham sentiment, his great reputation as a mountaineer was fully deserved.

Ten leisurely marches through the foothills took us across the Kuari Pass, which commanded a thrilling view of countless peaks of the Central Himalaya, several score more than 20,000 feet high, few of them named and all—*all*—unclimbed; and this in perhaps the most easily accessible part of the entire range. In another week, after passing through some spectacular gorges, the country becoming ever more desolate as we approached the

Tibetan border, we reached the Raikana Glacier, where, at 15,500 feet, we pitched our base camp.

Kamet (25,447 feet) had previously been reconnoitred and attempted no fewer than ten times; then more than any other mountain in the Himalaya. A straightforward route had been discovered up its eastern side, and two parties (Meade and his Alpine guide, Pierre Blanc, in 1913; Kellas and Morshead in 1920) had climbed to within 2000 feet of the summit. Thus, faced by few unknown factors, our task was one of logistical planning and steady persistence rather than climbing skill. The only serious mountaineering problem was a 1000-foot wall between 21,000 and 22,000 feet, and even this was not unduly exacting. Much had been said beforehand about our intention to employ "siege tactics" and to acclimatize ourselves thoroughly at various altitudes; but in fact it took us only a fortnight to reach the summit from the base camp. It was fortunate that we did not pursue our original policy, for the first storms of the monsoon broke a few days later. Of course we suffered a good deal from altitude, particularly on the final climb; and although that day was fine and windless, Lewa, one of the Sherpas, who went with us to the summit, had his feet so severely frostbitten that he lost all his toes.

Though, given reasonable luck with the weather, the outcome of our venture had been almost a foregone conclusion, we were none the less delighted to reach the summit of the first 25,000-foot mountain ever to be climbed. But by far the most enjoyable part of the expedition was the month that followed. First we made our way westward to the holy Hindu shrine of Badrinath. On the way I made my first acquaintance with the true splendour of Himalayan flora, which was to become a constant delight on later journeys. This was in the Bhyundar Valley, which had been visited only three or four times by earlier travellers. Crossing a pass from a barren region heightened the impact as we entered this remote coombe, encircled by lofty peaks, and walked for mile after mile through a dazzling profusion of primulas, irises, forget-me-nots, potentillas, dwarf rhododendrons, geraniums and blue poppies. From Badrinath we went northward beyond the range of the monsoon, and spent several glorious weeks in an unexplored area near the Tibetan border, crossing passes and climbing many peaks. Finally, we travelled down the Pilgrim Route and so returned to Ranikhet after nearly three months in the mountains.

I was not by nature an optimist, and despite much evidence of a kindly Providence, I never expected opportunities to occur. My scholastic failures had left me with a profound sense of inadequacy which my climbing successes did strangely little to dispel; this was because I still thought of my passion for mountains as highly eccentric, having no relevance to life. Certainly at that time my ambitions were set at a very modest level, circumscribed by a frugal, if pleasant, farming existence. I regarded the Kamet Expedition as a bright flash in the pan, a once-in-a-lifetime experience never likely to recur. But only a year later, in the autumn of 1932, there dawned a still more dazzling prospect: the Tibetan Government agreed to allow another attempt to be made to climb Mount Everest, and I received a cable inviting me to join the new expedition then being organised under the leadership of Hugh Ruttledge.

But the cable added a sinister proviso, "subject to medical approval." I had often been aware of an irregular heart-beat which had led me to suspect that something was amiss, though, like Darwin before he joined the *Beagle*, I was much too scared to have it examined. Now, however, I decided to go to a local doctor, hoping that he might be more easily persuaded to overlook the defect than one appointed by the Everest Committee. Under his stethoscope, however, my heart performed a wildly erratic syncopation; the doctor's worried frown seemed to confirm my fears, and I fainted. He said nothing to reassure me and declined to sign a certificate of physical fitness, though I got him to agree not to divulge his opinion; for I hoped somehow to evade further examination. After all, whatever the condition of my heart, I had reached 25,000 feet the year before and, more recently, had survived a strenuous expedition to Ruwenzori. When I arrived in England, however, I was appalled to learn that all members of the Everest party were required to undergo the R.A.F. medical test, then regarded as the most searching of all. Panic-stricken, I divulged my dread secret to my mother's doctor, who, to my intense relief, told me that my irregular heart-beat was due to dyspeptic flatulence, and signified nothing. Armed with this assurance, I faced the R.A.F. inquisitors in high spirits until they discovered an enlarged spleen due to malaria. Having denied that I had ever suffered a day's illness, this was a little difficult to explain; however, it was evidently not regarded as a hindrance to climbing Everest.

Though for some years the role I was lucky enough to play in the attempts to climb Everest from the north had an important bearing on my life, the story has been told too often to be repeated here. The journeys through Tibet were certainly the most enjoyable parts of those expeditions, and I am profoundly grateful to have seen something of that fabled land, to have known its charming people and their curious medieval culture before they were engulfed in the drab uniformity of Chinese Communism. In 1933 we took six weeks to reach the base camp; first marching across the snow-bound passes to Phari, then westward over a section of the vast plateau which stretches 1,500 miles along the northern flanks of the Himalaya and 800 miles across to the Tarim Basin in Chinese Turkestan: a million square miles of mountains, almost unknown to Western travellers! At a comfort-able speed of fifteen miles a day we rode through this world of wide hori-zons and ice-blue skies, always in sight of the great peaks, following valleys through the russet hills and along frozen rivers, the winter homes of huge numbers of wildfowl. At Kampa, Tengkye and Shekar, where we stopped for several days to collect fresh transport, we visited the *Dzongs* and *Gompas* and admired their austere design blending with the stark landscape.

In violent contrast to the simplicity of this ancient land came our mas-sive caravan of 350 pack animals carrying all the civilised amenities thought necessary for our welfare. Among the more unlikely items of equipment was a set of boxing gloves used for the promotion of bouts between vari-ous members of our retinue. Whether for the entertainment of ourselves or the Tibetans, these compared poorly with the displays of devil dancing and mounted archery staged by our hosts. Our cumbersome mode of travel separated us from intimate contact with the country, but, oblivious of this, we revelled in our strange surroundings and in the prospect of our great adventure. Not for a moment did we doubt its successful outcome. From Shekar we turned south and, with mounting excitement, entered the deso-late wilderness of the Rongbuk Valley.

The actual attempt on Everest from the base camp upwards was mostly a grim and joyless business. This was chiefly because of persistent physi-cal infirmity, varying between a feeling of mild ill-being and acute nausea, headache or exhaustion according to the altitude and our individual reactions to it. From the start nearly all of us suffered from coughs and colds, chest troubles and chronic sore throats, caused by the dust-laden winds of Tibet and perpetuated by the dry, freezing air and oxygen-lack. Food, despite lavish catering, was rarely enjoyable and often repulsive, and I doubt if we ever ate enough. Nor was our appetite for physical exertion much more robust, though this did not seem to make the long spells of enforced inactivity any less irksome. For we spent a very large proportion of our time in our sleeping bags, waiting for supplies to be carried up the glacier, waiting for the weather to clear, waiting for our red blood corpuscles to multiply; moreover, our working days were short, and it was generally too cold to sit around outside. I sometimes thought that bed-sores were a more serious hazard than frost-bite or strained hearts. These conditions were conducive to hypochondria, and they were, I think, largely responsible for some spectacular outbursts of ill-temper, for which we used to blame the altitude.

On our first sortie up the East Rongbuk Glacier we were inspired by the feeling of treading historic ground and by the strangeness and beauty of the forest of ice pinnacles; but with frequent repetition of the route to Camp 3, which held no vestige of difficulty, the effect of this stimulant was soon dulled. The North Col gave us a good deal of trouble, not by its technical difficulties but because a series of heavy windstorms again and again destroyed our work; and when, after two weeks of intermittent toil, we had fashioned a staircase up its icy slopes and fixed ropes over the steeper sections we felt the first satisfaction of solid achievement.

We varied a great deal in our adaptability to altitude, and upon this physiological characteristic, not upon mountaineering skill, depended the selection of the "assault pairs." Thus Frank Smythe and I, who acclimatised quickly and had the great advantage of having climbed above 25,000 feet before, were the first to be selected for a summit attempt. On the other hand, Jack Longland, probably the most competent climber among us, was consigned to a supporting role.

"High-altitude deterioration," a kind of creeping paralysis of our limbs and faculties, was by far the most unpleasant manifestation of life above the North Col. It was like a wasting disease, causing rapid degeneration of our muscles and progressive weakness and lethargy. It was a very disagreeable feeling and also rather alarming, for it made us increasingly doubtful of our ability to deal with an emergency or to judge how close we were to collapse. As with acclimatisation, we varied a great deal in the speed of our physical decline: Frank, for example, suffered less than most of us in this respect, and when he and I reached Camp 6 (27,400 feet) the disparity in our performance was already very marked. Nevertheless, when we returned to the base camp we were all extremely emaciated, and I have little doubt that this was one of the main causes of our failure to reach the top. In 1933 some of us spent nineteen consecutive days at or above 23,000 feet. When in 1938 Frank and I again camped above 27,000 feet, after only four days on and above the North Col, we were both far stronger than before, despite the fact that we had struggled through appalling snow conditions to get there.

Physiologists now tell us that the deterioration we suffered was largely due to dehydration resulting from excessive loss of moisture from the lungs, which in turn was due to continuous panting in the unusually dry atmosphere. In other words, if only we had drunk a great deal more than we did we would have maintained our strength. Certainly I remember being perpetually thirsty at high altitudes, but we were discouraged from drinking by the tiresome business of collecting and melting sufficient snow; and, of course, the weaker we became, the more we tended to neglect this chore. It is tantalising to reflect that, had we but known it, we had such a simple remedy to hand.

When we set out in 1933 none of us had any doubt that we would reach the summit, and we blamed our failure entirely upon the weather: the series of apparently unseasonable storms which frustrated our first attempts to establish the high camps, and the early arrival of the monsoon at the end of May. But in 1936 and 1938 we fared even worse; in both these years monsoon conditions were fully established at the beginning of May, which gave us no chance whatever of climbing the difficult rocks on the upper 1500 feet of the mountain. Subsequent experience of the mountain has shown that we were indeed unlucky to have struck a cycle of exceptionally early monsoons in the 1930s, which have never been encountered by any of the many post-war expeditions to Everest.

Yet the interesting question remains: even if we had met with favourable conditions on any of our pre-war attempts, could we have reached the summit without oxygen? The physiologists say "No." There is obviously an altitude limit of human survival without breathing apparatus, and it is argued that the fact that several parties turned back from about the same point, 900 feet below the top, is evidence that they had reached this limit. But, without exception, all those who climbed to that point were convinced that the summit could have been attained without oxygen if the snow and weather conditions had been good. Certainly it is hard to believe that the limit can be set within so narrow a margin: in the first place, the barometric pressure near the summit of Everest varies by the equivalent of a great deal more than 900 feet; secondly, there is plenty of evidence that people differ widely in their tolerance of oxygen-lack; thirdly, if deterioration can be substantially reduced by drinking more this would surely improve the climber's ultimate performance. I myself have little doubt that one day the physiologists will be proved wrong, just as they were in 1922 when climbers pierced the previous theoretical limit of human survival without oxygen by several thousand feet.

The pundits tell us that anyone climbing to these extreme altitudes without oxygen runs a serious risk of sustaining permanent damage to his brain cells. This may be so, but at the same time it should be remembered that some two dozen men, climbers and Sherpas, have gone above 27,000 feet without oxygen, some spending several nights there, and that, with one exception, none of them appears to have suffered any lasting ill effect from the experience. The exception was Pasang, who developed a cerebral thrombosis on the North Col a few days after carrying to our high camp in 1938.

The fact that we did not use oxygen on the attempts in the 1930s was due, in some measure, to prejudice; the rather irrational feeling that it was "not fair." Certainly Norton's achievement in reaching a height of 28,150 feet, despite the extreme exhaustion incurred by his earlier labours, gave us good reason to suppose that we could manage without it. But the main reason was our lack of faith in the heavy, cumbersome oxygen apparatus provided, and our fear of the consequences of its failure, which could well have been fatal. The fact that Mallory and Irvine had been using similar apparatus when they perished did not inspire confidence. It is interesting to speculate upon how we would have fared if we had had the oxygen equipment used by the successful 1953 expedition. When Wyn Harris and Wager made their attempt on May 30, 1933, conditions were by no means impossible, and I believe that, with such equipment, they would have broken through the couloir early enough to climb the final pyramid, then still clear of snow, and reach the top by noon. Two days later, after the snowstorm that delayed Frank and me at Camp 6, the issue would have been more doubtful, but even then there would have been a good chance of success. In 1936 and 1938 no oxygen equipment yet devised would have given us the strength and endurance to overcome the massive accumulation of powder snow covering those treacherous upper slabs.

To my mind the 1933 expedition, like its predecessors in 1922 and 1924, was far too large and grossly overburdened. The current belief that a vast and complex organisation was needed to carry a party of climbers to the Base and to establish the lower camps originated, no doubt, in military thinking; that it remained so long unquestioned was due to the fact that the "news value" of Everest always made it easy to raise large sums of money for an expedition, and also because almost unlimited animal and porter transport was always available. If a few cases of champagne or a couple of extra transport officers could smooth the rugged path of the climbers, why not provide them? And besides this attitude, a kind of mystique developed out of the very complexity of the affair which increased its apparent importance. I was convinced that a small party, lightly equipped and shorn of supernumeraries and superfluous baggage, would not only be just as effective but would have several positive advantages. Among these would be increased mobility and a greater sense of cohesion and purpose, which had been so conspicuously lacking in the early stages of the climb.

In 1933 none of my colleagues shared these views, which I plugged with nagging persistence and which they attributed to my abnormal asceticism. They may well have been right, for though I genuinely believed in the practical superiority of a light expedition, my strongest objection to a large one was that it destroyed the fundamental simplicity of mountaineering, which I have always regarded as one of its principal charms. The sight of our monstrous army invading the peaceful Tibetan valleys, the canvas town that sprang up at each halting place and the bustle and racket that accompanied our arrival and departure gave me a feeling of being chained to a juggernaut, and I longed to return to these lovely places free and unshackled by the trappings of civilisation.

Then why not do so? The very idea of a million square miles of mountains waiting to be explored was intoxicating. Of course, most of the vast area was politically inaccessible, but there was still enormous scope, even within the confines of British India and along its undemarcated frontiers. Could I not abandon farming to pursue a nebulous career as Himalayan traveller? The obvious barriers to this tempting project were lack of substantial private means and of any scientific training. For the first time I regretted not having gone to Cambridge to study geology. On the other hand, I had little or nothing to lose by the experiment. Much as I had enjoyed my frugal life in Kenya, I was well aware that it offered little prospect of success. So, without too much thought, I decided to follow this phantom star and let the future take care of itself. But I felt as though I were embarking upon a life of unbridled licence, and for some years I suffered from periodic spasms of guilt which caused me to envy my friends in their normal pursuit of settled security. I had yet to learn that to become an expert in any field, however outlandish, can open the most unexpected doors.

There was no difficulty about choosing my first objective. Nanda Devi (25,660 feet), the highest peak in the Garhwal Himalaya, was surrounded by a mountain barrier which had never been penetrated. The only breach in this remarkable wall was on its western side, where the Rishi Ganga river had carved a gigantic canyon, twenty miles long, to the Dhaoli Valley. We had passed its entrance on the way to Kamet in 1931. Since 1883, when Graham and his two Swiss guides had tried to force their way up this gorge, repeated attempts had been made, from every angle of approach, to reach the inner basin surrounding the great peak. Among those who had tackled the problem was Dr. T. G. Longstaff.

Tom Longstaff was a doyen among mountain explorers, and as such he had long been one of my heroes. In spite of his small stature and generous nature, he was an intimidating character, forthright and uncompromising.

I had seen him at La Bérarde in 1926, but had been far too diffident to approach him. Early in 1933 I had met him at the Royal Geographical Society, where several of the younger members of the expedition had gathered to hear his advice. He had concluded his remarks, with outstretched finger and flashing eyes: "The man who collapses above the North Col is a scoundrel; a scoundrel, sir!" Thus, when he kindly invited me to spend a week-end at his home to discuss my Nanda Devi plan I accepted with a good deal of trepidation. This was in no way lessened by the fact that the great man's family was composed of seven daughters, then in various stages of adolescence. To make matters worse, Ferdie Crawford, another member of the 1933 expedition and a close friend of the Longstaffs, had told the girls that I was a brilliant pianist and that they must persuade me to play for them. He warned them that I was extremely shy and would probably deny my prowess, and that they would have to insist very strongly to get me to comply. This they certainly did. Luckily, despite the years I had spent practising five-finger exercises in lieu of prayers, I could not play a single chord; and when at last I got them to believe me, their mounting anger was turned on Ferdie, who, having savoured his joke to the full, had drifted out of the drawing-room.

I received a great deal of help from Longstaff, who advised me to concentrate my efforts on the Rishi Ganga. Though on one of his expeditions, in 1907, he had tried to penetrate the gorge, he had not been able to press home his attempt; but he was convinced that it was possible. However, he was frankly skeptical about my budget, which he considered ludicrously small. I had made a careful estimate, and I believed that by travelling to India and back by cargo ships I could spend five months in the Himalaya with two Sherpas for an overall cost of £150. A certain amount of local transport would be necessary to carry us to our base of operations, but by cutting down equipment to the bare necessities and by living almost entirely on local produce, it would not cost much. Apart from this, the only expenses in the field would be the Sherpas' wages, 1s. 10d. per day each, and the cost of our food, which would consist mainly of flour and ghee (clarified butter). Frugal fare no doubt, but since it was the basic diet of the Sherpas, I saw no reason why I should not thrive on it as well.

Nanda Devi

There was, of course, the problem of raising the £150. At first I was confident that the project would be of sufficient interest for some newspaper to pay me a substantial part of the sum in exchange for a series of articles; but I was wrong. Though I took my proposition to the editors of most of the leading journals in London, I failed to elicit any response. How different it would have been today! An alternative source of income was lecturing about Everest. I had never lectured before, and the prospect appalled me, but I wrote an account of the recent expedition, 8000 words long, and learnt the whole thing by heart, including some corny jokes. Perhaps my earlier struggles with *The Odes of Horace* and *Cicero Pro Milone* had been of some benefit after all. The result was an exceedingly dull lecture, but it was repeated often enough to yield most of the money I required, and the experience helped to conquer my horror of public speaking. I also spent much of that winter learning the rudiments of topographical survey.

I tried hard to find someone to come with me, but before long it seemed clear that I would have to attempt the venture alone with the Sherpas. Maybe the prospect of living for five months on flour and ghee was a deterrent, but of those whom I invited only Dr. Noel Humphreys was enthusiastic about the project. Unfortunately he had recently undertaken to lead an Arctic expedition, and though he tried to find someone to take his place so that he could join me, his sponsors would not agree to release him. Then a man of fifty, he had led a life of Spartan simplicity, dedicated to exploration; his chief field of activity had been Ruwenzori. Starting with virtually no private means, he had become a qualified geographical surveyor and a trained botanist. He was also a mountaineer. Two years before, at the age of forty-eight, he had qualified as a medical doctor. To do this he had rented an attic in London for a nominal sum, where he had lived for four years at an average total cost of 24s. 6d. a week. His chief motive for becoming a doctor had been to further his career as an explorer. I spent delightful evenings in his attic discussing the many fields of exploration still untouched. A keen exponent of the art of travelling light, willing to undergo any privation to achieve his objectives, he was in complete accord with my views, and could not understand why I had any qualms about abandoning my pursuit of security to embark on a life with no discernible prospects. He provided the encouragement I desperately needed, and I owe a great deal to his sympathy and advice.

Early in 1934 I received a letter from Bill Tilman telling me that he, too, had given up the struggle to make a reasonable living in Kenya; that, after an unsuccessful spell of prospecting in Kakamega, where people were still hoping, now rather forlornly, to strike fresh deposits of gold he had bought a push-bike and, living almost entirely on bananas, had ridden it across Africa to the West Coast, where he had boarded a homeward-bound cargo ship. He suggested that I should join him for a fortnight's climbing in the Lake District. I replied with a counter proposal that he should join me on a seven-month trip to the Himalaya, and he readily agreed. His return to England was most opportune, and I believe that the course of both our lives would have been profoundly changed if he had arrived a few months later. For, while he would probably not have gone to the Himalaya during the next five years, thus missing the experiences which laid the foundation of much of his subsequent career, I for my part owe the success of the Nanda Devi venture very largely to his support.

For the plan I had devised, Bill was nearly the ideal partner: he was tough and always ready for any amount of hardship and privation; indeed, his ascetic tastes often made me feel a positive sybarite. Nearly ten years older than me, he had served in France from 1915 to 1918, winning the M.C. and bar, though he was only twenty when the war ended. Because I had had a great deal more mountaineering experience, he was apparently content to let me assume charge and take the decisions, and we always seemed to be in general agreement about our plans. He was a recluse and a misogynist, and he had no taste for the softer pleasures of life: he had never even been inside a cinema. By contrast, he had a sensitive compassion for animals and an effervescent humour which won the hearts of the Sherpas. Nevertheless, he was astringent company, with little use for small talk and none for abstract discussion; and, much as I liked him for his humour and admired his staunchness, our relationship remained practical rather than intimate. As we had done in Africa, we continued to address one another as "Tilman" and "Shipton"; and when, after another seven months continuously together, I suggested that it was time he called me "Eric" he became acutely embarrassed, hung his head and muttered, "It sounds so damned silly."

My previous experience of travel in Garhwal was, of course, a great help, and when we reached Ranikhet a day and a half was all that was needed to complete our simple preparations and start on our march across the foothills. With two to share expenses, I had recruited three Sherpas instead of two, and we had brought from England some biscuits, cheese and pemmican to supplement the local food. Our diet, however, was mainly composed of chupattis and tsampa; the former are pancakes made of flour and water, baked on a hot plate; the latter is roasted barley meal, which can either be made into a hot porridge, taken as a cold cereal or, following the Tibetan custom, mixed in tea. The Sherpas spiced their meals with a strong sauce, made with lentils or edible plants if these were available, or simply boiled chillies. Though Bill and I adopted this practice, we also ate a great deal of sugar. At first I found this simple fare very bleak, and sometimes, particularly at breakfast or when I was tired, even repulsive; though nothing would have induced me to say so in face of Bill's stoicism. But I soon became accustomed to it, and before long I ate my portion with ever-increasing relish. Apart from our ten tins of pemmican,

H.W. Tilman

which we kept for high camps, we hardly tasted meat, and though we probably suffered from lack of protein, we were not aware of this.

Later, Bill and I acquired a wide reputation for Spartan living, which gave rise to endless banter. In fact, though we had broken with contemporary tradition, we were merely following the example of countless pioneer travellers in various parts of the world: Simpson in Canada, Stefansson in the Arctic, Lawrence in the desert, each had found in close adaptation to his particular environment not only a convenient means of survival and of accomplishing his ends but a luxury sweeter and far more satisfying than any artificially contrived. Compared with such men we were mere novices; indeed, I often feel that I have never graduated from that category.

We soon had striking evidence of one of the many advantages of travelling light in the Himalaya. At Surai Tota, a village in the Dhaoli Valley, which we reached in twelve marches from Ranikhet, we engaged some men to carry supplies to our base in the Rishi Ganga. To avoid the lower section of the gorge, which was said to be impassable, we had to cross a pass over a flanking ridge; though this was only 13,000 feet high, it was still (May 22) under deep winter snow. The Surai Tota men, unwilling to face the heavy toil involved, deserted us as soon as we reached the snow-line. Luckily we had not discharged the ten Dhotial porters we had brought from Ranikhet, and they volunteered to come with us, carrying extra loads. These people were low-caste Hindus who lived and worked in the foothills; they had no experience of travelling in rugged, uninhabited country, let alone in snow. No doubt they were quite unaware of what they had let themselves in for, but their magnificent fortitude saved us from failure; for it was vital that we should reach our base several weeks before the onset of the monsoon. Had we been encumbered with anything but bare necessities we would not have stood a chance. As it was, for the next six days the issue hung in a delicate balance.

For most of two days we struggled through soft snow up to our knees, our waists and sometimes up to our armpits. Bill and I, lightly laden, went ahead to flog the trail, while the others followed with their heavy loads. Twice, after exhausting effort, we reached a saddle which we hoped was the pass, only to find a sheer drop of several thousand feet on the other side. The third time we were lucky, and descended into the gorge beyond. It was an astonishing place. The southern side of the valley was composed of tier upon tier of gigantic slabs, steeply inclined, which culminated, 10,000 feet above the river, in a host of spires set at a rakish angle, while beyond them stood a range of ice peaks. The northern side, the one we were on, was scarcely less precipitous, which made it impossible to see the way ahead for any distance. This, coupled with the immense scale of the gorge, made route-finding difficult. We would clamber 2000 feet up a buttress and then down a similar height into a gully beyond to gain a bare half mile of progress. Sometimes we reached an impasse which forced us to retreat to try another line. This was particularly disheartening for the Dhotials, their morale already badly shaken by the difficulty of the terrain; but we urged them on through all the daylight hours with the promise of rich rewards. The reason for our haste was that, with fifteen mouths to feed, each day spent in reaching our base meant three days less food for the work beyond.

Luckily the weather remained fine, for in mist or rain it would have been almost impossible to find a way. As it was, at dusk on May 28 we arrived at the Junction of the Rhamini Nullah (named by our predecessors) with the Rishi Ganga, which was the farthest point reached by Graham and Longstaff, and where we had planned to make our base. To emphasise our good fortune, a heavy storm broke a few minutes before we got there. The following morning we discharged the gallant Dhotials who, despite the hammering they had taken, left us with touching expressions of regret.

Now, after the anxieties of the past week, at the threshold of our adventure, we were in a splendid position. A stock-taking showed that we had food enough for five weeks, and thus ample time for our fascinating task of finding a way through the upper gorge into the untrodden sanctuary beyond. A strip of shore along the southern side of the river, overhung by cliffs, provided us with snug, weather-proof quarters, and a grove of birch trees with ample fuel. By an extraordinary chance, at this very point a vast boulder was wedged above the river, forming a natural bridge and giving us access to both sides of the gorge. After so much strenuous exercise Bill and I were very fit, while our recent trials had shown our three Sherpas to be men of very high quality.

Among the many delights of this Nanda Devi venture was that, for the first time, I was able to treat these people as friends rather than as hired porters and servants. Sharing with them our food and tent-space, our plans and problems, we came to know their individual characteristics and to appreciate their delicious humour and their generous comradeship in a way quite impossible on a large expedition. Having spent all their lives among high mountains, they naturally saw no purpose in climbing them; nor did they understand our desire to penetrate unexplored gorges and glaciers or to cross unknown passes, for all these objects abounded in their own land. But whatever task we undertook, they tackled with as much zest as though it was their own ambition to achieve it. With such colleagues leadership was hardly called for; indeed, in more than one tight corner it was theirs rather than ours that saw us through. We owed all our successes to their unfailing staunchness.

Angtarkay had distinguished himself on Everest in 1933 by weathering the three-day storm at Camp 5, which left most of us weak and dispirited, and then volunteering to carry to Camp 6. He was five feet tall, small even for a Sherpa, lightly built and with pronounced knock-knees. He had a diffident manner and a flashing smile. Both his diminutive stature and his retiring demeanour belied the remarkable force of his personality, which was manifest in any crisis or adversity. Though then illiterate, he was intelligent, balanced and capable of shrewd appraisal of men and situations. Indeed, he was a shining example of my contention (based, no doubt, on personal prejudice) that literacy is not a prerequisite of wisdom. He was to be my companion on seven more expeditions, and he acquired an international reputation which in no way spoiled him.

Properly speaking, the Sherpas are inhabitants of the Nepalese valley of Solu Khumbu, though racially they are pure Tibetans. A large proportion of the so-called Sherpas who have taken part in Everest and other Himalayan expeditions have in fact come from Tibet itself, and many of them had never even visited Solu Khumbu. Pasang Bhotia, as his name implies (*Bhot* means Tibet), was one of these. He, too, had reached Camp 6 in 1933, and I had known him better than most, as he had been appointed my personal "orderly" on the outward march. Tall and spare, with sensitive aquiline features, he was something of a dandy, and always contrived to look a great deal more presentable than the rest of us. Like the other two Sherpas, he wore his long hair plaited in a single pigtail with a red tassel at the end, and he was at great pains to keep it neat and sleek. He was a fine climber, and his graceful movements on difficult ground were delightful to watch. He was inclined to be temperamental, and his elan often needed restraint; but he was not easily discouraged.

Angtarkay

Kusang was Angtarkay's cousin. He had also been on Everest in 1933, though among hundreds of others, I did not even remember his face. Sherpas rarely know how old they are, but we judged him to be about twenty, several years younger than the other two. For this reason no doubt he was somewhat put-upon in the matter of work, performing the bulk of the camp chores, fetching wood and water, washing up and always carrying the heaviest load. But he seemed to delight in work of every kind, and he certainly never resented it. We were often grateful for his extraordinary ability to kindle a fire with the most unlikely material, while his complete composure in times of stress did much to steady our morale. He spoke little Urdu, our only means of communication with the Sherpas, but as he always knew what was required of him, this hardly mattered.

Elated though we were at having reached our base with such ample supplies, the prospect ahead was far from encouraging. Fifty yards beyond the shore the river issued from a perfect box-canyon, its vertical walls smooth and unbroken. The northern side seemed quite impassable; but luckily the cliffs overhanging our camp were split by a narrow cleft, which enabled us to reach a gully above and to climb 2000 feet up the southern side of the gorge. There we found the first of a series of ledges running westward above the canyon. We took nine days to find a way and to relay our food and equipment through the remaining four miles of the gorge. It was exciting work, for until the last moment the issue remained in doubt, and each section of the route appeared to rely for its continuity upon the slender chance of a rock fault in the right place. The last mile looked so unpromising that we tried to force our way along the bottom. It was lucky that we failed in this, for when the ice of the glaciers began to melt more rapidly the river became enormously swollen, and we would not have been able to return that way. Eventually we found the last frail link along the precipices of the southern side and entered the Nanda Devi basin with enough food to stay there for three weeks.

It was a glorious place, and, of course, the fact that we were the first to reach it lent a special enchantment to our surroundings. The Sherpas, whose appreciation of country was more practical than aesthetic, were particularly impressed with the extensive grass land, which, they thought, would provide unlimited grazing for yaks. The season was still early, and the flowers, though beautiful, were not yet so luxuriant as they had been lower down in the Rishi Ganga. We saw many herds of *bharal* (wild sheep) and though fresh meat would have been most welcome, I was not sorry that we had no rifle. Several long glacier valleys ran down from the great circle of mountains, between 21,000 and 23,000 feet high, surrounding the basin. In the centre of this mighty amphitheatre, standing 13,000 feet above its base, was the peerless spire of Nanda Devi, ever changing in form and colour as we moved.

It was soon clear that three weeks was not time enough to explore the whole basin, so we decided to concentrate on the northern half and return to survey the southern half in September when we hoped the monsoon would be over. The weather was mostly fine, and usually we slept in the open, even at our highest camps, for it deepened the sense of harmony with our exquisite surroundings. Though our main task was to map the country with a plane-table, we were able to combine this with some mountaineering. We climbed one peak of 21,000 feet and failed to reach the summit of another of 23,000 feet. We also reached three cols on the eastern and northern "rim" of the basin.

Towards the end of June the monsoon arrived, and we retreated down the Rishi Ganga in torrential rain. Though we had a lot of trouble with swollen side-streams and had to be very careful negotiating the more difficult passages, we knew every yard of the way and, with little to carry, we made rapid progress. The gorge was even more splendid in foul weather than in fair. Particularly I remember one night of violent storm when I was snugly wedged in a little recess between two boulders listening to the hiss of the rain outside, and to the thunder which, echoing along miles of crag, maintained an almost unbroken roll. Lightning flickered incessantly upon the vast precipices and upon cloud banners entwined about ridges and corries. The sense of fantasy was heightened by the semi-consciousness of fitful sleep. At times, it seemed, I was perched on an eagle's nest above an infernal cauldron, infinitely deep; sometimes I was floating with the mist, myself a part of the tempest. On July 1, our food exhausted, we regained the Dhaoli Valley, after an absence of six weeks.

During July and August we made two complete crossings of the Badrinath Range, the first outside the pages of Hindu mythology, to effect a direct connection between the three main sources of the sacred River Ganges. The second of these journeys proved tougher than we had anticipated, and we landed ourselves in an awkward situation.

From the head of the Satopanth Glacier, west of Badrinath, we reached a saddle, 18,400 feet high, on the crest of the watershed. We arrived there in thick mist and falling snow, but early the following morning, a brief clearing revealed that we were on the brink of an ice precipice plunging 6000 feet into the valley below. But this looked so green and enticing that we decided to attempt the descent. It proved no less difficult than it had appeared, and it was not until the next day that we reached the foot of the precipice, having cut off our retreat by roping down one section in our eagerness to reach the Elysian fields below. The valley, however, was no primrose path; instead it was a formidable gorge filled with dense, trackless forest, where progress was terribly slow and laborious. The rain was heavy and incessant, and our sleeping bags became as saturated as our clothes. The sides of the gorge were precipitous and often it took us an hour to cover twenty-five yards, while we rarely achieved more than a mile in a day. Much of our trouble was caused by side-streams, which were generally at the bottom of deep ravines and always in spate. One held us up for two days before we found a place where we could bridge it. Before long our food ran out, and for a week we lived on tree-fungus and bamboo shoots, happily then in season. Eventually we reached a tiny hamlet where we obtained four pounds of flour, a cucumber and a handful of dried apricots. Though these provided a memorable banquet, even more welcome was the forest track which led us down to the Kedarnath pilgrim route.

At the beginning of September we returned to the Rishi Ganga. With no problem of route-finding and with local porters to help us, we got through the gorge in eight days from the Dhaoli Valley. By then the monsoon was over, and we enjoyed a long spell of fine weather. The geography of the southern section of the basin was relatively simple, and it did not take us long to complete our survey. We found a practicable route up Nanda Devi itself by way of its southern ridge, but though we climbed some way up it, we were not equipped to make a serious attempt on the summit; for one thing our boots were now full of holes and almost devoid of nails.

Our ambition was to find a way out of the basin over some part of the encircling ranges which had so long proved impregnable. With little choice in the matter, we determined to concentrate our efforts on the lowest depression (18,000 feet) on the southern wall, which Hugh Ruttledge and his Italian guide, Emil Rey, had attempted to cross two years before. Angtarkay, Kusang and I climbed a peak of 22,360 feet immediately above this col, and from there we saw the 6000-foot precipice forming its southern side. Though I fully appreciated Ruttledge's decision to abandon his attempt to climb it, we thought it might be possible to descend. In fact, it proved to be even more difficult than the precipice we had descended into the Kedarnath valleys seven weeks before, though this time we had fine weather, plenty of food and the certainty that when we reached the bottom we would be only a couple of days march from habitation. It was perhaps the most exciting of our adventures, and certainly provided a wonderful finale.

The march back to Ranikhet, in golden autumn weather, through new and beautiful surroundings, gave us time to reflect on the crowded events of the last five months. We had achieved far more than I had dared to hope. I appreciated as never before not only the joys of unencumbered travel but also the deep satisfaction of exploring unknown ranges; and from then on I became far more interested in this than in climbing peaks. It might be argued that, by relying upon such slender resources, we had run too many risks; for the bulk of the time had been spent in uninhabited regions, where even a relatively minor mishap could have had grave consequences. But it should be remembered that, before the advent of radio and helicopter, such risks were inherent in most exploratory journeys through wild country; certainly those we ran seem paltry compared with the appalling hazards faced, quite deliberately, by polar travellers only a few decades ago when the art of survival was sometimes their only asset. The expedition cost £286 for the two of us, including all our travel; £14 less than my original budget.

From Ranikhet I travelled to Southern India to visit my sister and her husband, and thence to Ceylon to recapture some of the enchantment of that lovely island which had sustained me in the first bleak years at school. The return voyage in a small cargo ship provided something of an anti-climax; for twenty-four hours out from Colombo the vessel developed engine trouble, and thereafter proceeded at three knots the rest of the way to Port Said. The only passenger on board, appalled by the prospect of endless weeks of boredom, I set about the task of writing a book on our recent expedition. I soon realised the heavy toil involved and the stern discipline needed to cudgel my sluggish intellect to produce a coherent account of even a simple and inspiring theme; and I doubt if in other circumstances I would have had the drive to persist beyond the first chapter. As with all my subsequent books, I resolved that this should be my last. Since then the effort has never grown any less demanding; and though there have been flashes of satisfaction, exultation even, when a passage seemed to do justice to a cherished experience, these have been rare moments amid the general welter of exasperation.

Reaching England in mid-December 1934, I spent the next few months based in my mother's house in London, completing the book, lecturing and acting as a guinea-pig to Dr. Zilva of the Lister Institute, who was conducting some experiments in the retention of vitamin C, in exchange for some elementary instruction in dietetics. Bill and I also devoted the little time necessary to complete our plans for the following summer, which we hoped might include an attempt to climb Nanda Devi. The success of our recent venture had received flattering recognition in geographical and mountaineering circles; the Gill Memorial Award of the Royal Geographical Society, amounting to £52, enabled me to discharge most of my debts, and it seemed that we might count on some modest financial backing for any fresh project. Such encouragement and a staunch colleague to share my plans did much to dispel my earlier misgivings, though I could not entirely suppress my puritan conscience.

It would be false to give the impression that my life at that time was entirely devoted to the pursuit of adventurous travel. In fact, I led a fairly sociable life with a circle of friends quite outside my main field of interest. Money was much tighter than it is today, even allowing for its greater purchasing power, and it was easy to find my level among contemporaries who could afford only modest forms of entertainment. Though my chosen way of life made it impossible to contemplate marriage, it did not prevent my falling in love from time to time as I had done since the age of twelve. This, of course, presented problems and caused me, as a defensive measure, to adopt a light-hearted attitude towards sex, not quite in keeping with my temperament. I could not, alas, discuss these matters with my mother, whose views were even more strait-laced than most women's of her generation. These were presumably responsible for my sense of guilt and habit of reticence which had developed in puberty and were never entirely eradicated. Apart from this, my mother and I got on well together. She accepted my eccentric pursuits with her usual calm; and though she must have suffered a good deal of anxiety, she was careful not to show it. With my sister in India, she was no doubt glad to have me with her for a few months each year; and for my part, it was very nice to have a home to return to.

Early in March came the news that the Tibetan Government had granted permission for further expeditions to Everest in 1935 and 1936. As it was too late to organise a full-scale expedition that spring, the Mount Everest Committee decided to defer the attempt until the following year. It seemed a pity to waste this rare opportunity and, as the Committee still had a balance of some £1,400 at its disposal, I offered to take a party of six climbers to the mountain that summer for an overall cost of £200 each. My avowed objectives were to find out whether the monsoon snow on the north face became sufficiently consolidated during July and August to warrant an attempt at that season; to test likely candidates for the main expedition and to give them some experience of high-altitude conditions; and to extend the explorations of the 1921 Reconnaissance Expedition. But I had a private motive: my dislike of massive mountaineering expeditions had become something of an obsession, and I was anxious for the opportunity to demonstrate that, for one-tenth of the former cost and with a fraction of the bother and disruption of the local countryside, a party could be placed on the North Col, adequately equipped to make a strong attempt on the summit. The Committee accepted my proposal, and I began to recruit my party, which naturally included Bill. I expected him to be delighted by this chance to go to Everest, but in fact he was far from pleased with this change of plan. Though he did not say so, I suspected that the root of the objection was that, while he had been forced to accept the stark necessity of my company, the prospect of having five companions was scarcely tolerable.

It is never easy to predict how people will react to one another on an expedition. This was well illustrated by a curious experience I had at this time. Lawrence Wager was then organising an expedition to Greenland, and I spent a week-end with him discussing food, equipment and other matters. Talking of the composition of his party, he told me that he had come to the conclusion that it was a great advantage to include one member so universally disliked that the others, with a common object for their spleen, would be drawn together in close comradeship. Though an expedient employed by most successful dictators, I was astonished to hear it proposed in this context, particularly by someone as temperate and as warm-hearted as Wager. He went on to tell me that he had found the perfect subject for his experiment in Michael Spender, a brilliant surveyor and an excellent traveller, but a man whose overbearing conceit had made him most unpopular on each of his several expeditions. Happily he did not seem to notice, let alone resent the fact.

Shortly afterwards I was startled to hear that the Royal Geographical Society had decided to attach Michael Spender to my party to make a stereo-photogrammetric survey of the northern aspect of Everest. So it seemed that it was I who would be conducting Wager's experiment in human relations! I was a little apprehensive, but too intrigued with the idea to raise any objections. But the outcome was very different from what I had expected; for in Michael I found a delightful and stimulating companion, and we became close friends. He had an extraordinary originality of outlook, totally unfettered by conventional thought. A year after leaving Oxford with a double first, he had abandoned a promising career in commercial research in a quest for "reality," which still lacked clear focus partly because of the great diversity of his interests. It was easy to see how he had made himself disliked, for he had an arrogant manner and a provocative way of expressing wildly unorthodox views, which effectively disguised the fact that he himself did not necessarily hold them. He was sensitive and honest enough to be well aware of his faults and sometimes revealed surprising humility.

Whether my liking for him influenced the rest of the party, or whether they were an exceptionally tolerant lot, or whether Michael himself had mellowed, he certainly did not assume the role of scapegoat. Nor was this needed, for, perhaps because of the width of our field of operations which meant that the party could be frequently split into small units, each with its separate objective, there was remarkably little friction—so often caused by people treading on each other's toes. In any case, the presence of Dan Bryant would have made dissension difficult to sustain, for any ostentation or humbug became the target of his gentle mockery, which discouraged any of us from taking himself or his grievances too seriously.

Dan joined us from New Zealand, where he was one of the most distinguished of the younger climbers. Tough and thoroughly competent, he had a delicious brand of humour and a huge fund of anecdotes, largely derived from his acute observation of people. Among his best was the description of his meeting with Bill in Darjeeling and the two days they spent there together in almost complete silence before the rest of us arrived. No one enjoyed the yarn more than Bill, who, after that initial encounter, responded to Dan's charm with unwonted conviviality. Poor Dan! Despite his exceptional fitness, he had the greatest difficulty in acclimatising to altitudes of more than 18,000 feet, and for weeks on end, long after the others had adjusted

Michael Spender

themselves, he was prostrated with acute headaches and nausea. This meant, of course, that he could not qualify for a place on the main expedition; but he treated the whole thing as a joke and never gave the slightest indication of the bitter disappointment he must have felt. He was certainly a wonderful ambassador for New Zealand climbers, and the impression he made upon me was to have a decisive influence upon events eighteen years later.

There was another prophetic incident. From a hundred applicants, we chose fifteen Sherpas to accompany the expedition from Darjeeling. Nearly all of them were old friends, including, of course, Angtarkay, Pasang and Kusang; but there was one Tibetan lad of nineteen, a newcomer, chosen largely because of his attractive grin. His name was Tensing Norkay—or Tensing Bhotia as he was generally called.

We left Darjeeling towards the end of May 1935, and pausing for a fortnight to explore the Nyonno Ri range, we reached the Rongbuk Monastery on July 4. There we were joined by another Sherpa, Sen Tensing, who was with me on many of my subsequent expeditions. Most Sherpas are staunch individualists, but none more so than Sen Tensing. He was so delighted with the clothes we gave him that he could hardly bear to take them off. Down in the valleys under a blazing sun he could be seen fully attired in a windproof suit, gloves, goggles, puttees and a balaclava helmet, ready to battle with a blizzard. This penchant for dressing the part of the complete mountaineer earned him the nickname "Foreign Sportsman." He had once been a lama, and was forever intoning prayers in a deep bass voice.

Two days later we left Rongbuk, and in less than a week established a camp on the North Col, stocked with sufficient supplies for a fortnight and enough for a further three weeks at Camp 3 below. My plan was to carry a camp to 26,000 feet, and from there to make a close examination of conditions on the upper part of Everest, which, of course, was plastered with monsoon snow. We had found the slopes below the Col to be surprisingly firm and apparently stable, and we had some hope that the snow above might also have become compact. The weather, however, was bad, and after four days of storm, during which we made some short climbs up the northeast spur, I decided to withdraw and wait for an improvement. Two hundred feet below the Col, we were dismayed to find that an enormous avalanche had swept the line of our ascending tracks. The snow that we had thought perfectly safe had slid away to a depth of six feet over an area a quarter of a mile wide, and it was only by luck that we and the Sherpas had not gone with it. It was obvious that the same thing might happen on any part of the slope, and that the only sensible course was to leave the North Col alone.

It was disappointing to have to abandon one of our main objectives, but I for one was not heartbroken; for it gave us time to embrace wider horizons which would otherwise have been beyond our reach. As it was, we were free for more than two months to wander far afield, following untrodden routes, crossing new passes into unknown valleys and revelling in the constant change of scene. In a veritable orgy of mountain climbing we reached the summit of twenty-six peaks, all more than 20,000 feet; as many, in Longstaff's phrase, as had been climbed "since the days of Adam." On four occasions we went above 23,000 feet, and each time we experienced a sudden deterioration in snow conditions, which provided evidence of what might be expected at extreme altitudes during the monsoon. We also tried to reach the Western Cwm, hoping to discover an alternative approach to the summit of Everest which would avoid the treacherous slabs of the upper part of the north face. But, though from several points along the watershed we looked into the mysterious defile and saw the now famous ice-fall below it, we found it impossible to get there except by first descending into the forbidden valleys of Nepal. The best part of the expedition was the time we spent exploring in the glorious country to the east of Everest.

Though he did not suffer nearly so much as Dan, Bill was also very slow acclimatising to altitude. Each time we had been above 20,000 feet in 1934 he had become sick. In 1935, though he was as active as any of us, and though he seemed to have raised his "ceiling" to about 23,000 feet, his performance approaching that level was not good enough to warrant his inclusion in the 1936 attempt on Everest. As with Dan, it was a hateful decision to take, and it seemed cruel that these two, so eminently suitable in every other way, should be excluded by a small physiological peculiarity. In Bill's case, however, it proved to be a great stroke of luck, for instead of taking part in the abortive attempt on Everest in 1936, he joined an Anglo-American expedition to Nanda Devi and, with Odell, achieved perhaps the most outstanding mountaineering success of those pre-war years by reaching the summit. Whether his astonishing reversal of form was due to psychological or to physiological causes, we shall never know. The whole process of acclimatisation is very mysterious.

I had hoped that the achievements of the 1935 expedition, which were generously applauded, would convince the "Establishment" of the virtues of a light, mobile party. In this I was sadly disappointed, and when it became clear that the 1936 attempt was to be launched on the same massive scale as before, I considered resigning my place in it. Having tasted the joys of simplicity and freedom in two long seasons of unrestricted travel, I felt so out of sympathy with the enterprise that I certainly should have had the strength of mind, the integrity, to refrain from joining it, even though it might mean missing the moment of success. No one, of course, was to blame for the dismal failure of that expedition: it was due to the diabolical weather conditions, the breaking of the monsoon a month before its normal time, that we climbed no higher than the North Col.

| 5 |

THE KARAKORAM

THE KARAKORAM, WHICH LIES BEYOND the Himalaya to the north-west, is the greatest concentration of lofty mountains in the world. Studying the maps with a view to going there, I had been so intimi-dated by the vast scale of the country that I had hesitated to take the plunge. Could our "shoe-string" methods, however successful in the more compact ranges of the Himalaya, possibly achieve worthwhile results among glacier basins, some of which could enclose an area the size of Sikkim, in regions weeks away from the nearest habi-tation? Frustration, however, can be a powerful spur; it was during the long days spent weatherbound on the East Rongbuk Glacier in 1936 that I resolved to undertake a major exploratory journey in the Karakoram the following year. The decision was to change the whole course of my life.

The most obvious objective was the exploration of the unknown region, several thousand square miles, surrounding the basin of the Shaksgam River, immediately beyond the main continental divide. Represented on the map of the Karakoram by a challenging blank, it lay across the undemarcated frontier between Kashmir and Sinkiang. At that time mounting tension in that Chinese province due to Soviet intrigue was causing the Government of India much con-cern, and they were reluctant to allow travellers to approach the area. However, on my way back from Everest I went to Simla with my

proposition and managed first to get the backing of the Surveyor General
and then to persuade the External Affairs Department that there was little
risk of my party being captured in the Shaksgam valleys and some benefit to
be derived from better knowledge of the frontier region. The matter settled,
I went as guide with an official survey expedition to the Nanda Devi area,
and returned to England in December.

Bill and I used to boast that we could organise a Himalayan expedition
in half an hour on the back of an envelope. For my first Karakoram venture,
with no experience of local conditions, scarcely able to visualise the immense
distances involved, the job was rather more exacting, and a lot of study was
needed before I could reduce the details of my plan to a sheet of foolscap. I
decided on a party of four, and was extremely lucky in its composition. Bill,
despite his resounding success on Nanda Devi, was willing to join my more
pedestrian enterprise. Michael Spender had won a Leverhulme Scholarship,
and my expedition offered him an excellent opportunity for research into
new methods of geographical survey, the subject of his study. John Auden, of
the Geological Survey of India, had already worked on the southern side of
the Karakoram and was delighted with the chance to project his researches
into the less accessible region to the north. It was quite fortuitous that the
brothers of two celebrated poets were thus included in the party.

My budget, including three return passages to India, amounted to £855.
The very contemplation of such a sum made me feel like a financial tycoon,
but I had little difficulty in raising it, largely from grants by the R.G.S., the
Survey of India and the Royal Society. With complete confidence I entrusted
the selection of seven Sherpas to Angtarkay. His freedom from the common
Oriental addiction to nepotism was shown by the fact that one of his team
hailed from a place in Tibet two months' march north of Lhasa. I intended
also to engage four men from Baltistan for work in the Shaksgam, bringing
our total strength to fifteen.

Towards the end of April 1937 we foregathered in Kashmir, where we
spent a week in leisurely preparation before exchanging a life of luxury for
the sterner pleasures of the wilderness. Then, with our caravan of twelve
pack animals, we marched up the Sind Valley to the Zoji La. Though only
11,500 feet high, the pass was still blocked by winter snow and we had to

cross it by night to avoid avalanches. Beyond it there was an abrupt change of scene: from the soft colours and gentle shapes, the woods and meadows of the Vale of Kashmir, we entered a world of stark grandeur, of harsh, rugged outlines, of sombre gorges and sleek, powerful rivers. At intervals along the barren valleys, wherever irrigation was possible, there were oases of intensive cultivation, the terraces of young corn vivid green beneath a pink haze of apricot blossom. Many were small isolated patches; some extended for miles, and there our way would lie through shady orchards, the path flanked by ribbons of mauve and white iris, before we plunged once more into the hard glare of the mountain desert.

In two weeks, after marching more than twenty miles a day, we reached Skardu, capital of Baltistan, where we bought supplies of sugar, rice, ghee and kerosene. We then crossed the Indus, which marks the geographical boundary between the Himalaya and the Karakoram, and travelled up the difficult gorge of the Braldu River to Askole, the last village, which we reached on May 24.

At Askole we had reached the most critical stage of the expedition. Immediately ahead lay the mighty barrier of the main Karakoram; everything depended on our ability to find our way across it in the least possible time, and to transport our equipment and one and a half tons of food over to the uninhabited region beyond. But besides the food, which was to keep our party of fifteen alive for nearly four months, we had to take food for the men who were carrying it, and still more for those who were carrying theirs. On top of this we had to make provision for the porters on their return journey. Working on a somewhat hypothetical time-scale, it was a simple arithmetical sum which I had done some months before and had reached the appalling conclusion that we needed to start with 104 porters, each carrying sixty pounds. We also had to buy nearly two tons of flour, but despite the desolate appearance of the valley, this presented no problem. Recruiting the porters was another matter. We had brought seventeen from Skardu, four of whom were to stay with us in the Shaksgam, and we had to engage the remaining eighty-seven in Askole.

The inhabitants of the Braldu valley, for all their remoteness, were accustomed to expeditions bound for the giant peaks at the head of the Baltoro. For us this was a source of embarrassment. The summer journey up the glacier to the various base camps was familiar to the porters and

Karakoram—unknown pass

involved them in little hardship. In the past nine years three of these climbing expeditions had been run on a huge scale, regardless of cost, and had employed upwards of 600 porters who, apart from inflated rates of pay, had acquired rich perquisites and massive loot from abandoned equipment and stores. Accustomed to such largesse, it was natural that they should look askance at our Spartan outfit; and when it dawned upon them that something much more arduous was in prospect than the customary summer trek up the Baltoro, our call for volunteers met with blank refusal. After many hours of futile argument our prospects seemed utterly hopeless. Then suddenly the mood changed and we found ourselves besieged by a crowd of applicants eager to be enrolled. Presumably a few of the more thoughtful spirits had realised that, as we were obviously too poor to employ the entire male population, they had better take what they could get while the going was good; panic was kindled, the rest followed their lead with the speed of an avalanche and the day was won.

Until the middle of the nineteenth century the people of Baltistan and Hunza used to cross the main range to Sinkiang for trade or plunder. It was said that the practice was stopped largely because of a vast increase in the ice of the glaciers. Personally I think a more likely cause was the shrinkage of the ice; for glaciers in a state of rapid decline are usually much more difficult to negotiate than those which are expanding. Whatever the reason, within a few decades tribal memory of these remarkable journeys had faded to mere legend, and we only know of their historical reality from the records of early travellers in Baltistan, such as Godwin-Austen, who met men who had actually performed them. In 1937 the people of Askole flatly denied that a practicable route across the range had ever existed.

The only one of these ancient passes of which we had any precise knowledge was the Old Mustagh Pass, which was crossed by Younghusband in 1887 after his discovery of the Shaksgam River at the end of his famous journey from Peking. He had found it very difficult to descend on the Baltoro side. In 1929 the crossing was repeated from the Baltoro by a party from the Duke of Spoleto's expedition, headed by Professor Desio. He reported that it had become still more formidable owing, apparently, to the recession of the ice, which had left more of the precipice above the glacier. Even if the difficulties had not further increased during the past eight years, it was far from certain that we would be able to negotiate the pass so early in the season, when the winter snow was still unmelted; particularly with a large, heavily laden caravan. However, from the head of the Trango Glacier, a lower tributary of the Baltoro, Desio had seen a saddle leading in the same direction as the Old Mustagh Pass, which he thought would provide an easier passage across the range. Thus we were faced with a choice between a pass known to be very difficult and another said to be comparatively easy but which had not yet been attempted. It would have been wise, no doubt, to have made a thorough reconnaissance before committing ourselves to either. But this might have taken at least ten days and, for reasons that I will explain later, it was vital that we should reach the Shaksgam without delay.

With the critical choice of route yet undecided we set out on May 26 and, in three marches, reached Paiju, a patch of willow jungle near the snout of the Baltoro. The weather was bad and there was much heavy rain, which seemed incongruous in this arid valley. Our prospects appeared as bleak as our surroundings, for we could see that a great deal of snow was falling at higher levels and we desperately needed fine weather during the coming weeks. To make matters worse Bill and Sen Tensing became ill with high fever. With our army of porters to be paid and fed (we were now consuming 220 pounds a day) we could not afford to wait; so it was decided that John and two Sherpas should remain in Paiju with the invalids, while Michael and I pressed on with the main body. If they had not overtaken us by the time we crossed the range I was to return, leaving Michael to begin his survey. It was an unsatisfactory compromise, but the best we could devise.

As a result of these complications we made a late start the following day and, clambering slowly over the wilderness of boulders forming the lower Baltoro, we failed to get as far as we had hoped. But we found a pleasant camp site with abundant juniper wood, and the Balti porters, still on familiar ground, were in good spirits. That evening the weather cleared and for the first time we saw the fantastic forest of spires surrounding us; immense columns of granite rising smooth and sheer for 6000 or 8000 feet and flanking the glacier for many miles on either side. A short way on, we turned left into the narrow defile of the Trango Glacier. Mainly because of the situation arising from Bill's and Sen Tensing's illness, I had decided to gamble on Desio's reported saddle, which, if feasible, seemed likely to provide a shorter route than the Old Mustagh Pass. Everything now depended upon the correctness of Desio's assessment, for had it proved wrong, we would not have had sufficient resources for another attempt to cross the range with substantial supplies. I cannot say that I enjoyed the tension that mounted during the next few days.

The bad weather returned and snow fell. The Baltis, reluctant to venture up the unknown glacier, apparently afraid that we were leading them into a region from which they would not be able to return, went painfully slowly and needed constant goading. Their morale sank to a low ebb, and in these wintry conditions they seemed incapable of looking after themselves. At the end of each day's march they sat around helplessly and refused to do anything to protect themselves from the weather. Certainly the conditions were tough, but matters were made a great deal worse for them by their craven behaviour. The seventeen Skardu men, on the other hand, were very staunch, and it was left to them and the Sherpas to construct shelters, make fires and cook for the helpless, shivering multitude, often working far into the night. Luckily we had brought plenty of juniper wood, carried by the porters whose food loads had been consumed.

Farther up, the remains of the winter snow on the glacier were leg-deep; though it was usually firm until mid-morning, after that the going became terribly laborious. Coming upon an unexpected fork in the valley, we could no longer pretend that we knew the way. Michael and I spent an exhausting day reconnoitring the right-hand branch, only to find that it ended in a semicircular precipice crowned by a hanging-glacier terrace. Returning to camp, tired and thoroughly depressed by the thought that we had wasted a valuable day, we found that the Baltis, whose spirit had seemed at breaking point the night before, were rather more cheerful as a result of their rest.

The weather, too, had improved, and the next morning, making an unusually early start, we followed the other branch of the valley and reached a side glacier rising gently to a col which appeared to be on the main divide. Praying that we were not mistaken, I promised the Baltis that I would discharge them as soon as we reached it. This was rash, but their morale was now so shaken that they would not have tolerated further uncertainty. Indeed, for several days they had been clamouring to be paid off and allowed to return. It was still early in the day, and we were tempted to press on towards the pass, but the snow was already so soft that we decided to halt 1000 feet below it and risk a change in the weather and the effects of another night's exposure on the temper of the men. We were on a bleak, comfortless ledge, 17,000 feet high, and at sunset it became bitterly cold. However, there had been time to construct deep snow shelters for the porters, and they survived the night, apparently none the worse.

When at 9:00 the next morning we reached the col we were dismayed to find that it did not lie on the crest of the range. All was not lost, however, for a mile away across a crescent basin of snow we saw another saddle, some several hundred feet higher and accessible. Though we would certainly not be able to induce the Baltis to go there, at least we seemed to be within reach of our goal. They were still some way behind, so, without waiting for them to arrive, we plunged down and waded through deep snow until we were half-way across the basin. This was, in fact, the top of the hanging-glacier terrace that Michael and I had seen two days before. The Skardu men followed without comment; but when the Baltis breasted the top of the col and saw us half a mile farther on they sent up a howl of protest. It was a mean trick, no doubt, but it worked, and eventually they joined us, bringing their loads, which saved us half a day's relaying. Many of them lay in the snow holding their heads and groaning, but when we had paid them their wages plus a substantial bonus their headaches seemed to vanish and, with the rest, they started back with a great deal more zest than they had displayed since leaving Askole. The seventeen Skardu men needed no persuasion to remain with us, and shouldering as much of the abandoned loads as we could carry, we struggled to the second saddle. Happily this proved to be the true pass, and soon after nightfall, tired but enormously relieved, we camped in the upper basin of the glacier flowing north from the main continental divide.

Michael began his survey while the rest of the loads were brought across the pass. This task was just completed when the last of our major worries was set at rest by the arrival of John and the invalids. They had recovered from their fever (we never discovered the cause), but were still very weak, and it had been a hard struggle to reach the pass. On June 14 we reached broad gravel flats below the glacier and there, in a little patch of scrub, we established our main base, nine miles from the Shaksgam River. We selected four of the Skardu men to stay with us, and the rest returned across the pass.

Of the many highlights of my life, none have stayed more fresh in my memory than those threshold situations such as the night before our attempt to climb Mount Kenya or the arrival at our base in the Rishi Ganga or that which we had now reached after so much suspense and anxiety. No doubt the sheer happiness of these moments is later enhanced by the retrospective knowledge of the success they preceded but certainly that evening, warmed by the unaccustomed luxury of a blazing camp fire, I was blissfully aware of our position. To the east and west stretched an unexplored section, eighty miles long, of the greatest range in the world. We had food enough for three and a half months, and a party equipped and fully competent to meet the opportunity.

Our first task, however, lay in the Aghil mountains beyond the Shaksgam River. This range had been crossed by Younghusband fifty years before when he discovered the Shaksgam; but as he was unable accurately to plot his route across this vast wilderness, the exact whereabouts of his pass had since remained something of a mystery. In 1926 a Survey of India expedition under Major Mason attempted to reach it from the east. After overcoming great difficulties they found a very large river which, as it was flowing in the right direction, they assumed to be the Shaksgam. They followed it downstream until they were stopped by the enormous volume of water racing through its gorges; but not before they had discovered their mistake. They named it Zug—or false— Shaksgam. We hoped both to fix the position of Younghusband's Aghil Pass and to solve the riddle of Mason's river. Our time was woefully short; for by the middle of July the Shaksgam itself would be so flooded by the melting of the vast glaciers of the main range that it would become impassable. To be caught on the wrong side when this occurred would mean that we would have to wait there until late autumn for the river to subside.

Partly as an insurance against starvation in such a situation we had brought a rifle. Though we never had to rely on it for our survival, it was well worth its weight; for throughout the summer we found many herds of *bharal* which, whenever we had time for hunting, provided us with poor sport but a welcome supply of fresh meat. We also saw foxes and small mountain wolves, and at our base we were sometimes visited by *kyang*, a rare species of wild ass. These delightful creatures would approach to within two or three hundred yards of our camp and stand gazing at us by the hour.

Carrying three weeks' food which, with our equipment, was as much as we could manage without relaying, we set off up the Shaksgam. The great square valley was enclosed by high limestone cliffs, slashed across with twisted streaks of yellow, red and black strata which gave it a weird, rather awesome appearance. The river flowed over gravel flats a mile wide, sometimes concentrated into a single channel as it swirled around a bend in the valley, sometimes split into a dozen streams. At wide intervals we found thickets of willow and tamarisk, natural counterparts of the cultivated oases of Baltistan. Apart from these the valley was utterly barren. Here and there its sides were split by cavernous ravines scored by glacial torrents. At the entrance to one of these we found a collection of ancient stone shelters which gave us the clue to the route, and climbing through a narrow defile, we emerged on to a grassy plateau which cradled a small lake, edged with drifts of mauve primulas (*denticulata*), and dipped gently northward. This was the Aghil Pass, made famous by Younghusband's journey in 1887, but not seen since by Western travellers. On the far horizon, across the wide gulf of the Yarkand River, stood the gaunt mountains of the Kuen Lun. Beyond these lay the strange country of the Tarim Basin in Chinese Turkestan, which, had I but known it, was one day to become as familiar to me as my native land.

While Michael worked near the pass, fixing its geographical position and mapping its surroundings, John explored to the west, and Bill and I with some of the porters struck eastward in search of the Zug Shaksgam. We started by climbing a 20,000-foot peak to discover the lie of the land, then crossed a saddle almost as high. Though the country beyond was extremely rugged and complicated, the glaciers were relatively small, and a lot of scrub in the valleys provided ample fuel. This and a spell of perfect weather enabled us to travel very light and, sleeping in the open where darkness found us, we were able to cover the difficult ground rapidly. So when we reached the great river we had just enough time to follow it upstream to Mason's farthest point and then trace it down to its confluence with the Yarkand River, near the northern side of the Aghil Pass. When, with the rest of the party, we recrossed the Shaksgam it was already so swollen that we realised we had returned none too soon.

The next ten days were spent exploring the glaciers flowing north and west from K2, the second highest peak in the world. At the foot of its northern face we found a huge amphitheatre with a slender buttress rising from the level floor in one prodigious sweep of 12,000 feet to the summit dome. The air was clear and very still as we watched ice avalanches break from a hanging glacier so far above us that no sound broke the silence of the cirque. When the survey of this small sector of the range was complete we were free at last to turn our eyes towards the most intriguing problem of all.

When in 1892 Sir Martin Conway crossed the Hispar Pass he saw a vast basin of snow and ice, with "a series of mountain islands rising from it, and with endless bays and straits." He called it the "Snow Lake" and estimated its area at 300 square miles. Since then it had only once been seen, by the Workmans, who, ten years later, crossed the Pass in the reverse direction, though like Conway, they had not explored the strange basin. As a result, there had been a great deal of speculation about the nature of the "Snow Lake," and it had been suggested that it might be an ice-cap—a phenomenon almost unknown outside polar regions—in which many of the vast glaciers by the Karakoram had their origin. As its southern fringes, traversed by Conway and the Workmans, represented the limit of exploration in this region, the map of the main continental divide faded into the unknown with this intriguing enigma.

From our base we looked up a very large glacier, later named the Skamri, to some unknown mountains far away on the western horizon. By theodolite observations Michael calculated the position of these peaks and found that they lay barely twenty-five miles east of the Hispar Pass. This suggested that the glacier had its origin somewhere near the "Snow Lake," if not actually in it, and that it would lead us directly into the very heart of the mysterious region.

On July 18 we started, with two months' food, to work our way up the glacier, carrying the loads in relays. The surface was a chaotic wilderness of ice pinnacles characteristic of many of the glaciers on the northern side of the range, and though we could avoid much of it by following moraine

Shipton at Snow Lake

terraces on one side or the other, our progress was tantalizingly slow. But this gave Michael time to carry his survey forward as we advanced, and it was fascinating to watch his map develop as each side valley, each distant ridge fell into place like the pieces of a giant jig-saw. On August 1, my thirtieth birthday, we broke through to the upper basin of the glacier, which, opening before us like a vast fan, offered a wide choice of routes.

Now that we were able to move freely over smooth ice we made a depot of most of our supplies and went forward in lightly laden groups to explore the various branches and to seek passes into whatever country lay beyond. It was exciting work. In ten days we reached the perimeter at several points over a wide arc and, in spite of much bad weather, discovered enough about our more distant surroundings to form a long-term plan.

We were at the very hub of the largest unknown region of the Karakoram, with major glaciers radiating from it in every direction and all within our reach. It was clear that, with so much to explore, we could best use our superb situation by dividing the expedition into three independent parties, each pursuing a separate objective and eventually returning to Kashmir by a different route. John and the four Skardu men, carrying our light photo-theodolite, crossed one of the passes we had discovered, which led them south into the Panmah glacier system and thence to Askole. Bill and two of the Sherpas, taking only the barest necessities, travelled westward. After crossing a long series of passes they reached and traversed Conway's "Snow Lake," which turned out to be not an ice-cap but one of seven contiguous glacier basins occupying the major part of the region. Finally, they broke through the great rock wall south of the Hispar Pass to Arundo in Baltistan.

On the way they explored the "Cornice Glacier," which had been seen and named thirty years before by Hunter and Fanny Workman, whose categorical statement that the glacier had no outlet gave rise to one of the most acrimonious debates ever to occur at a meeting of the Royal Geographical Society. As no one had been there since, the issue had remained unresolved. Bill, though unlikely, perhaps, to be actuated by motives of chivalry, always delighted in a chance to confound the scientific sceptics, and had been very anxious to confirm the Workmans' unique discovery. He was disappointed, therefore, to find that the topography of their glacier conformed to the normal pattern. Some years later I found in the archives of the Survey of India the sketch map that he had made on his remarkable journey: the areas representing the "Snow Lake" and the "Cornice Glacier" were titled respectively "Martin's Moonshine" and "Fanny's Fantasy."

Michael and I and the remaining five Sherpas travelled to the north-east. We were less mobile than the others, for we had with us the heavy survey equipment and, as ours was likely to prove the longest journey, a larger share of food. We spent a fortnight unravelling an exceedingly complicated range of mountains lying between the Skamri Glacier and the Shaksgam, and then turned west to complete the mapping of the main divide. On several of the glaciers in this region we found hundreds of dead ducks lying on or embedded in the ice. Presumably they had perished during migratory flights between Central Asia and India; and the fact that the corpses were in varying stages of decomposition suggested that these flights occurred annually. It seemed strange that the birds should follow a route across the most extensive ice sheets in the entire range, and we wondered if it could have been chosen by their remote ancestors before the glaciers, or perhaps even the range, existed. I hoped one day to return there at the right season to see this extraordinary migration.

In mid-September we reached an open valley beyond the main range where we met the first strangers we had seen since leaving Askole, nearly four months before. One afternoon four men with some yaks passed close to a deep willow grove which hid our camp. With whoops of joy the Sherpas sprang out upon them, and though they tried to bolt, they were too slow or too terrified to escape. But when, instead of being cut to pieces as they had doubtless feared, they found themselves invited to take tea with us, they relaxed and warmed to our friendly overtures. It transpired that our guests were Shimshalis from the remote Hunza village of Shuijerab, now only one day's march away across the Shimshal Pass. As they spoke only Burushaski, a language totally different from any Indian dialect, conversation was diffi-cult. But the Sherpas are adept at dealing with such situations, and before long we had achieved a surprising measure of mutual understanding. But it was not enough to satisfy the Shimshalis, who were intensely curious to know who we were and whence and why we had come. One of them, Mohi Bacha, kept clutching his tongue in a gesture of despair at its impotence.

As our supplies were running low, the youngest Shimshali was sent back across the pass to fetch food. A few days later he returned with a large caval-cade, armed with ancient muskets and headed by the *Lambadar* (headman) of Shimshal himself, who greeted us with distant courtesy, but made it plain that we were under arrest. This did not surprise us; nor, since our captors came from the right side of the frontier, were we much perturbed. At least it provided a simple solution to our transport problem. Soon, however, we found that one of the escort had a smattering of Hindustani, and with his help we managed, though with some difficulty, to convince the *Lambadar* that Michael and I were English. He was obviously relieved and at the same time strangely embarrassed.

Later we heard that he had already sent a swift messenger to the Mir of Hunza with the news that five Chinese had entered his domain with two servants, and that all seven of the intruders had been captured. The Mon-golian features of the Sherpas and their pigtails had doubtless prompted the first assumption; our beggarly appearance explained the second. The

Skamri Glacier

Mir immediately informed the British Political Agent in Gilgit, who tele-
graphed the tidings to New Delhi. In those days raids across the frontier
were not uncommon, though it was virtually impossible to seize the raiders.
The *Lambadar* had been greatly puzzled by our calm demeanour and had
certainly suspected a trap. He now departed, leaving some of his retinue
with instructions to give us every help. A few days later, having completed
the survey of the region, we followed him on horseback across the Shimshal
Pass to begin our long journey home.

At Shuijerab we were welcomed by the *Lambadar* as though we were
royal visitors; he treated us to a banquet, consisting mainly of vast quantities of mutton and yoghurt, and did his best to persuade us to prolong
our stay. He then escorted us to Shimshal, three days' march farther down
the valley. While we were resting there two Hunza levies arrived; they had
been sent by the Mir as soon as he had received a second despatch from the
Lambadar correcting his previous error. The Hunzas have a great relish for
pomp and ceremony; themselves a proud and dignified people, they delight
in social panache. The two levies were doubtless thrilled with their mission and looking forward eagerly to the reflected glory of escorting distinguished strangers, honoured guests of their prince, through the land. They
had obviously expected to meet two elegant sahibs; and when, instead,

The Lambadar *of Shimshal*

they saw two disreputable ruffians emerging from the *Lambadar's* house, with long, tousled hair and ragged beards, clad in filthy, tattered garments and broken boots, their dismay was all too plain. Their salutes froze half-way to their caps, the customary greeting, *Salaam Aleikum*, died on their lips and their faces displayed the disgust they felt. For nearly two days they preserved a stony silence and evidently found our proximity quite repulsive; then they began to soften towards their eccentric charges, and soon we were on cordial terms. Whether this change of heart was due to pity or a gradual realisation of the extent and nature of our recent travels, it was hard to tell. Happily, many years later, their tolerance was rewarded when, with the impressive retinue proper to a senior government official, I passed through their native village on my way back from Kashgar, and they gained much kudos among their fellows by claiming my acquaintance.

Our brief encounter with the Shimshalis marked the beginning—a delightful one—of our gradual return to the fleshpots, which progressed in stages of increasing affluence through the month-long trek back to Kashmir. After so long in the wilderness their high pastoral villages seemed almost suburban, and we did not appreciate their extraordinary isolation until we had seen the monstrous gorges dividing them from the main Hunza community. For mile after mile the way led along a slender track cut across the face of sheer conglomerate walls, thousands of feet high. The deep, vertical chasms formed by side ravines were spanned by fragile rope bridges slung from the boulders embedded in the matrix of those ancient alluvial deposits. Hardened to rugged country, we were none the less astonished at the courage and ingenuity, the dogged tenacity, of the men who, centuries ago, had pioneered this fantastic route through to the remote upland pastures. Mostly we were in the grim confines of the canyon, but sometimes the track led over high ridges, and on clear days we saw the massive ice ramparts of Dastoghil and Momhil Sar, the northern bastions of the Karakoram.

We escaped from the gorge one moonlit night by a climb of 8000 feet up an arid precipice and descended the next morning through meadows and pine woods to the valley of the Hunza river. Four more marches took us to Baltit, capital of this unique principality, where we stayed two nights as guests of the Mir. Almost the whole of the intervening day was spent on a shady lawn in the palace garden indulging our gross appetites with unlimited fruit and gazing up at the 24,000-foot spires of the Kanjut peaks or out across miles of terraced orchards, now ablaze with autumn colour.

Our host, Sir Muhamhad Nazim Khan, K.C.I.E., was a very old man, and we saw less of him than we had hoped. Forty-five years before his elder brother, Safdar Ali, had fought and lost a war against the British, which had been caused by his people's light-hearted indulgence in the sport of plundering caravans plying their trade between Kashmir and Sinkiang. When the war ended, Safdar Ali fled and Nazim Khan succeeded him as Mir, and had since remained a staunch supporter of the British Raj. From Baltit our way led through Gilgit, where we had our first news of the outside world for more than five months. Twelve days later we reached Srinagar, and there, for a delicious week amid exquisite surroundings of autumn Kashmir, we savoured the long-anticipated delights of beds and baths, clean clothes and idleness.

The Shaksgam expedition had been immensely rewarding. Never before had I seen anything like the wild grandeur of those desert mountains, their stark simplicity and their boundless range. Every phase, every step of the way, whether in known or unknown country, had opened another door upon a new aspect and a fuller understanding of that fantastic world; yet such was its scope that the more familiar it became, the more powerful was its impact upon the imagination. To have captured so much of it in a single season, and yet to feel that we had won but a bare acquaintance, was at once tantalising and deeply satisfying.

Plans for a second and still more ambitious Karakoram expedition had begun to take shape long before we had turned towards home. Our meeting with the Shimshalis had suggested the idea of spending a winter around the Shaksgam exploring the Aghil range, which was still largely unknown. By acquiring a herd of yaks and living in the manner of Central Asian nomads, it would be possible to move freely about the main valleys while the great rivers, the bugbear of summer travel, hibernated in their glacier founts. Skis would be used for sorties into the higher regions, and polar equipment needed to combat the cold. The previous summer would have been spent mapping the southern part of the main range; the following spring would find us far to the eastward heading for the Aling Kangri range, totally unknown, though believed to contain peaks of more than 24,000 feet. In Ladakh or Tibet? Who could tell?

In 1938 Everest intervened once more—this time a light expedition led by Bill—and it was not until 1939 that I had a chance to launch my spacious project. By then, of course, international politics were set upon their collision course, and despite the recent promise of "peace in our time," few of us really believed that war would be averted. With repeated assurances by scientists during the Thirties that the next war, if it came, would make the carnage of 1914–18 seem like a light-hearted skirmish, there were many who believed that it would result in the total destruction of Western civilisation. However, there seemed to be little purpose in waiting around for this eventuality, and I decided to go ahead with my plans, hoping that the disaster might at least be postponed for a couple of years. In spite of the general uncertainty, I had no difficulty in raising funds from the same sources as before, with additional grants from the British Museum and Kew. I even succeeded in borrowing an extremely expensive photo-theodolite from a firm in Germany, free of charge. Unfortunately, though I very nearly persuaded Michael to join me, neither he nor Bill was prepared to commit himself for eighteen months; while John could not again be spared by his department. However, I had little trouble in finding suitable companions, Peter Mott, Scott Russell and

Edric Fountaine, to replace them. All three had Arctic experience, which would have been extremely useful.

We left Kashmir in June and marched through Gilgit to the Hispar Glacier. The main purpose of our summer programme was to extend the existing triangulation northwards so as to provide a large number of fixed points which would be visible from the Aghil range. We had with us a small radio set to get periodical time signals necessary for the fixing of our position by the stars; to preserve precious battery-power we had intended not to use it for any other purpose. The Surveyor General of India had asked us also to make a detailed map of the great Hispar, Biafo and Punmah glacier systems, a big job which took most of our time and energy. We had planned to move to our winter base beyond the Shimshal Pass early in November.

At the beginning of October Scott was at our main depot on the Hispar Glacier, conducting some experiments in plant physiology, his special field. Feeling lonely perhaps, he broke our rule of not using the radio for frivolous purposes, and was punished by the appalling discovery that the war had begun; indeed, it had already been in progress for a month. With the expedition still scattered over a wide area it was some weeks before we all heard the grim tidings and could be brought together to discuss what we should do. Edric argued, I believe without much conviction, that as nothing much seemed to have happened so far, we should continue at least with our winter programme. He pointed out that Shackleton had been faced with a similar situation on his way to the Antarctic in 1914 and had not turned back. But we knew in our hearts that we had no choice: apart from any other consideration, none of us could have faced seven months of complete isolation at such a time. Even so, it was hard to make the break; the more so because it then seemed certain that, whatever the outcome of the conflict, we would never again experience this way of life. For my part I found solace in the realisation of how incredibly lucky I had been in making nine expeditions to the greatest mountains on earth, which had yielded a wealth of experience and happiness that I could hardly have dreamed of ten years before.

| 6 |

KASHGAR

THERE WAS CERTAINLY NO SENSE of urgency abroad when we returned to Kashmir in November 1939. No one seemed eager for our services, which, at our request, had been placed at the disposal of the British and Indian Governments by the Political Agent in Gilgit. Indeed, the response to our somewhat magniloquent offer suggested that we would be lucky to find any employment at all, in or out of the armed forces; and we began to regret our decision to abandon the expedition. While trying to decide what to do next we lived for three golden weeks in a houseboat moored alongside the Residency in Srinagar. Then, for the second time in Kashmir that year, I fell in love. It would be both unchivalrous and untrue to suggest that either time or place itself was responsible, but certainly no setting could be more perfect.

In December Edric and Scott returned to England, while Peter and I went to Dehra Dun to work on the completion of our Karakoram map at the headquarters of the Survey of India. Three months later the maximum age for joining the Army was raised from thirty to thirty-five, and I went to the Officers' Training School in Belgaum in Southern India. Not one of nature's soldiers, my performance there was hardly more distinguished than it had been at my earlier schools. Among other unfortunate lapses, I got into serious trouble over a matter concerning my room-mate.

He was an Anglo-Indian who had been a railway guard in civil life. He had received previous military training in a territorial regiment and was extremely keen and very efficient—certainly far more so than I; also he was most likeable and obviously a good leader. Moreover, he had been recommended for a commission by the divisional commander of his district. Half-way through the course, he was suddenly informed that he must leave the School as he was not considered to be "Officer material." I was convinced that this was only because of his colour, and so incensed by the monstrous injustice of his expulsion that I tried to induce the rest of our company to join me in a protest. When this became known I was brought before the Commandant, who informed me that I was guilty of mutiny which, according to Army law, I suppose I was. Nevertheless, at the end of the three-month course I was grudgingly given a commission and sent back to Dehra Dun for further training.

In August 1940 a telegram arrived from the Government of India offering me the post of British Consul-General in Kashgar and asking me to come to Simla at once. Had someone invited me to go to the moon, I could hardly have been more astonished, and for the next few days I was in a turmoil of incredulity, elation and doubt. Having abandoned all reasonable hope of ever seeing the mountains of Central Asia again, the immediate prospect of a two-month trek through the Karakoram, across the great Asiatic watershed and over the Pamirs was alluring enough; the idea of becoming closely acquainted with the Tarim Basin, which three years before on the Aghil Pass had seemed so utterly inaccessible, was wildly exciting. On the other hand, so far as I could see I was totally unqualified for the job; secondly, it hardly matched my purpose in joining the Army; thirdly, in times of supreme crisis such as these one's gregarious instincts are strong, and the thought of such complete isolation in a potentially hostile land was a little daunting. In Simla I was told, both by the Secretary for External Affairs and by the Viceroy, that the situation in Sinkiang, dominated by Russian influence, was delicate, and that the Kashgar post had become very important because of the enigmatical position of the Soviet Union in regard to the war. I raised the matter of my lack of qualification, but as this was dismissed as apparently irrelevant, I accepted the job.

The Kashgar post was founded in 1888 by Younghusband. The first incumbent, Sir George MacCartney, who held the appointment for twenty-five years, was entitled "Agent to the Resident in Kashmir," but later he was promoted to Consul and then to Consul-General to match the increasing Russian diplomatic representation in Sinkiang. The ostensible reason for the post was to foster the age-old trade across the Karakoram Pass (at the eastern end of the range) from Kashmir, and to protect the interests of a small but prosperous Indian community engaged in it. But, in fact, its establishment was part of that strange, semi-clandestine web of activity, intelligence and counter-intelligence, intrigue and diplomatic manoeuvre, known as "The Great Game" whose purpose, from the point of view of British India, was to observe, and where possible to contain, the advance of Russian imperialism in Central Asia. Since MacCartney's day the Consul-General had generally been a member of the Indian Political Service, though I was by no means the first outsider to be appointed.

I engaged two Sherpas, Lhakpa Tensing and Rinzing, to come with me as personal servants; both had been with me on several expeditions. In Gilgit we were joined by two new members of the Consulate staff; one of them, Sirdar Raza Ali, was my Indian secretary. Between us, with our baggage and stores for two years, we had a majestic caravan of fifty pack animals as we rode up the valley towards Hunza. Raza Ali had brought his wife, and on the first day she rode demurely behind her husband, clad in the tent-like robe of deep purdah. On the second morning, cantering along in front of the caravan, I was astonished to overtake a beautiful girl, with flowing black hair, dressed in a smart riding habit. It was some time before I realised, not without a pang of disappointment, that this was the same lady. During the next two years she continued to alternate between these two extremes, and when I came to know them better I discovered that she did so to satisfy her own whims and not those of her husband, a charming and very tolerant man.

Ten days later we reached Misgar, the last village at the head of the Hunza Valley, where the Government of India maintained a radio post.

From there we crossed the Mintaka Pass to the Taghdumbash Pamir (Sari-kol) in Chinese Turkestan. Here the vast gorges and towering precipices of the Karakoram gave place to rounded mountains and wide valleys, where even with pack-ponies, we had little difficulty in travelling thirty miles a day. My delight in seeing this new land was clouded when, on the second day, we were met by a squadron of Chinese cavalry and conducted to the fortress town of Tashkurghan, where we were locked in a filthy *serai* for four days. During this time we were treated with rough discourtesy by the Chinese officials, searched again and again, even in the linings of our clothing, and excluded from all contact with the local people. It was hardly the kind of welcome that might reasonably be expected by the accredited representative of a friendly country, but I already knew enough about the situation in Sinkiang not to be much surprised. The Indians behaved with admirable restraint and good humour, which certainly made things a lot easier.

Eventually we were allowed to proceed on our journey and, to my great relief, without an escort. For the next ten days our way led through the high Chinese Pamirs, between mountains of 24,000 and 25,000 feet: wild, majestic country, sparsely inhabited by Kirghiz herdsmen. Now that we were far from their Chinese rulers, whom they had always detested, these people greeted us with the spontaneous hospitality almost always to be found among nomads. We spent each night at one of their encampments; always they seemed delighted to see us, insisted on our sleeping in their warm, comfortable *akois* (dome-shaped tents) and sharing their food. Late one evening we crossed the Chichilic Pass, the mile-wide dale between its two summits already deep in the snows of autumn. I was riding alone, far ahead of the caravan, when two snow-leopards, the first I had ever seen, walked out from behind a rock not fifty yards ahead. They paused to look at me, then ambled slowly across the snow, now dyed with the sunset colours, without a sound to stir the absolute stillness. Six days later we emerged from the northern foothills of the range into flat desert; the great mountains, our abode for so many weeks, dimmed and vanished in the dust haze behind.

Southern Sinkiang consists of the Tarim Basin, a vast, oval plain surrounded by high mountain ranges: the Kuen Lun on the south and south-east, the Pamirs on the west, merging into the Tien Shan, which stretches in an arc, 900 miles long, to form its northern rim. The rivers draining from these mountains, though many are fed from some of the largest snow-fields outside Polar regions, can do no more than water a narrow fringe, an oval chain of oases nearly 2,000 miles long, before they disappear into the arid interior of the Basin, the formidable Takla Makan Desert. They are the life-blood of the country, for on the plains there is practically no rainfall, and agriculture is entirely dependent upon irrigation. Though the country has been under Chinese rule for five centuries (the word Sinkiang means "New Dominion"), the people of the oases are mostly Turki, closely akin in race, language and Islamic faith to the Ottoman Turks. They are placid, easy-going folk, but they have a turbulent history of war and civil strife, largely instigated by minority groups, such as Mongols and Tungans.

Kashgar, at the eastern extremity of the great ring of oases around the Takla Makan, I found similar to most of the other towns—Yarkand, Khotan, Aksu—of Southern Sinkiang. Surrounded by a massive wall fifty feet

Shipton in the Tien Shan, 1947

high, its narrow streets were lined with the open-fronted shops of metal workers, potters, cloth merchants, bakers and fruit sellers. In the centre was a large market square and a mosque with a dome of blue tiles. On the ramparts, high above, stood an old Chinese temple, in curious contrast to the indigenous architecture of the rest of the town. The streets and the square were always thronged with people, mostly riding donkeys; for the Turkis never walked, even to cross the road, if they could help it. For an Oriental town there was a remarkable absence of squalor and poverty. The men wore long, padded coats, black leather riding boots and embroidered skull caps, black and white or brightly coloured; but some had white turbans denoting that they had made the pilgrimage to Mecca. The women were dressed in similar clothes to the men; some, but by no means all, were veiled. They were a handsome crowd, and surprisingly cheerful considering the harsh, often cruel, tyranny of their rulers. By 1940 Southern Sinkiang had changed but little in the past several hundred years. That great scourge of modern civilisation, the internal-combustion engine, had only recently appeared; it was still a rarity, confined to the two main highways to Urumchi and Khotan. All other journeys were made by pony or camel, or on foot.

The British Consulate-General, my home for the next two years, was in a large walled compound outside the town. The staff included an assistant surgeon, John Selvey, who acted as Vice-Consul; Indian and Chinese secretaries; an accountant; numerous *chaprassis* (office servants); a platoon of Hunza gatekeepers in scarlet uniforms and a dozen mail runners. These last operated the first leg of our weekly diplomatic courier service, one of the more bizarre features of this extraordinary establishment. Riding in pairs on tough little horses, Union Jacks stuck in their saddles, the couriers took our mail bags at high speed across the Pamirs to Tashkurghan, where they exchanged their burdens with others operating the section across the Mintaka Pass to Misgar; and so on through Gilgit to Srinagar. Though they travelled by double, even treble, stages throughout the journey, it took at least a month for the bags to reach their destination. Our telegrams were handled by the radio station at Misgar, and it happened occasionally that we actually got a reply within thirty-five days. During the whole of the fifty years since the post was founded, through many rebellions and spells of administrative chaos, this remarkable service had continued to operate with mysterious immunity from outlaws, insurgents and hostile governments. In spite of the hardships involved, particularly in winter, the job of courier was jealously coveted, for the pay was high, and each pair was only required to make the journey to Tashkurghan and back once every six weeks. For the rest of the time they were free to recline in idleness, a condition dear to the hearts of most Orientals—and many Europeans.

My own house was a large, castellated mansion with spacious rooms, comfortably furnished and superbly carpeted. It had no modern conveniences, such as electricity and running water, but with plenty of servants this was no hardship. Owing to the difficulty of transport, it had long been the practice of my predecessors to leave behind all the amenities they had brought with them or acquired locally. Among the treasures that I inherited were a *droshki* or Russian carriage; a beautiful black stallion named "Tungan," which had been given to the wife of a former Consul-General by the local governor as a placatory offering after she had been shot in the shoulder during the Tungan rebellion of 1937; an excellent E.M.G. gramophone with hundreds of records, classical and "pop"; enough toilet paper to last twenty-three years, and a fine cellar of French wine which had been ordered direct from the growers. Best of all was the enormous library, which reflected the manifold tastes and interests of the original owners—history, poetry, botany, detective fiction, Shakespeare, Muslim law—and included a comprehensive collection of books on Central Asian travel, some signed by the authors, grateful for the hospitality they had received.

Two of the reception rooms opened through French windows on to the terraced garden shaded by massive plane trees and tended by six gardeners. The view extended northward across the river to a line of buff-coloured loess cliffs topped by clusters of flat-roofed mud houses, and beyond over fields and orchards, willows and poplars to the edge of the oasis, five miles away. From there the desert rose gently to yellow hills, fluted and scored like the "Bad Lands" of Arizona. When the air was clear the western ranges of the Tien Shan were visible through a gap in the hills. From the roof, where, like many of my neighbours, I kept a flock of tumbler pigeons, I could see the great ice peaks of the Pamirs forming a glistening arc to the south and south-west. But on most days, perhaps eight in ten, the view was restricted by a dust haze, like a misty day at home, and I could not see beyond the edge of the oasis.

In winter the scene was often drab, as, with no evergreens and scarcely any grass, everything was brown and grey. Sheets of ice lay on the rice-fields and along the meandering river flights of mallard, pochard and grey geese passed to and fro in search of unfrozen springs; in the late spring they migrated to India, perhaps by way of those huge glaciers we had explored in 1937. By the middle of March a bloom of misty green showed in the willows, closely followed by the fruit blossom in scattered drifts of pink and white. In April the young lucerne and corn appeared in the fields and, with the trees in new leaf, the countryside was swept by a flood of emerald. So swift was the change that scarcely three weeks separated deep winter from the fullness of summer. Our vines and fig trees were dug from the ground, where they had been buried for protection from the frost. By mid-May the fruit began to ripen: first apricots, then, in continuous series, strawberries, mulberries, cherries, nectarines, figs, peaches and grapes. And the melons! Nowhere else in the world can there be anything to compare with the melons of the Tarim Basin. I counted twenty-six varieties; some of the sweetest measured four or five feet in girth. They played an important part in the cultural and commercial life of the people. Melon stalls served as wayside cafés where the thirsty traveller could refresh himself by paying a few cents for a juicy slice. In any market there were as many melon sellers as all the other vendors put together. In a Turki house melon was the first thing to be offered to a guest. Traders made weeks-long journeys into the mountains to exchange them with the pastoral nomads for butter, meat and skins. They were stored in cellars throughout the winter, with the result that they were available for nine months of the year.

For all the luxury and intense interest of my surroundings, my first year in Kashgar was not a happy one. Though Sinkiang was nominally a province of China, the Central Government, far away across the Gobi Desert, had exercised virtually no control over its affairs since the Chinese Revolution in 1911, when local power had been seized by a remarkable man called Yang Tseng-Hsin. Under his adroit and, on the whole benevolent, rule it had enjoyed unwonted peace and prosperity for nearly two decades. Then, in 1928, Yang was murdered and Sinkiang relapsed into a state of chaos which gradually crystallised into a three-cornered civil war, with each contending faction holding part of the Province. It seemed that they all received a measure of Soviet backing, presumably pending a decision as to which of the three leaders was likely to prove the most malleable puppet. Eventually one, Sheng Shih-t'sai, was chosen as the most promising, and with strong support in the shape of modern weapons, he defeated his rivals and suppressed sporadic outbreaks of resistance throughout the Province, some of them full-scale rebellions. By 1940 it seemed certain that Sinkiang would soon be absorbed into Russian Turkestan, an event foretold by Lord Curzon as long ago as 1901. It was already a police state on the Stalinist model.

All commerce with India had been stopped several years before, and it seemed strange that the presence of Indian traders and a British Consulate were still tolerated, and our courier service allowed to operate. We could only suppose that until the Russians were ready to annex the Province they preferred to maintain the fiction of Chinese suzerainty, which would best be achieved by avoiding an overt break with a neighbour friendly to China. Meanwhile we and the traders, as "imperialist dogs," fulfilled the useful role played by the Jews under Hitler and the bourgeoisie in the French Revolution: a focus for hatred, a whipping boy for discontent. Anyone whom the authorities wished to remove was denounced as a secret agent of the British Consulate-General. I discovered later that our sinister "influence" had spread far and wide: to distant towns where no member of our staff had been seen for a quarter of a century; among Khasak tribesmen in remote mountain valleys, who had never set eyes on our establishment. The resulting boycott was sometimes tiresome, but, on the whole, surprisingly ineffective, for we were on excellent terms with the local people. Far worse was the systematic persecution of the wretched Indians, who were flung out of their homes, imprisoned, even flogged, at the slightest provocation, real or invented. Many of them had spent all or most of their lives in Sinkiang, and they clung to their position with pathetic tenacity, hoping that conditions would improve. The futile struggle to protect their lives and property was certainly the worse aspect of my job. Our own position was precarious, particularly in view of the treaty, signed the previous year, between Russia and Germany; but with London being pulverised daily, and the whole Western world on the edge of an abyss, one could hardly complain of insecurity.

In spite of my love of wild, remote places, I am not very good at coping with long periods of isolation, unless they are accompanied by vigorous activity. I am in fact a gregarious creature and crave the company of my fellow men—and of women. I delight in discussion, the more intimate the better, and I am by no means averse to gossip. Accustomed since childhood to analysing my own feelings and motives, I greatly enjoy probing those of my friends. In Kashgar, denied these simple pleasures, surrounded by an atmosphere of hostility and suspicion, I had spells of crushing loneliness.

It was not because of this, however, that a month after my arrival I wrote to the girl I had fallen in love with in Kashmir a year before, asking her to marry me. Her reply, which came ten weeks later, left me in no doubt about her feelings or her delight at the prospect of coming to Kashgar. Meanwhile I had got provisional permission from the Government of India to travel to Gilgit the following spring (1941), and it was arranged that we should meet there, and be married by the Political Agent. For a while all cares and forebodings were swamped by the flood tide of my happiness. Then came her telegram, three weeks old, with the bald statement that it was off. I sent letter after letter across the ranges, pleading and protesting. Week after week I waited at least for the cold solace of an explanation, and as each successive mail arrived without a word my dejection deepened. Eventually I heard from a mutual friend that she was married and that the cause of her defection had been the opposition of her mother, a powerful character, who had strongly disapproved of my eccentric way of life. I was certainly no stranger to the bitter taste of jealousy, and had often tried to convince myself that it was possible by despising it to negate its corrosive poison. Nevertheless, I had a long, hard struggle to extricate myself from the slough of self-commiseration that now engulfed me. In other circumstances I might have been tempted to follow Lhakpa Tensing's example by seeking consolation with a local mistress, for the Turki girls were very attractive. But the delicate political situation demanded immaculate behaviour, and I was too scared of the possible consequences.

Happily, even in moments of deep depression, I never quite lost touch with the magic of my surroundings. Each morning I woke with a sense of wonder that I was there, in the very heart of Central Asia, in a dream world of mountains and deserts and measureless distance. Each morning I rose just before dawn: one of my ponies, Tungan or his stable mate, was ready saddled, and in the first twilight I started on a ten- or twelve-mile ride; cantering over the wide river-flats where in winter wild duck congregated in their thousands and where the mist rose in the frosty air from a hundred ice-girt pools; along the twisting lanes, lined in early summer with deep banks of iris; or out into the desert towards the foothills of the Tien Shan, where, on clear days, I could look back across the purple-shadowed plain to the great arc of the Pamirs, sparkling in the early sunlight. In those two hours before breakfast I held daily communion with this antique land, its outward appearance unaltered since the days of Marco Polo. It was easy then to forget the menace of change.

Well aware of my capacity for idleness and with no one to impose the ordinary disciplines of life, I made myself conform to a strict routine; my morning rides were part of this. Mostly my work was divided between trying to help the Indian community, which was mainly concentrated in Kashgar, Yarkand and Khotan, and collecting political and other information which provided material for my weekly despatches to the Government of India and the Foreign Office. My spare time was largely filled by reading, writing and learning colloquial Mandarin from Mr. Chu, my Chinese secretary. To pay for these lessons I submitted to frequent games of chess with Mr. Chu; I detest the game, but it seemed to give great pleasure to my opponent. Apart from voluminous letters, which must have astonished my friends, I wrote a book of memoirs (*Upon That Mountain*) and a brief history of Sinkiang covering the past hundred years, culled largely from the massive archives of the Consulate. In the winter and early spring most of my week-ends were spent duck shooting with John Selvey and some of the Hunza gatekeepers.

Like most of the mountain tribesmen around the north-west frontier of India, the Hunzas were passionately fond of polo. Their version of it bore some slight resemblance to the game played at Hurlingham in that the players were mounted on ponies and hit the ball with sticks; but it was a much more rugged affair, contested on any reasonably level strip of ground of indefinite size, by any number of players who cared to join either side. They were not allowed to clout each other over the head with their sticks, but apart from this there appeared to be no rules. Any man able-bodied enough to climb into a saddle and not willing to participate would have been regarded as despicably effete. On my various journeys through Baltistan and Hunza I had always managed to avoid the ordeal on some pretext or other; though when Michael Spender and I were in Gilgit on our way back from the Shaksgam we had escaped only by the merest chance—which was fortunate, since Michael could barely retain his seat on a gently ambling pony.

Hunza staff of the Kashgar Consulate-General

Polo had been played by the staff of our Kashgar Consulate since time immemorial, but shortly before my arrival my predecessor had put a stop to it after a fatal accident. When I had been there six months I received a formal request from the Hunzas, led by a delightful character named Musa Beg, to resume their favourite sport. I hadn't the heart to refuse, even though they made it clear that I would be expected to take part in the opening game, a prospect I found terrifying. The game was played on a small field, iron-hard and surrounded by a high wall. There were ten of us on either side, so the ground was grossly overcrowded. The ponies were unschooled, and as soon as the match started they were maddened by the confined space and by the roars of the onlookers. For two minutes my only concern was to keep my seat on my wildly bucking mount. Then Musa Beg was thrown; his foot caught in the stirrup and he was dragged two lengths of the ground before his terrified pony could be stopped. He never regained consciousness and died of a fractured skull early the following morning. After this dreadful tragedy no one suggested playing polo again.

In some parts of the Tarim Basin an even wilder equestrian game was played. Its object was to pick up the carcass of a sheep and pitch it over a wall at one end of the field. Usually, several dozen riders competed, each against the rest; and when one had achieved the difficult feat of hoisting the carcass from the ground, all the others would strive to snatch it from him so as to score the goal themselves. The only time that I witnessed this astonishing contest I was invited to act as referee and, luckily, not to take part. On that occasion there were only a few minor casualties. A more popular and profitable sport was hunting gazelle with eagles. This was done in teams of eight or ten horsemen, each with one of the great hooded birds perched on his arm. They would ride out from an oasis in the early morning to surprise the animals when they came down from the hills to drink at some spring. The initial stalk was followed by a swift chase across the stony desert, which demanded skilful horsemanship; and when they were within 300 yards of their quarry they would unhood and release the eagles, which then caught the gazelles and broke their necks with their powerful talons.

The German invasion of Russia in the summer of 1941, whereby the Soviet Union became a reluctant ally of Britain, removed the main threat to our position in Kashgar, and my relations with the Soviet Consul-General became slightly less frigid; indeed, on two occasions we actually went shooting together. But it was many months before the local authorities began to relax their persecution of the Indian community.

In September four young Norwegians turned up in Kashgar. The first intimation I had of their arrival was when I received a letter from the local governor enclosing their passports and asking me to furnish visas to enable them to travel to India. Learning from the messenger that they were confined in the jail, I declined to issue the visas until they came in person. When after nearly a week of negotiations they were allowed to come I was glad that I had insisted, for they were obviously in need of a spell of comfort and good food; one had dislocated his spine and was in much pain. Aged between nineteen and twenty-one, they had a remarkable story to tell. Nine months before they had escaped on skis from German-occupied Norway to Sweden, and from there they had made their way through Finland, Russia and Soviet Turkestan to Northern Sinkiang. When, after this formidable journey, they reached Kashgar they had asked to be allowed to go to the British Consulate, but were told that it had been closed several years before; this despite the fact that they could actually see from their jail the Union Jack which flew above my house. They did not know that Russia and Germany were at war, and their first reaction to the news was perhaps a measure of the hardship and privation they had suffered on their journey; for instead of expressing the hope that the Germans, from whom they had escaped, might at last have met their match, they were delighted by the thought that the Russians would be defeated, which at that time seemed highly probable. In face of repeated protests from the Governor, I kept them in my house for a month. Though it was one of the rare occasions in my life when I have been in the position to offer liberal hospitality, I believe I enjoyed their stay at least as much as they did. Eventually I provided them with ponies and supplies, and they left with two of the mail couriers on the long journey to India; the lad with the injured spine encased in a stiff leather corset cunningly contrived by John Selvey.

The provincial capital, Urumchi, lay east-north-east of Kashgar, a thousand miles away. Until 1935 the only communication between the two cities had been by cart or by pony or camel-caravan; the usual time for the journey was two months each way. Since then motor transport had made its appearance, and by 1942 there were a few lorries plying back and forth, covering the distance in two or three weeks; though the bulk of the traffic still went by the old means. One of the first to make the journey in a motor vehicle was Sir Eric Teichman, who in 1935 brought a Ford V-8 30-cwt. truck from Peking to Kashgar, where he sold it to our Consulate and went on to India on horseback. It was then discovered that one of the gatekeepers, a Pathan named Mir Hamza, was something of a mechanical genius; so he was put in charge of the truck, which, with loving care and makeshift tools, he maintained in perfect running order for the next thirteen years. He was a strange character. Though quite illiterate, he spoke several languages, had travelled widely and lived by an extraordinary diversity of employment, including opium smuggling and other profitable trades. Still barely forty, he had settled down in his menial job in Kashgar, where he seemed utterly content.

Ever since I had come to Kashgar I had been trying in vain to get permission to go to Urumchi to urge the Provincial Government to put an end to the persecution of the Indian community, and to try to start negotiations for the reopening of the trade route over the Karakoram Pass. Repeated representations had been made by our Ambassador in China which, not surprisingly, had been no more fruitful. After the invasion of Russia an approach was also made through our Embassy in Moscow asking the Soviet Government to intercede with Sheng Shih-t'sai, the Provincial Governor, on our behalf, but this move had met with a cold rebuff. In an attempt to break the deadlock I suggested that I should be succeeded by a member of the Foreign Service in China, who would travel direct to Urumchi from there.

In July 1942 I received word from Delhi that Michael Gillett had been appointed and that he was expected to arrive in Urumchi at the beginning of August. Though it was largely the object of the manoeuvre, I was none the less surprised when my request to be allowed to go there to meet him was immediately granted. Still more astonishing was the sudden friendliness of the local authorities, who did everything they could to facilitate my journey. I left Kashgar in the Consulate truck on July 28, taking Mr. Chu, Mir Hamza and Lhakpa Tensing with me.

Though I would have preferred to travel on horseback, the 1000-mile drive to Urumchi was fascinating enough. For the first 200 miles we drove along a rough desert trail close to the foothills of the Tien Shan; after that we followed the line of oases fringing the northern edge of the Takla Makan. There was no motor road in the Western sense, but a series of country lanes, deeply rutted and pitted and linked by stretches of open desert. We were often ploughing through soft sand at 3 m.p.h., and very rarely got into top gear. At each of the towns where we stopped for the night we were entertained by the local Chinese magistrate with a show of hospitality quite unlike anything I had previously experienced in Sinkiang. On one occasion, when I complimented our host on an excellent Chinese dinner he had provided, he replied solemnly with evident compassion that it was very sad that good food was not to be had in Europe. He was not referring to wartime conditions.

Leaving Aksu at dawn one morning, we had a superb view of Khan Tengri (23,600 feet) and other peaks of the Central Tien Shan, rising above the morning mist which hung over the rice-fields. From Kara Shahr, the home of the Mongol Kalmuk tribes, we crossed a range of barren mountains and descended 7000 feet through a narrow gorge into that extraordinary basin known as the Turfan Depression. Though in the very centre of the landmass of Eurasia, and thus at the farthest point on the earth's surface from the sea, it lies 1000 feet below sea-level. In the summer it is so hot that the inhabitants live in cellars beneath the houses. From there we crossed a wide gap in the Tien Shan to Urumchi on the vast steppes of Dzungaria, or Northern Sinkiang. By driving thirteen hours a day we had completed the journey in a week, beating the previous record, so I was told, by five days.

Outside the city we were met by a large delegation of senior government officials headed by Mr. P'eng, Sheng's deputy. With them were Michael Gillett, who had arrived a few days before, and Mr. Chaucer Wu, the finance minister of the Kuomintang, the first high-ranking official of the Central Chinese Government to visit Sinkiang for more than thirty years. After the formal reception Michael and I were driven to our quarters, a comfortable suite in the Foreign Affairs Department. Two years of limited society had left me with an insatiable appetite for talk. Michael bore my ceaseless chatter with kindly tolerance, though he sometimes had to drive me from his room in the early hours of the morning to get some sleep. Compared with the lovely unspoilt towns of Southern Sinkiang, I found Urumchi an ugly, sprawling place, combining the worst aspects of jerry-built Western architecture with the more squalid features of the Eastern way of life. We were entertained with great courtesy, provided with a car for drives into the country, taken to bathe in some nearby hot springs, to the Chinese opera and occasionally to see a Russian film at the Anti-Imperialist Cinema.

Our official talks were conducted in a friendly atmosphere. Mr. P'eng appeared genuinely shocked by my lurid account of the maltreatment of Indian nationals; he assured me that the local officials in Kashgar and Yarkand had been responsible for this and that it would cease forthwith. He said that his Government was anxious to reopen the caravan route to India, not only for normal trade but also as a means of bringing military supplies to aid China's war effort against Japan. We soon began to understand the reason behind this unwonted cordiality and for the sudden show of friendliness I had met before leaving Kashgar. It was clear that the Chinese, taking advantage of Russia's dire plight in the west, were in the process of ridding Sinkiang of Soviet domination. We were fascinated to know what part the notorious Shen Shih-t'sai was playing in this dramatic *volte-face*. Having ruled the Province with ruthless tyranny for nine years, he was loathed by the native population; having submitted completely to Soviet direction and ignored the orders of the Chinese Central Government, he cannot have been much more popular with his fellow countrymen. Unfortunately we never met him. Mr. P'eng's repeated explanation that he was indisposed carried little conviction.

We had intended to stay in Urumchi for a fortnight before returning to Kashgar; but Mr. P'eng was very reluctant to let us go and kept delaying our departure on the grounds that there were still many matters to discuss. It seemed that our presence in the capital lent some kind of moral support to the political manoeuvres in progress. When, after nearly a month, we showed signs of becoming restive Mr. P'eng suggested a week's expedition to an ancient Taoist monastery by a lake, aptly named the Heavenly Pool, among the high mountains of the Tien Shan. We travelled on horseback with an armed escort, stopping the nights with Khasak nomads on the way. There I first tasted *kumis*, fermented mare's milk, an excellent drink with about the same alcoholic content as beer.

It was mid-September before we were able to leave Urumchi. On the eve of our departure we were given a farewell banquet attended by some 200 people. Most of them sat at long tables ranged along either side of the hall, while Mr. P'eng and his half dozen guests dined at a round table in the centre. Because of a prohibition order in force at the time, those at the long tables, mostly government officials, had nothing to drink but water, while at our table the only liquid available was Russian brandy. Each of the officials toasted us in turn; each demanded *Kan Pei* (bottoms up), blandly ignoring the inequality of the contract. At the outset, I had agreed with the Soviet Consul-General, sitting on my right, that we should support each other through the ordeal; but presently I noticed that before each toast he emptied most of the contents of his glass under the table. However, as principal guest, I thought that more robust behaviour was expected of me, and I accepted each challenge with a full glass.

By the fifteenth course I was feeling on top of the world, and looking forward keenly to my part in the evening's entertainment, the thought of which had earlier spoilt my appetite. But shortly afterwards, when Mr. P'eng rose to make his speech of welcome, I began to feel very ill. I must have looked it, too, for our host, a kindly man, interrupted his speech to say that if Mr. Shipton would care to go out for a breath of fresh air he was welcome to do so. With stupid arrogance I declined the invitation, and soon it was my turn to reply. Controlling my nausea with the help of some more brandy, I rose to my feet, noticing as I did so that Mr. Chaucer Wu, my left-hand neighbour, was asleep with his head on the table. I had intended to begin my speech with a few apposite remarks about Central

Asia being the birthplace of many cultures. Plunging straight into my subject, I announced, "The dawn of civilisation." This weighty remark was translated into Chinese by Mr. Chu and thence into Russian, and I clearly had the rapt attention of my audience. I said again with great solemnity, "The dawn of civilisation." Mr. Chu, taking this for a rhetorical gambit, again translated it into Chinese, whence it was again rendered into Russian. When I repeated the phrase a third time my secretary reminded me that he had already translated it twice. I replied hotly, "Well, say it again." This he did, and I sat down amid loud applause. It was the shortest, and probably the most successful after-dinner speech of my life. After that I lost contact with the proceedings, and when I regained consciousness I was walking along a garden path on Mr. P'eng's arm. Michael assured me that I had made a dignified exit, even keeping time to the regimental march played by the band to speed the departing guests.

It was with very mixed feelings that I left Kashgar in the middle of October 1942. For all the loneliness, hostility and frustration I had experienced during the past two years, I was still under the spell of this enchanting land, which I could hardly hope ever to see again. Of the two Sherpas I had brought with me, Rinzing decided to return to his native Tibet, but Lhakpa, who seemed thoroughly content with his Turki mistress, elected to stay. The Foreign Office had arranged for me to return to India by way of Soviet Turkestan; so I travelled westward through the Russian Pamirs to Osh and thence on the Turk-Sib Railway through Tashkent Samarkand and Bukhara to the Persian frontier near Ashkabad. From there I went by way of Meshed and Baluchistan to Delhi. The whole journey took less than a month; half the time I had taken to reach Kashgar. From Delhi I flew to London, arriving there for my first experience of wartime England on December 6.

Ten days later I was married to Diana Channer, whom I had met in Kashmir on my way to the Karakoram in 1939. The daughter of an officer in the Indian Forest Service, she had spent much of her childhood in jungle camps, and among the many things we had in common, she shared my love of wild country. She was serving in the A.T.S., so that we could snatch only a few brief spells together before I was sent to Persia for nearly two years, and again before my next assignment in Hungary. In September 1945 our first son, Nicky, was born.

Early in May 1946 I was in Vienna, doing an excessively frustrating job with U.N.R.R.A., when I got a telegram from London, asking me to return to my former post in Kashgar. I was scarcely less astonished than on the first occasion, and even more thrilled; for this time I had fewer reservations about accepting. I knew that Diana would be delighted at the prospect of making the fabulous journey to Kashgar and the unique experience of living there. Moreover, it provided our first chance since our marriage three and a half years before of being together for more than a few weeks, and a splendid setting for a delayed honeymoon. The only serious problem was what to do with Nicky. To take a baby less than one year old on horseback for two months of rugged travel seemed a hazardous venture. Also there was the lack of adequate medical facilities in Kashgar and the fact that, even at the end of my two-year appointment, he would not be old enough to remember the experience. So we decided that Diana would come with me for a year, leaving Nicky in the care of a woman who ran an excellent home, near Diana's parents, for a dozen children in similiar circumstances. Many of our friends were deeply shocked by our decision, and poor Diana was made to feel like a criminal. Whether our action was right or wrong, Nicky is now, at twenty-three, an unusually integrated and tolerant person.

When I went to the India Office to discuss my appointment I found that there were problems of a different kind. The previous autumn there had been a revolt by the Kirghiz nomads of Sarikol, the district north of the Mintaka Pass. There seemed little doubt that many of the so-called rebels as well as the arms for the uprising came from across the Soviet border. Most of the small Chinese garrisons had been annihilated, though some had managed to escape to Gilgit, and the rebels had advanced over the Pamirs to the oases south of Kashgar, cutting the main trade route across the Karakoram Pass from Ladakh. Though occasional reports had been received from Kashgar through the Chinese radio, the situation was still obscure, though it seemed clear that neither of the routes from India was yet open. Michael Gillett, who had been due to come home on leave the previous summer, had stayed in Kashgar until March 1946, when he had set out to reach Central China by way of Urumchi and the Gobi Desert. He reached London in June.

After much discussion it was decided that Diana and I should sail for India on July 26, hoping that by the time we arrived there the situation might have clarified; but when we reached Delhi on August 10 there was no further news. The diplomatic courier service between the Kashgar Consulate and Gilgit, which normally passed through Sarikol, remained closed, and it was assumed that the country south of Yarkand and Khotan was still in the hands of the rebels. The atmosphere at the Secretariat was depressing. The Calcutta riots were at their height, and all Government departments were beset by a mass of urgent problems in that delicate period before the granting of Indian independence. Over-worked officials were also oppressed by uncertainty about their own future; and it was hardly surprising that the question of how to get a Consul to the remotest of all their posts did not seem to them of prime importance.

When we had been in Delhi a week, however, news arrived from Ladakh that a caravan of Turki traders had left Leh for Khotan across the Karakoram Pass. We decided to follow this bold lead and to attempt to travel by that route. At least by the time we reached Leh, in a month's time, we might hope for news of how they had fared. So, thankful to leave the heat and fevered atmosphere of the capital, we travelled to Srinagar. There, in surroundings romantically familiar to both of us, we spent a week living in a houseboat and preparing for the journey.

The two routes from Kashmir to Sinkiang were about equal in length; by either, the normal time allowed for the journey to Kashgar was nearly two months; though, travelling light, it could be done in less. Neither has been in use for nearly twenty years. Though the route via Gilgit and the Mintaka Pass was much easier, nearly all the trade was carried over the ancient caravan route, eastward to Leh, capital of Ladakh, and then north across the Karakoram Pass to Yarkand and Khotan. This was mainly because supplies of fodder for the pack animals was more plentiful in Ladakh than in Hunza, but also because it would have been impossible to take camels, or even large numbers of heavily laden ponies, along the narrow ledges across the vast precipices of the Hunza gorge. With two passes of 18,000 feet and several more almost as high, nearly half its length through totally uninhabited country, it was certainly one of the most remarkable caravan routes that has ever existed.

We started on September 1. The first phase of the journey, a march of two weeks to Leh, was easy and wholly delightful. A comfortable path made walking easy, and at each eighteen-mile stage there was a rest house in one of the lovely oasis villages where we lived off the fat of the land. The way led over the Zoji La to Kargil, which I had passed through on my way to Skardu in 1937. Then turning east, we crossed a barren little pass to Ladakh. Though the nature of the landscape was the same, there was an astonishing change in the cultural atmosphere. It was as though we had stepped straight into Tibet. Villages of white- and red-faced houses, with slightly inward-sloping walls, climbed the hillsides; monasteries, gaunt and severe yet very beautiful, stood upon lofty crags as though they had grown out of the living rock. The Ladakhis—in features, in speech and dress, in their laughter and their charming courtesy so free from suspicion and reticence—were indistinguishable from the Tibetans I had known and admired. Is it their religion that moulds the character of a people, or is it that their native character fashions the religion of their adoption? If it be the former, then there is indeed much to be said for Tibetan Buddhism.

Set in a deep enclave in the Indus valley, Leh was the junction of several important trade routes: from Kashmir, from Kulu, from Gartok and the Tibetan Plateau, from Chinese Turkestan. Though its bazaar was the meeting-place of many races, its Tibetan appearance had remained intact. As we approached the town on September 15 we were met by a large deputation of merchants who evidently welcomed our arrival as a sure sign that the route over the Karakoram Pass was now open, though of course we knew no more than they of the situation beyond the ranges. The actual carrying trade was performed by Turkis from Yarkand, who transported the merchandise at an agreed rate for camel- or pony-load. Many of these people had been stranded in Leh by the Sarikol revolt nearly a year before, and by now they were seriously short of money and supplies. At the end of July, as we had heard in Delhi, a party of them, bolder or more desperate than their fellows, had started on the journey; it was not yet known how they had fared. The rest were now anxious to join us, in the naïve belief that the presence of the British Consul-General would be sufficient protection from any marauding bands of Kirghiz rebels we should happen to meet.

Though still undecided whether or not to go on, we made all the necessary preparations: hiring transport animals, buying fresh stores and sheepskin coats and hats against the intense cold we were likely to meet. Meanwhile we were joined by three new members of my staff: Rafaqatullah Khan, my secretary; Allen Mersh, the doctor; and Mohammad Shah, his assistant, who had followed us from Srinagar. On September 20 I received a telegram from Delhi telling me that a radio message had come from Kashgar to the effect that the caravan that had left Leh in July had been attacked by rebel bandits beyond the Karakoram Pass and robbed of all their baggage and animals, and advising me not to attempt that route, but to proceed to Gilgit in the hope of

Turki traders

travelling through Sarikol. It also said that Dr. Binns, the retiring consulate doctor, and his wife and two children had left Yarkand nearly a month before on their way across the Karakoram Pass to Leh.

The news faced us with a teasing dilemma. It would take us a month to get to Gilgit, possibly some weeks to arrange for onward transport there, and well over a month more to reach Kashgar. Moreover, if the rebels were still operating as far east as the Karakoram Pass, surely Sarikol, their orig-inal base, would be still more dangerous, particularly when the rigours of approaching winter forced them back to more habitable regions. Indeed, this suggested a potent factor in favour of the Leh route. The country beyond the Karakoram Pass was so severe, so totally devoid of grazing and other necessities to support even the tough Kirghiz nomads, that the rebels could not remain there indefinitely and it seemed likely that by mid-October they would have already retreated. On the other hand, to be stranded at 16,000 feet in late autumn, without pack animals and possibly without food, in country devoid of fuel, several weeks' march from the nearest habitation, faced by scores of river crossings impassable on foot, would be a grim situa-tion. I discussed the problem with the Turkis. They heard the news of their unfortunate colleagues with disconcerting calm; they agreed that we would be much less likely to meet with bandits so late in the year, but said that it was up to me to decide whether or not to go, and that in any event their fate was in the hands of Allah.

One thing was clear: we could not leave the region without discovering what had become of the Binns family. If they had run into trouble they might, at this moment, be struggling on towards Leh in desperate need of help. I decided therefore to go forward with the whole caravan as far as Pan-amik, the last inhabited place on the southern side of the ranges. If we had not met them by the time we arrived there I planned to ride forward with a light party by double marches in search of them.

On September 20 we left Leh accompanied by several other caravans, their leaders still happily deluded that our official presence would afford protection. Our entourage also included a sad little band of unarmed Chinese soldiers, headed by a Captain, who had escaped to Gilgit from the Sarikol massacre a year before, and had come to Leh hoping to find a safe way home. I had been reluctant to accept this responsibility, which could have been compromising, but was unable to ignore their pathetic appeal. Our first obstacle was the Khardung La, an 18,000-foot pass immediately north of Leh; a steep little glacier on its far side gave us a foretaste of the difficulties ahead. From there we descended into the valley of the Shyok River and reached Panamik on September 25.

We were intensely relieved to find that Dr. Binns and his family had arrived there that very morning, and were enjoying the exquisite pleasure of being once more in an inhabited country, in warmth and comfort, among trees and fields after a month of rugged, lonely travel. Their caravan had been attacked and shot at in one of the valleys north of the Karakoram Pass. Though quite unaware of the plunder of the unfortunate trading caravan, which must have occurred a few weeks before, they naturally assumed that their assailants were Kirghiz rebels. They took cover, waved handkerchiefs in token of submission and waited for their captors to come and claim their booty. Luckily, though the shooting continued for nearly half an hour, no one was hit, and when the attackers arrived they turned out to be a body of Chinese troops who had been sent to the area in search of bandits and had mistaken the caravan for their quarry. The Binns children were thrilled with the escapade. The Chinese had had good reason for shooting first and asking questions after, for another body of troops on a similar mission had been ambushed and badly mauled. However, with stronger forces patrolling the area south of Yarkand and with winter coming on, it seemed virtually certain that all rebel bands had now withdrawn, and we decided to continue our journey.

From the fertile valley of Panamik, the track climbed a slab of rock, 2000 feet high, so steep and smooth that from a distance it looked scarcely passable for a mountain goat. Beyond it we entered a wilderness of rock and ice surrounded by lofty peaks; and by the evening of the second day we reached the foot of a glacier cascading in a series of steep ice-falls from the Saser Pass (17,480 feet). The only way through was up a narrow gully of large moraine boulders between the ice and a vertical cliff. Though this type of ground is familiar enough to any mountaineering expedition, never before had I dreamed that it would be possible to climb it with heavily laden animals. There was no vestige of a path, and as the ponies clambered up the great boulders, their hooves scraped and slithered agonisingly in their efforts to gain purchase and retain their balance on trembling, bleeding legs. As we helped the muleteers to drag the unfortunate creatures up the gully, and often during the weeks that followed, I had to keep reminding myself that we were not engaged in a desperate attempt to establish a base camp on some high peak or to reach some unexplored country, but that we were travelling along a regular trade route on our way to take up a civil service appointment.

After many hours in the gully we reached a point where the angle of the glacier eased sufficiently for us to take to the ice. Here, as on the rocks below, the camels, with their soft, cloven feet, had much less trouble than the ponies. Camels are not usually associated with glacier travel, and to see how well they performed in this exotic environment was one of the many surprises provided by this astonishing journey. The descent from the Saser Pass was no less exacting than the climb up to it. Travelling northward, with the animals still fresh and well fed, the crossing was not so bad; but for caravans coming from Turkestan it was near the end of the journey, and then the poor creatures were often too weak from fatigue, hunger, altitude and exposure to survive this last effort. In the valley leading up to the Pass we had seen the first of the corpses, skeletons and heaps of bones which formed a continuous line for hundreds of miles until we reached the first oasis beyond the ranges. Later, riding ahead of our caravan, we would often find ourselves following this gruesome trail as the only guide to the way. It was estimated that an average of 15 per cent of the ponies and camels died on each journey.

The Saser Pass led us again into the Shyok valley, 160 miles upstream from the place where we had crossed it near Panamik. Instead of following the valley we plunged almost immediately into a ravine, so narrow that the opposing walls almost met 1000 feet above our heads, so dark that we seemed to be in a vast cavern. For the next ten days we travelled through a labyrinth of gorges and across high, barren ridges; utterly sterile, completely devoid of plant and animal life, it was the most forbidding country I had ever seen. Though we never dropped below 15,000 feet, we were now far from the great ice peaks of the Karakoram, and except for occasional distant views, there was nothing to distract the eye from the stony wastes, the interminable screes, the crumbling ruins of rock, mountain skeletons without form or identity. Despite the great elevation, there was little snow, though we passed some glaciers, hideously deformed, blackened with debris, coiled like repulsive serpents in sunless chasms. Here, surely, was the origin of the name Karakoram, which means "black gravel" in Turki, and is so absurdly inappropriate to the vast snowfields and sparkling peaks of the great range. Nothing is known of the men who, centuries ago, first ventured across this monstrous wilderness in search of trade or conquest. It is easier to imagine the toil, hardship and frustration they must have endured than to understand what inspired the courage and tenacity needed to discover a way.

Aware of their dwindling supplies of fodder, the Turkis were eager to travel as fast as possible, and in spite of the rough terrain, we usually covered between twenty and thirty miles a day. The weather was fine and still, but the October nights were so cold that it was difficult to start early in the mornings, which often meant that we did not camp until after dark. The crossing of the Karakoram Pass, for all its height of 18,250 feet, was one of the easiest stages of the whole journey. Beyond was the valley of the Yarkand River, which we followed for three days, fording its powerful current as many as thirty times in a single stage. Two more passes took us over the mountains of the Kuen Lun range, where we met with some heavy snowstorms, and eventually down through desert foothills to the first oasis of the Tarim Basin. There, the main part of our journey over, we spent a whole day resting in the shade of a willow grove, devouring grapes and delicious melons, while the Turkis were engaged in tortuous negotiations with the Chinese customs post.

As on a long sea voyage, many weeks in the mountain wilderness, remote from the habits and concerns of our former world, had made us intensely sensitive to our new environment. I had thought that I remembered it well, yet I was astonished at the impact made by the revival of half-forgotten memories: the peculiar moonlit feel of the landscape caused by the sunlight diffused through the dust haze; the way the shadows melted into the mud walls of the houses; the ethereal quality of the loess cliffs, of distant poplars dancing on the mirage-mist; a hundred sensations of sight, sound and smell, too intermingled for distinct analysis.

Then, at last, Kashgar, and the welcome of old friends. The ancient wall; the market thronged with life and colour; the view from our terraced garden over the tranquil river to the stillness of the desert hills beyond; the long lines of camels strung together, moving sedately to the deep clang of bells; the pigeons tumbling overhead; the mill in the willow grove across the valley, where the boy still blew his horn to announce that his father was ready to receive fresh supplies of grain; how wonderful to find it all unchanged. So much of life's experience remains shut away in watertight compartments simply because its essence is incommunicable. What luxury now to have someone close to share this with!

The political atmosphere was very different from five years before. The suspicion and cold hostility of the Chinese authorities was gone, and the local people, no longer in fear of reprisals, were free to express their natural friendliness. The Sarikol "revolt" had ended, and soon our diplomatic courier service was restored, bringing the vast quantities of mail which had accumulated in Gilgit for more than a year. Later, during our long journeys among the Kirghiz nomads of the Pamirs, we were left in no doubt whatever that this so-called rebellion had in fact been an invasion from across the Soviet frontier. The object had obviously been to spark off a general uprising throughout the Province which could have led to the re-establishment of a Soviet-dominated regime. It had failed largely because the Turki population of the plains had remained loyal to the Chinese, with the result that the garrisons of the oasis towns south of Kashgar, who at one time were in desperate straits, were able to repel the attackers and drive them back into the mountains. All the Kirghiz we spoke with were very bitter about the whole affair, since they had lost a great deal of their stock, either slaughtered to feed the invaders or driven over the frontier.

Not surprisingly, the Soviet Consulate was not very popular, and while we basked in the sun of general esteem, they suffered some of the hostility and restrictions we had experienced before. A year later an unfortunate incident occurred when three members of their staff, chased by an angry mob, dashed into our compound to seek refuge. Unhappily some of their pursuers, evading our Hunza guards, ran in too, and beat up the fugitives on British territory; as a result, I received a strong note of protest from the Soviet Consul-General. Apart from this temporary setback, however, our relations with the Russians were, on the surface at least, very friendly, and there was a good deal of reciprocal entertaining. Unfortunately this was marred by competitive drinking, impossible to avoid without giving offence. Our parties with the Chinese were more relaxed and much more pleasant.

After the rigours of the journey we were content for a while to settle down to domestic life and enjoyment of the local scene. On special occasions, such as Christmas or some Muslim festival we gave a *tamasha* for the consulate employees and as many of the neighbouring population as could squeeze into the compound. This comprised a feast of *pilau*, cooked in enormous cauldrons, followed by displays of Turki and Hunza dancing. From time to time Diana gave purdah parties for the wives and daughters of the staff. I was, of course, banished from the house when they were in progress, but I gathered that they were by no means dull. When it was clear that Sarikol was peaceful once more, Rafaqatullah Khan arranged for his wife to come from India by way of Gilgit, and he went to Misgar to meet her. Unlike Raza Ali's wife, she was kept in strict purdah.

Some months later Lhakpa, who was then employed as a *chaprassi*, came into my office one morning with the astonishing news that Mrs. Khan was outside asking to see me.

"Whatever does she want?" I asked.

"I don't know," said Lhakpa, with a sly grin, "but I think she wants to complain that her husband is maltreating her."

This was most embarrassing, but I thought I had better hear what she had to say. So in came the small, tent-like object, and sat in a chair opposite me, sobbing bitterly. As she spoke neither English nor Urdu, I summoned another *chaprassi*, Amir Ali, who spoke her native Pashtu. Her pathetic sobs seemed to make her almost inarticulate, but in spite of this Amir Ali appeared to have no difficulty in understanding her broken speech, which he translated into Urdu. Her husband, she said, was treating her with great cruelty, beating her daily; she could stand it no longer, and implored me to arrange for her to go back to India. I replied that I was sorry, but that I would have to get her husband in to answer the charge. This evoked what sounded like a frightened wail, but she remained seated while the *chaprassis* went off to find Mr. Khan.

Left alone with this invisible, sobbing creature, I suppressed an impulse to walk over and lift the veil, and pretended to write busily, eerily aware of being watched by her unseen eyes. I was relieved when the door opened and Mr. Khan entered, looking, I thought, distinctly sheepish. I explained what had transpired and asked for an explanation.

"It is quite ridiculous," said Mr. Khan. "Everyone knows that I am very fond of my wife. I have never maltreated her, and I can bring witnesses to prove it. Will you please send for Sheikh Sahib (the accountant)."

As the lady was in strict purdah, I did not see what light Sheikh Sahib could possibly throw on the matter; but I agreed, and he was summoned. He told me that he considered the Khans a devoted couple and that his own wife thought that Mrs. Khan was happy. His testimony did not seem to be getting us very far; and I was wondering where we went from here, when suddenly I heard a disturbance outside the open door, and in came

a second tent. There was a moment of stunned silence—I was later able to appreciate its theatrical timing—then, pointing to the new arrival, Mr. Khan yelled: "But *this* is my wife. That woman is an impostor."

My head reeled. I banged the desk with my fist and shouted, "This is fantastic," whereupon the first tent calmly lifted her veil to reveal Diana's face, and reminded me that it was April 1.

Ten days before, Mr. Khan had approached Diana diffidently:

Kirghiz woman

"Madam, cannot we pull C.G.'s leg?" and propounded his plan. They had, of course, to include Lhakpa and Amir Ali in the conspiracy. Diana, a born mimic, and helped by her convulsive sobs, had no difficulty in simulating Pashtu, of which neither of us knew a word. The whole act had been well rehearsed and brilliantly performed. No one enjoyed the frolic more than Mrs. Khan, who asked if it might be repeated the following year; which rather suggested that she had missed the point.

As an important part of my job was to see as much of the country as possible and to find out what was going on, we took full advantage of our freedom to travel, and made frequent journeys of one, two or three weeks, sometimes in the mountains, sometimes to distant towns such as Aksu or Uch Turfan. Each time we discovered new aspects of this bewitched land; each journey yielded a deeper impression of its boundless horizons. Yet it was always a delight to return, tired after long days in the saddle, to the comfort and tranquillity of our home.

Most of our week-ends were spent in the foothills of the Tien Shan, hunting ibex or *ovis poli*, or simply exploring: for even on a short trip it was easy to reach valleys never before visited by Western travellers. On these local excursions we made friends with some delightful Kirghiz families. This proved most useful, for we generally took one of their men with us on our longer mountain journeys, which made it much easier to establish friendly relations with the nomads and to persuade them of our innocent intentions. It was particularly important in remote regions near the Soviet frontier; our failure to do so on one occasion resulted in our being shot at and captured by a platoon of Chinese cavalry sent to intercept "a party of Russians" reported to be wandering in the area.

On several week-end expeditions we tried to reach a huge natural arch in a range of jagged peaks north-west of Kashgar. A distant glimpse of it on my way to Osh in 1942 had roused my interest, which was greatly increased when we discovered it to be the subject of a local legend. It was believed to be a ghostly pergola, which vanished when approached, over a beautiful garden of flowers and fruit trees inhabited by spirits and inaccessible to mortals. We made three attempts to reach it from the south, but each time we became entangled in a maze of sinuous passages cutting deep into the heart of the range and ending either in sheer cliffs or in dark caverns. Later, we found a way of approaching the range from a wild region to the north. The arch was invisible from that direction, and none of our Kirghiz friends knew of its existence. But the canyons on that side were easier to penetrate, and eventually our search was rewarded when we came upon the enormous vault spanning a chasm 1000 feet deep. Though alas, there was no sign of the celestial garden, we were well satisfied to have found one of the greatest natural arches in the world.

It was one of the rare periods when Sinkiang was politically accessible to Western travellers, and as Urumchi could now be reached by air from Central China, we enjoyed occasional visitors from the outside world. Bill Tilman came twice; which, considering that I was married, might have been regarded as a touching tribute to our friendship but for the unique attractions of the mountains I had to offer. We climbed together in the Pamirs and Eastern Tien Shan. Among the most rewarding of our guests were Bob and Vera Ransom from San Francisco. Bob was an attorney who had been employed to defend the Japanese in the War Crimes Trials in Manila. After that, he and his wife had visited Peking and then flown to Urumchi. Acting as usual on the spur of the moment, they came from there to Kashgar by lorry, hoping to travel on to India, but with little idea of what this involved. Bob, widely travelled and with otherwise liberal views, had strong anti-British feelings, not uncommon among even the most enlightened Americans; and as they approached Kashgar he and Vera had discussed the problem of how to avoid meeting "this bloody British Consul." However, they were compelled to face this distasteful ordeal by their need for Indian visas.

We had been warned of their approach and, though happy in our exile, were excited by the prospect of fresh company. They came at tea-time one hot afternoon in early October and were conducted by the scarlet-coated Hunza guards, not to my office but to our sumptuous drawing-room, where they were greeted with thoroughly un-English warmth by Diana. It happened that I had a frostbitten foot sustained two months before while climbing with Bill at 24,000 feet in the Pamirs; and when I hobbled in on crutches, making a casual reference to my infirmity, our guests were clearly shaken by this evidence of the rigours of the journey ahead of them. Bob's prejudice was not revealed until, three days later, I took him with me to an official Chinese banquet, where, under the disinhibiting influence of a great deal of vodka, he treated me to an eloquent résumé of the disagreeable traits of my fellow countrymen. Nevertheless, we became and have remained firm friends.

The Ransoms stayed with us for a fortnight. Their lively response to everything they saw and their wide range of interests were immensely stimulating and gave us the feeling that the days were not half long enough for the full enjoyment of their company. Their characters contrasted sharply: Bob was vital, dynamic, restless, while Vera was placid, imperturbable and utterly content with the present; she also had the rare quality of complete naturalness. Our nightly discussions, always protracted until 2:00 or 3:00, covered a great variety of topics, though we often reverted to the subject of Bob's *bête noire* in a vain attempt to persuade him that as a nation we were not really more arrogant, hypocritical and oppressive than others. Before they left I gave him letters of introduction to twenty of my friends in England; and though perhaps we had implanted a germ of tolerance, it was one of these that wrought his eventual conversion. For their long trek over the ranges to Gilgit and Kashmir we provided them with an escort of Hunza guards.

Diana had originally intended to remain in Kashgar for one year, but she was so happy there that she decided to stay for a second winter and to leave in April 1948. Even then she was bitterly reluctant to end the unique experience of the past eighteen months, to break with a way of life never to be repeated. Owing to the war in Kashmir, I persuaded her to fly from Urumchi to Central China; but she was very sad to miss the chance to see the fabulous principality of Hunza. As a servant of the old Government of India my position was now rather ambiguous, for after Partition in 1947 India and Pakistan each laid claim to the Kashgar Consulate, and with it my allegiance. However, there was nothing that either could do about it, and distance helped me to deal tactfully with the conflicting instructions I received from both. As I was under contract to serve for two years, I agreed to stay until October.

As the day of my departure approached, I sank into a nostalgic daydream. My two spells in Kashgar, four years in all, had yielded a richer harvest of experience than any other period of my life; and behind my regret at leaving was the still persistent sense of wonder that it had really happened. This was now heightened by the realisation that I might well be the last Westerner for many decades to travel in the Tarim Basin; certainly the last ever to know it in its age-old form and with such intimacy. For it was all too clear from the way events were shaping in China that sweeping change could not be long delayed.

| 7 |

KUNMING

WHEN I RETURNED TO ENGLAND at the end of 1948 I was again at one of those crossroads, common in the life of a vagrant. My choice of occupation, though diverse, did not seem to be very wide. There was teaching: friends in the profession encouraged me to think that there might be an opening here; I should at least have learned a modicum of geography by now and, remembering my early scholastic attainments, there was a bizarre fascination in the idea of my becoming a schoolmaster. Diana and I thought seriously of emigrating to New Zealand, a country which, by all accounts, offered many of the things we enjoyed. Finally, there was the possibility of acquiring a small piece of land on which to raise chickens or pigs or establish a market garden. My sojourns abroad, however much I may have enjoyed them, have always stimulated a longing for the English countryside, and now the notion of owning a piece of Dorset or Wiltshire, however minute, had a strong appeal. So, in spite of repeated warnings against such a venture, we spent much of that winter, based at Diana's parents' home in Warminster, searching for a suitable property. Of the scores that we saw only one attracted us. This was a house near Winterslow of eccentric design, at the end of a mile of earth road and set in pleasant woodland, seventeen acres of which was included in the price of less than £3,000. We would have bought it but for the surveyor's report that the house was riddled with dry-rot.

In April 1949, still no nearer a solution to our problem, I received two offers almost simultaneously: one was from the Foreign Office of the post of Consul-General at Kunming in Yunnan, the southernmost province of China; the other came from the Government of Pakistan inviting me to return to Kashgar as their representative there. The second of these was very tempting, but on reflection I realised that there were factors which would make it unwise to accept. Having just left the joint employ of India and Pakistan, I could hardly return in the service of one to a consulate claimed by both. Moreover, the rapid advance of the Communist rule over China made it almost certain that Sinkiang would very soon come under its sway, and though this also applied to Yunnan, the extreme isolation of the Kashgar post made the prospect a great deal more intimidating. As it was, I had some misgivings about exposing Diana and Nicky (now three and a half years old) to a completely unpredictable situation in Kunming; for Diana was determined that neither of them should be left behind. However, there at least medical facilities and modern means of communication would be available, and there were other friendly consulates to lend moral support; so, after some discussion, I accepted the Kunming post.

Early in July, after a delay occasioned by Nicky getting measles at the last moment, we set out for Hong Kong. We made the journey by flying-boat in six days, staying the night and most of the preceding afternoon at each stop. To my mind this was a much more agreeable method of travel than by modern jet aircraft, which hurtle us half-way round the earth in one continuously gruelling ordeal. We spent a week in Hong Kong shopping and enjoying the charms of that lovely island city. The mass immigration from China had hardly begun, and no one could have predicted that, within a year, the already dense population would have more than doubled. While we were there the news came of the spectacular dash of H.M.S. *Amethyst* down the Yangtze. Although the growing menace of Communist China caused apprehension, it did nothing to stem the flood-tide of business activity in Hong Kong. From the hectic bustle of the city we once escaped into the tranquil hills of the New Territories,

strangely like the Scottish Highlands. We were sorry when the time came
to fly on to our new home.

During the war Kunming had acquired considerable importance as the
eastern terminal of the Burma Road. Thus inflated, it now sprawled far
beyond the walls of the ancient city of Yunnan-fu, surely robbing it of much
of its former charm. But it was beautifully sited near the northern shore of
a lake, twenty miles long and surrounded by green mountains. The climate
was ideal, for it was at an elevation of 6000 feet and only just outside the
tropics. The British Consulate-General was close to the northern wall of
the old city. It was an ugly, two-storied building surrounded by a high wall
with little room for a garden; a sad contrast to our palatial abode in Kashgar
with its sweeping views and its spacious, terraced gardens. Diana, Nicky and
I occupied the upper floor, where I also had my private office. The Consular
offices were on the ground floor, at the foot of a staircase of polished stone,
and with a number of chairs outside the doors for members of the public
waiting to transact business.

Soon after my arrival this staircase was the scene of a small incident
which must have made a curious impression on those who witnessed it.
Working upstairs one morning, I found that I needed a certain file from
the office below; so I ran down to fetch it. Eight steps from the bottom
my foot slipped and I completed the descent on my tail-bone. I uttered a
number of obscene expletives and limped into the office, scarcely noticing five missionary ladies sitting in a sedate row outside. Having returned
upstairs, I found that I had brought the wrong file, so I hurried down
again. My foot slipped on the same step and I gave an exact replica of my
previous performance, oaths and all, to the open-mouthed astonishment
of my little audience.

The Vice-Consul was Bertram Hemingway, a man in his late fifties,
who had lived most of his life in China and spoke the Peking dialect fluently. He and his wife lived in a separate house close by. We had an excellent Chinese secretary, Mr. Chou. It had been decided to establish a radio
station in the consulate and, towards the end of July, Frank Pile, a young
man belonging to the Diplomatic Wireless Service, arrived to install and
operate it. He was to maintain a twice-daily contact with Singapore and

thence with Hong Kong; and as his schedules were in the morning and evening, we decided that he should live in the Consulate and have his meals with us.

For many decades the dominant foreign influence in Yunnan had been French, owing to the proximity of their former colony, Indo China (now Vietnam). The French Consulate-General still maintained a very large establishment, which included press, cultural and commercial attachés, all of them married, and a doctor. There were also American and Burmese Consulates. For a time we were involved in an almost continuous social round, very different from our isolated life in Kashgar. Everyone was most friendly and the parties were pleasantly informal. There was an atmosphere about them of hectic gaiety, perhaps because we all felt apprehensive about the future. I recall the occasion when the British Consul-General's wife, anxious, no doubt, to dispel our national reputation for cold reserve, danced a can-can on the table with the French Vice-Consul. It was hard to believe that it was the same girl whom I found a few hours later demurely entertaining a group of missionary wives to morning coffee.

There was a large number of missionaries in Yunnan, of many nationalities and representing almost every Christian denomination. One of my first duties was to preside at the civil marriage of a young Canadian missionary couple. This was held in the consulate office, and was followed immediately by a religious wedding in our drawing-room. By an extraordinary oversight I had failed to explain the programme to Diana, with the result that, when the service was nearing its climax, she tripped briskly in bearing a tray of cocktails.

The various consulates used to take turns at arranging Sunday outings for the entertainment of our combined staffs, and two weeks after our arrival M. de Courten, the French Consul-General, organised an adventurous voyage, in a flotilla of rubber dinghies, down a river flowing from the lake. It was a huge success, and set a standard which, I realised, was going to be hard to equal. I had already bought a horse and reverted to my old Kashgar habit of riding a dozen miles before breakfast. These rides took me into some enchanting valleys north of the city. It was limestone country, and the small mountains were steep, beautifully shaped and very green. One morning, following a track over the hills, I came upon a circular basin about one mile across. It was completely surrounded by mountains with a solitary rocky hill in the centre of its level floor. From a point on the perimeter, a river emerged from the mountains, meandered across the flat ground, passed clean through the central hill by way of a large tunnel and eventually vanished into another cave on the opposite side of the basin. As the tunnel through the hill was curved, I could not see through it.

Here was a splendid solution to my problem of providing a Sunday's entertainment for my colleagues. This strange topographical phenomenon was well worth a visit, while an attempt to make a passage through the tunnel would be an amusing adventure for my guests. So, two Sundays later, we set out by jeep, followed by most of the combined consular staffs and their wives. A short journey by road followed by a pleasant two-mile walk over the hills brought us to my basin. Everyone was intrigued with the place and eager to explore the tunnel. It proved to be an impressive cave, high-vaulted and echoing. For much of the way we had to use torches, and in some places we had to wade through thigh-deep pools, which evoked shrieks of pretended distress from the women. A couple of hours sufficed for a leisurely exploration, and we emerged in time for a heavy lunch on the river bank. This, and some excellent French wine, brought by the de Courtens, together with the warm silence of the basin produced a general feeling of torpor in the party.

Frank Pile and I, however, were keen to investigate the cavern by which the river issued from the mountains flanking the basin, and six of the others agreed, reluctantly, to come with us. So, shortly after 2:00, we entered the passage, carrying two torches. It was the size and shape of a railway tunnel, and its floor was wholly occupied by the river, knee-deep and flowing gently over a sandy bottom. After wading along it for some twenty minutes we reached a point where the passage contracted to a narrow defile and the water became very deep. The others decided that they had come far enough, but Frank and I wanted to explore just a bit farther. We took off our shirts and watches for our friends to take back and, clad in shorts and gym shoes, started swimming through the defile, holding one of the torches clear of the water. Some thirty yards farther on we entered a large chamber with a shingle beach at the far side, where we scrambled ashore and looked around us.

At first it seemed that we could go no farther; but soon we noticed a small opening in the wall at the top of the beach. We squeezed through this into a small passage and scrambled along it. It was rough going: sometimes we clambered over huge boulders partly blocking the way; sometimes we were forced to crawl on hands and knees or squeeze through narrow clefts; sometimes we came to a drop of eight or ten feet in the floor of the passage. We saw no openings on either side, so we anticipated no difficulty in finding the way back. After half an hour of this I was beginning to think that it was time to return, when we heard the sound of rushing water. It grew louder, and a few minutes later we emerged into a large transverse tunnel, carrying a raging torrent. This was clearly the place to turn back, for apart from the fact that our appetite for subterranean exploration was now fully satisfied, the river was much too boisterous to wade. Before turning back we noticed a brass bell firmly wedged in a rock cleft, its outer surface deeply encrusted with calcium.

Scrambling over the slimy walls of rocks and squeezing through the holes seemed, on the way back, even more strenuous than before. I assumed that this was because I was tiring, and I longed to get out into the sunlight. Half an hour had elapsed and we were expecting at any moment to reach the large chamber where we had finished our swim when, to our surprise, we again heard the sound of rushing water. We thought at first that it must come from the river flowing to the mouth of the cavern; I was puzzled, for I distinctly remembered noticing the silence in the large chamber. Maybe it was just some curious trick of acoustics. But the sound increased rapidly as we advanced, and presently, to our dismay, we found ourselves back in the big transverse tunnel. There could be no doubt that we were in the same place, for there was the bell.

Considerably shaken, we turned and hurried back along the passage. This time we tried to take more notice of our surroundings, but the obstacles were so numerous, so similar in their repeated sequence, that it was impossible to identify them with any certainty. Moreover, we had approached them from the reverse direction on our inward journey. Another half-hour of scrambling, crawling, squeezing, and then—there it was again, that infernal dull roar, mounting to a delirious crescendo as we emerged once more into the transverse tunnel.

The situation now had the quality of a nightmare. Twice we had failed to find the way back, and already our small pocket torch was weakening. All we could do was to keep calm and try again. This time we were determined to take great care, examining each slit and cranny as we went lest any should lead to an alternative passage; if we found one, one of us would explore it for some distance while the other remained behind. As there were frequent patches of mud along the floor of the passage, it should not be difficult to identify the correct branch by our footprints. We worked methodically; but, try as we would, we could find no alternative passage. Certainly we did not spend as long on the job as we would have liked, for the light from our torch was fast diminishing, and the need for haste was obvious. As it was, the third circuit took us a full hour to complete.

Utterly forlorn, we sank down on the rocks beside the bell, our nightmare hardened to grim reality. Our torch now only gave a faint glimmer, which would barely last another ten minutes. Even had it been possible to wade in the torrent, it would have been mad to attempt to make our way up or down the transverse tunnel in complete darkness. There was nothing to do but wait for rescue.

We switched off the torch to preserve its feeble light. In normal circumstances one rarely experiences total darkness; it now seemed to have a solid quality. For a while we fell into futile speculation as to how we could have lost our way, and I was tormented by the thought of my crass stupidity in embarking upon such a venture without proper equipment. More important, however, was the question of what our friends would do. The ugly thought did not escape us that anyone coming to our rescue might also get lost. It was possible that the whole mountain was honeycombed with passages; in which case we had at least been lucky to return each time to the same place. The others might assume that we had found another exit, possibly some miles away over the mountains, and might wait until dark before returning to the jeeps. In that case they would probably not be able to organise a search until the following morning. Then at least, we thought, they would have the foresight to equip themselves with adequate light and a means of blazing a trail through the passages.

Often in the first hour or so we thought we heard voices, and we yelled ourselves hoarse; each time the sounds turned out to be some extra echo of the torrent. Inactivity and the damp atmosphere chilled our nearly naked bodies, and it was not long before our teeth were chattering. We wrestled and massaged and pummelled each other to restore warmth. It was an exhausting occupation, and eventually we lay down clasped in each other's arms. Frank fell asleep and I dozed. Suddenly I was wide awake with the conviction that I had heard a sound above the noise of the water. As I listened a rumble came from Frank's tummy. I cursed and nestled down again, determined now to stay awake.

Some time later, I again thought I heard voices and let out a mighty yell, which echoed through the cavern. This time there was an answering call. As we scrambled to our feet I shouted to whoever it was to wait for us and to keep on calling. In this way I hoped to minimise the danger of their falling into the trap that had enmeshed us. By the dim glow of the torch we made our way along the passage. After twenty yards we came to one of the places where we had to go on hands and knees. As we were crawling along, I noticed that the calls, much louder now, were coming from directly above. The passage was so restricted it was difficult to screw my neck round and look upwards. Sure enough there was a dark hole in the roof. We clambered through it and found ourselves in another passage only eight feet above, where we met de Courten and Larry Lutkins, the American Consul.

This, then, was the solution to the puzzle. All the way from the chamber we had been climbing over boulders and other barriers, many of them more than ten feet high. This "hole" had appeared as no more than another steep drop in the floor of the tunnel like dozens of others, and we had slipped through it without noticing that it took us into the lower passage. Each time we tried to find our way back we had crawled beneath it without looking up. One mystery remains, however: how did Frank and I go three times round the *lower passage* without seeing the opening which brought us back to our starting-point?

It was past midnight when we reached the mouth of the cavern. Rain had been falling since nightfall, but all my guests were still there, huddled round a fire under an overhanging cliff. I had certainly provided them with a memorable day's entertainment. Our rescuers told us that they had just decided to abandon the search when they heard my shout. It is said that Providence looks after babes and drunks; sometimes, it seems, she goes to unreasonable lengths to extend her protection to fools.

Nicky was obviously enjoying Kunming. For a child of barely four, he lived a remarkably independent life. We had engaged an *amah* to look after him, but he soon had her well under his control. The gardener had five small boys, named according to the Chinese custom, "Venerable One," "Venerable Two," and so on, and with them he spent much of his time in the local bazaar, where he acquired a wide circle of acquaintances. After a few months he spoke Chinese more fluently than English.

Diana was busy improving the austere décor of our house. Housekeeping was a simple matter, for our excellent Chinese cook did all the marketing. He produced a daily list of his purchases written in Chinese, which he took to Mr. Chou for translation. One day, perusing the list, Diana was intrigued to see, clearly stated in the secretary's neat handwriting, that one of the items bought was two pounds of dragon's liver. She went to the office to consult Mr. Chou, who regarded the list with a puzzled frown: "Yes," he said solemnly, "that is odd! We don't have dragons in Yunnan." The cook was summoned, and after some discussion it transpired that the relevant Chinese character had been misleadingly drawn. After all, it was not dragon's liver that he had bought.

For a long time China's customs service had been staffed very largely by Europeans. Shortly after our arrival I received a call from Mr. West, an Englishman who was about to retire from the department after thirty years' service. He wanted to find a home for his bitch Peggy. At the age of twelve she was still an excellent gun-dog, but too old to face the journey to England and the quarantine. I was glad to accept her. West told me that he was hoping to travel down the Burma Road to the Shan States, just across the border, where he had many friends who had invited him to visit them before returning home. As I thought it important to see something of the Province before the tide of Communism engulfed it and while it was still possible to travel, I offered to take him in my jeep and trailer. We set out towards the end of August, taking Mr. Chou with us. I arranged for Diana and Nicky to follow a few days later with some missionaries going to Tali, half-way down the Burma Road and a few miles north of it. I was to pick them up there on my way back.

It was a beautiful drive, across a series of fine limestone valleys and ridges. The first night we stopped at a wayside inn which provided rice and vegetables cooked in deep fat, and accommodation in a dark, unfurnished shack with a mud floor. Towards evening on the second day we were descending from a plateau into a steep, twisting defile, when there was a loud report immediately in front of us. I thought that one of the tyres had burst, and clutched the wheel, expecting the jeep to drag over to one side. A moment later there was a second report, this time accompanied by a splash of gravel in the road ahead and followed by a shrill whine. Then I realised that we were being shot at. When I had stopped the engine we heard shouts, and presently we saw a number of gesticulating figures on top of a high ridge. Mr. Chou thought that they were telling us to come on; so I took off the brake and the jeep rolled forward. A volley of shots, which spattered the road around us, made it quite clear that he was wrong. We got out of the jeep and climbed the steep hillside with our hands above our heads, an operation which I found far from easy. We assumed that our captors were bandits, a species common in Yunnan. But they turned out to be a party of Communist guerilas. They for their part had thought, from the amount of baggage on our trailer, that at least one of us would prove to be a high-ranking Kuomintang officer, and their disappointment was plain. We were subjected to a brief and courteous interrogation and then asked if we had read the works of Mao Tse Tung. Judging the question to be largely rhetorical, I said that I had; and they allowed us to depart with apologies for the inconvenience they had caused.

On the third day we reached the town of Yung P'ing, some thirty miles east of the Mekong. At the inn that evening I talked with a tall, blond young man who had been sitting with a group of Chinese lorry drivers. He was a German Jew named Wolfgang Karfunkel. When still a boy he and his father, a doctor, had escaped from a Nazi concentration camp and, after a remarkable odyssey, had reached China, where his father had established a practice in Chungking. A few years later his father had died, and since then Wolfgang had been making his living as a lorry driver. He was then on his way to Paoshan, a town between the Mekong and the Salween.

We started very early the next morning, for we hoped, in a long day, to cross both the great rivers and to reach the Burmese frontier. We were beginning a descent of several thousand feet into the Mekong basin, now filled with cloud, when the first light appeared in the eastern sky; at the same time the full moon, enormously enlarged, was setting behind the distant mountains. Ever since I can remember, the combination of dawn and a setting moon has always given me a peculiar thrill. An hour later we had reached the bottom of a large tributary valley and were driving along the right bank of the stream towards its junction with the Mekong, where there was a suspension bridge spanning the gorge of the main river. We had intended to halt there for breakfast.

When barely 200 yards from the junction, but still unable to see the bridge, which was screened from view by a steep ridge on our right, we heard the sound of gunfire. I stopped and, looking up, saw some soldiers scrambling down from the ridge towards us. They were in a frenzy of excitement, and when they arrived some of them clambered on to the jeep. One was a young officer who ordered me to turn round and drive back. Indignant at such brusque treatment, we began to argue the matter, but as he was obviously prepared to use force if necessary, there was nothing to do but comply. As the road was narrow, it was a lengthy operation, for the trailer had first to be detached. Meanwhile, the officer, somewhat calmer, explained the situation. The troops under his command had been guarding the bridge, where, at dawn, they had been attacked by a force of Communist guerillas, and the battle had been in progress ever since. The enemy had captured the far end of the bridge, where they had mounted three machine-guns. It was lucky that we had stopped when we did, for if we had gone another 200 yards we would have presented an easy and obvious target for their fire.

By now some more soldiers had arrived, two of them wounded, bring-ing the total to fifteen, which was about as many as the already loaded jeep and trailer could take; so there seemed little point in delaying our departure. As we drove away, the sound of heavy firing from across the ridge showed that the battle was still going on; but as we had abducted the commanding officer of one side, the issue was not likely to be long delayed. Somehow our intervention seemed rather unethical, but we had had little choice in the matter. Grinding along in bottom gear, it took us a long time to climb out of the valley. Before reaching the plateau we met Wolfgang and his colleagues, who, on hearing our news, decided to turn back, and were thus able to relieve us of most of our load of soldiery. We all returned to Yung P'ing, where we spent the rest of the day. In the eve-ning we heard that the bridge had been completely destroyed. As it had provided the only means of crossing the Mekong, this ended our attempt to reach the Shan States.

We arrived at Tali shortly before Diana and Nicky, who were surprised to find us already there. We had intended to go north to Likiang on the road to Tibet, by which, less than a year later, the Communists invaded that once happy land. But, as there was an epidemic of bubonic plague throughout the district, we decided to return home. Some months later the epidemic spread to within fifty miles of Kunming.

Our journey back was not uneventful. On the morning after leaving Tali we were ambushed by bandits. They were the genuine article this time, and a tough, ruthless bunch they looked as they searched our baggage for any-thing worth taking. We told them that several miles back we had passed a military convoy coming in the same direction. This happened to be true, but it seemed to make them so angry that I began to regret having imparted the information. Evidently, however, they must have believed it, for suddenly they abandoned their search and disappeared into the forest, leaving us to continue on our way.

At noon, our nerves still slightly jangled, we reached a small village where we stopped to have lunch at an inn. While the meal was being prepared Nicky went to play in a small garden behind the inn, and when it was ready I went to fetch him. He was nowhere to be seen. I called, but there was no answer. I ran to the end of the garden, which was bounded by a wide irrigation canal, spanned by a low wooden foot-bridge. As I crossed it, noticing that the water was deep and swiftly flowing, I heard a gurgling sound. There, under the bridge was Nicky, well out of his depth, hanging on to a strut. He had fallen in and swallowed too much water to be able to shout. Three hours before, our possessions had been saved by a stroke of luck; now, another had saved our son.

In the autumn of 1949 tension in Kunming began to grow. One after another, with little resistance, the cities of Central China had fallen to the Communists; and with each stronghold taken the victorious Red Army was further strengthened by the capture of military equipment supplied to its opponents by the United States. The Nationalist Government had already withdrawn to Formosa, and with the fall of Chungking, virtually the only province left to them on the mainland was Yunnan. It was difficult of access, and the Red Army was still a long way off, so there was no immediate likelihood of attack; but there were persistent rumours that a Communist *coup d'etat* was imminent or that the Provincial Government was preparing to defect. Nearly all our Chinese friends claimed to be anti-Communist, though it was difficult to know what they really felt. The only exception was Dr. Han, a forthright woman and an ardent patriot, who believed that China was in desperate need of a dynamic ideology to drag her from the slough of corruption and apathy which the Kuomintang had failed to dispel. These sentiments were also expressed in public demonstrations, mostly organised by students, which the local authorities did little to suppress. But for the majority of people accustomed all their lives to conflict and misrule, with a stoic endurance of repeated calamity, the prospect of yet another change of regime was a matter of small concern.

We were often surprised by the apparent complacency of the rich. Some of them had no doubt salted away part of their wealth in foreign banks, but those we met showed no sign of anxiety to escape the retribution which to us seemed inevitable when the Communists took over the Province. We could only suppose that it was due to their faith in the immutability of the Chinese way of life, their inability to imagine a regime in which money could not buy privilege. Great fortunes had been made immediately after the war. Many of the supplies sent up the Burma Road had found their way into the black market, and the bazaars were still full of a wide range of these goods, from tins of peanut butter to army uniforms and walkie-talkies. One member of the Provincial Government had bought, at little cost, a huge stock of motor tyres left by the allied forces. He then succeeded in passing a law making it compulsory for the wheels of all ox-drawn carts to be equipped with rubber tyres for the preservation of the highways. As his was virtually the sole source of supply, he soon became very rich indeed.

There were, however, many people eager to leave China while it was still possible, and Bertie Hemingway and I were inundated with requests for Hong Kong visas. Among those who most feared the impending change of regime were the small foreign traders and business people, particularly if their dealings were of a doubtful nature. There was a memorable occasion when I returned from my morning ride to find twenty-three Russian prostitutes waiting for visas outside the office, all ready, even at 8:30 a.m., to use their practised blandishments on me. Most of them had come from Shanghai to Kunming during the boom period after the war. Unfortunately I was unable to oblige them, for I had been instructed to issue no more visas without the explicit permission of the Hong Kong authorities. Their anger at my refusal stemmed, no doubt, as much from affronted professional pride as from the frustration of their purpose.

The massive material support given to the Kuomintang by the United States had naturally incurred the wrath of the Communists, and America had become the chief target of their enmity. Larry Lutkins had been instructed by his Government to remain in Kunming as long as possible, but to be sure to leave China with his family and his American staff before Yunnan fell into the hands of the Communists. De Courten and I sympathised with his predicament, and the three of us met frequently to exchange information and assess the current rumours. Luckily we were on friendly terms with Lu Han, the Provincial Governor, and although, of course, he was not prepared to divulge his intentions, he promised to warn Lutkins secretly when it was time to go.

Weeks passed without significant incident, and by the end of November we had become so accustomed to false rumours that we paid little attention to them. On the morning of December 5 there was an ominous hush over the city. Before breakfast Diana and I set out for a walk along the ancient wall; but outside our gate we were met by a friendly policeman who warned us to stay indoors. I tried to telephone to de Courten, but the line was dead; so for the rest of the day we remained in ignorance of what was afoot and, save for our radio contacts with Singapore, in strange isolation. Apart from the occasional sound of gunfire the eerie silence persisted.

The next morning we awoke to find that the city had resumed its normal life as though nothing had happened. The only difference was that it was now under the rule of the "People's Government" instead of the Kuomintang. In staging their *volte-face*, the Provincial Government had met with little opposition locally. Poor Lutkins was distraught; for the past twenty-four hours he had been trying desperately to get in touch with Lu Han to remind him of his promise, but had failed to do so. That evening, however, he received a message that the Governor had arranged for him and his family and staff to be flown to Hong Kong the same night. By this act of courtesy, Lu Han showed either great courage or a faulty assessment of his new masters; for in a totalitarian state not even the most highly placed officials can afford to take such liberties.

A week later two army corps, which had remained loyal to Chiang Kai Shek, attacked Kunming, and for some days the city was subjected to sporadic shell-fire. At the same time aircraft from Formosa began a daily bombardment. The fighting was largely centred upon the airfield, three miles from the town, which apparently changed hands several times. I reported on the situation twice daily to Hong Kong via Singapore. One morning, when the battle was at its height, I received a signal from Hong Kong informing me that a civil plane with an American crew would be departing for Kunming at 9:00 a.m. As the message was non-priority, I had not decoded it immediately, so it was already 10:00 before I was aware of its alarming import. So far as I knew the airfield was still being hotly contested, the runway was probably blocked, and if it were in the hands of the insurgents the plane, on landing, would undoubtedly come under heavy fire. I asked Frank to try to make contact with the pilot in flight; as he had no idea of the wavelength, his chances of doing so were very slight, but he kept trying while I hurried off to see General Chang, the Garrison Commander.

Considering that the General was involved in a battle peculiarly critical to his personal welfare, he received me with remarkable courtesy. He listened sympathetically to my tale, but was not optimistic of its outcome; for although his troops had recaptured the airfield, the runway had been largely blocked by wire, and he doubted if they could be restrained from shooting at any aircraft attempting to land. Our deliberations were cut short by the daily air-raid, which began punctually at 11:00. Some bombs fell uncomfortably close to the building we were in, and I was hustled into a shelter beneath the garden. I did not see General Chang again, but in the afternoon I was informed that the American plane had landed, that it had not been fired on and that its crew of four had been taken into custody. I was allowed to see them, and they told me that before leaving Hong Kong they had been assured that Kunming had been retaken by Nationalist forces and had reverted to its former status. So much, I thought, for my carefully drafted reports! I could not, of course, arrange for them to return to Hong Kong with their plane, but I managed, by giving a personal guarantee that they would not try to escape, to persuade the authorities to allow them to rent an apartment in the town and to move about freely. They remained in Kunming for nearly three months, and were then allowed to depart down the Burma Road. During that time we saw a great deal of them, for they often dined with us and generally joined in our Sunday outings.

A colleague of theirs in the same company was less fortunate. Due to a similar miscalculation, he was captured in the south of Yunnan shortly afterwards. A few days before leaving Hong Kong on his ill-fated flight he had been married. He was incarcerated in Wenshan for eight months and then moved to a prison in Kunming. By that time we had no influence whatever with the local authorities, and so were powerless to help him. However, from time to time Bertie Hemingway was allowed to take him small gifts of food and other comforts and occasionally to exchange a few words with him through the prison bars. He was subjected to an intensive course of brain-washing, and later appeared to be going out of his mind.

Meanwhile Bertie maintained a harrowing correspondence with his bride. When I eventually left Kunming he had been a captive for eighteen months. I never heard what became of him.

Not long after the arrival of the American airmen the attempt to capture Kunming was abandoned; but the daily air-raids continued until the end of December. After their punctuality had been noticed a large part of the population used to evacuate the city at 10:00 each day and wait outside until the planes had departed; so there were few casualties. Our servants joined the daily exodus, generally preparing a cold lunch for us before going; but we cooked our Christmas goose and plum pudding ourselves, to the accompaniment of exploding bombs, none of them very close. The townspeople always referred to the bombers, simply and without rancour, as "American"; this was long before they had been subjected to the intensive anti-American propaganda which was to follow a few months later. Thus it was a simple matter for the Communists to focus the hatred of the masses upon one "Super Enemy"—always a desirable objective for a totalitarian regime.

These excitements passed, and with the arrival of the New Year (1950) our lives resumed for a while their former tranquillity. On the surface little had changed, and our relations with the Provincial authorities were as cordial as before. There was always plenty to do at week-ends. Often we made day-long walks over the azalea-covered hills, their strange shapes and changing colours a perpetual delight. Usually I took a gun with me to shoot pheasants, which were plentiful but so difficult to flush that, but for the tireless efforts of Peggy, we would have hardly seen any. Peggy had developed a peculiar and most useful trick: while she was hunting her tail wagged in the normal manner, but as soon as she found the scent her tail whirled like a Catherine wheel and gave me infallible warning that a pheasant was about to fly out of a nearby thicket. They were mostly Mongolian pheasants, the species common in England, but there were others, including the beautiful Lady Amherst pheasants with enormous tails; I did not shoot these, as they were rare and not very good to eat.

Sometimes we spent Sundays on the lake in a hired boat, watching the activities of the cormorant fishermen. They lived in large punt-shaped boats, with thatched cabins amidships. The cormorant teams occupied a space in the bows, while the young, untrained birds were accommodated in the stern, though they spent much of the time in the water tethered by long lines. In the breeding season the birds nested beside the cabin. When fishing, the boat was poled along until a shoal was sighted; then the adult birds were pushed off the bows into the water, where they began diving. Each bird had a metal ring round its neck to prevent it from swallowing its prey. When it caught a fish it would return to the boat where it was hauled aboard and its catch removed from its savagely protesting beak. It was then given a small eel or a strip of flesh narrow enough to pass through its constricted throat, and pushed back into the water for another sortie. Some of the fish the birds caught weighed as much as five pounds. Usually there were several boats operating in the same vicinity, and as the birds often swam several hundred yards before catching their fish, the various teams became intermingled; but they always returned to their owners. They were unable to fly.

Wolfgang Karfunkel was now living in Kunming, where he had found employment as a mechanic at a very meagre wage. He spent much of his spare time with us, particularly at week-ends; he was excellent company, disarmingly naïve, but always cheerful and enthusiastic for whatever entertainment was proposed. He introduced us to Mrs. Li, the German widow of a Kuomintang colonel. The death of her husband had left her in poor circumstances, and under the new regime it was clear that she would lose her tiny pension; but she never complained of her lot and faced her future, which seemed to us very bleak indeed, with remarkable courage. She had two sons, Karl, eighteen, and Toni, fourteen. Toni was a charming extrovert, full of zest for open-air pursuits. Karl was a serious-minded youth and already a dedicated Communist. Despite the fact that I was an Imperialist dog, it was evident that he had some liking for me, and he never lost hope that one day he would succeed in persuading me to see the light. It was, of course, an essential part of his faith that before long the whole world would come under Communist rule, to its inestimable benefit. Later, he kept me well informed on propaganda techniques and other matters of current interest. I also learned from him many illuminating facts about life in Britain, of which he had much positive knowledge: that, for example, a school teacher in England received less pay than a Chinese coolie. Nothing I said could shake his belief in the truth of his information.

In the middle of March 1950 the first units of the Red Army reached Kunming. There had been ample warning of their approach, and the Provincial authorities arranged for a mass welcome to the conquering heroes on the road three miles east of the city. To our surprise, Bertie and I received invitations to join the Governor's party on the saluting base. Though we attended the ceremony and made our presence known, we thought it tactful to do so in a less exalted position, since the Peking Government did not recognise our official status. The marching columns were greeted with appropriate enthusiasm. They were an impressive body of men, mostly from the northern provinces of China. I was told that many of them, though they had taken part in the capture of several of the major cities, had not heard a shot fired in anger.

This event marked the official take-over of Yunnan by the "People's Government," and most of us expected it to be followed by sweeping changes. These, however, were slow in coming, and for some time the only noticeable novelty was the intensification of anti-American propaganda. Huge placards appeared in the town depicting the diabolical figure of General McArthur, with bloody claws holding a dagger poised above the corpses of women and children.

I was convinced that it would not be long before I received orders to close our radio station and hand over our equipment, even if it were not seized in a less courteous manner. I was wrong; and for the next twelve months we continued our daily transmissions to Singapore. Why we were permitted to do so remains a mystery; for as a rule the Communists were particularly averse to radio transmitters, and all similar stations had been closed immediately they came into power; the local authorities must have been aware of the existence of ours, and I am satisfied that our cypher messages were not monitored. The only explanation I can offer is that when we opened the station I did not ask permission but merely notified the local authorities of my intention. As I had anticipated, I received no reply, and my letter was probably destroyed. It is possible, therefore, that as there was no official record of it, no orders had been received from above to close the station, and so no action was taken. After all, a totalitarian state is at least as prone to bureaucracy as any other. The recent revelations concerning the defection of Philby, then one of the chief executives in the British intelligence service, now suggest a more sinister and more plausible explanation.

Letters from England continued to arrive occasionally; though I never knew by what means. They were addressed "British Consulate-General" without the name of the street; but we soon received orders from the Chinese authorities that this practice must cease forthwith, as we had no official status. To save time, I cabled the Foreign Office a list of our regular correspondents and requested that they should be informed of our postal address. Whoever dealt with the matter in London must have consulted an old directory, for our friends received the address of a building in Kunming which had housed the Consulate some fifty years before. It did not matter, however, for when the letters arrived the local post office employees simply scratched out the wrong address and wrote above it in bold Chinese characters "British Consulate-General."

Gradually the new regime tightened its grip on the Province and the pattern of life changed. One by one our acquaintances in the old Provincial Government were removed from office and disappeared. According to some reports, Lu Han had been summoned to Peking to take up an important position there; others said that he had gone there to answer charges of crimes against the People. We had little real contact with the new authorities, who treated us with cold disdain. We were forbidden to go beyond certain points on the main roads, about three miles from the city; but we were never prevented from walking or riding as far as we liked in the mountains to the north. Often I rode forty or fifty miles in a day, starting at dawn and returning at sundown, and always succeeded in reaching valleys I had never seen before; each seemed more beautiful than the last, for in the crags and gorges, the meadows and lakes, the forests and limestone caverns, I found an infinite variety. I never took any food with me, for I could always find something to eat at the peasant farms and mountain hamlets I passed. My most unusual meal consisted of hornet grubs fried in oil. I found them delicious; perhaps because I was very hungry after riding from 5:30 until 11:00 without breakfast.

Though the townspeople appeared to respond more or less satisfactorily to Communist indoctrination and anti-American propaganda, the peasants and the inhabitants of the villages were less easy to rouse. Most of them were illiterate, and as they were chiefly concerned with extracting a meagre living from the soil, politics had little meaning; one government was much the same as another, and hitherto none had done much to alleviate their poverty. A few months after the arrival of the Red Army an intensive campaign was launched to overcome this rural apathy. One method adopted was the holding of People's Courts in the villages, which everyone in the locality was obliged to attend. When they were not too far away the students and schoolchildren of Kunming were brought to witness them, partly to swell the throng and partly to further their ideological education. I heard many accounts of the proceedings, none more graphic than Karl's; as a student, he had attended several of the courts.

Most of the offenders were local landlords, large or small, accused of oppressing the people. First, one of them, his hands tied behind his back, would be led into an arena formed in the village street, where he would be made to kneel. A master of ceremonies would then ask if any of the crowd had anything against the man; whereupon one of the throng, perhaps a woman, would step forward and describe how he had extorted money from her family, or seduced her daughter, or seized an ox. She would work herself into a fury, which would culminate in her smiting the man across the face with her shoe. She would be followed by others who would allege similar misdeeds. Meanwhile the audience would be roused to a passion of indignation against the prisoner, and when at length the master of ceremonies intervened to demand the verdict of the People's Court they would howl "Death." The unfortunate wretch would then be shot in the back of the head, his body removed and the next victim led into the arena. By all accounts, the conduct of the Courts seems to have been well stage-managed, and presumably they had the desired effect of inspiring the peasants with revolutionary fervour; but whenever I visited the outlying farms and villages I found the people so charming and friendly that it was hard to believe that they had really played much part in these bestial orgies.

Considering the traditional reverence of the Chinese for their dead, it was surprising to find that the bodies of paupers were buried on waste ground just outside the city, in graves so shallow that they were often dis-interred by pariah dogs. Returning from one of my morning rides, accom-panied by Sola, a puppy I had acquired some weeks before, I noticed him trotting alongside me carrying a dark object in his mouth. At first I paid no attention, and we were approaching the gates of the Consulate before I realised that it was a baby's head. I leapt off my horse and tried to persuade Sola to drop it; but, mistaking my action for the start of a game, he bounded joyously along the street with me in hot pursuit. Luckily there was no one to witness the macabre scene, and the local Press were thus denied a superb anti-Imperialist scoop. The chase ended within the Consulate compound, and I was faced with the task of disposing of Sola's grisly trophy.

In May Wolfgang Karfunkel married a Chinese girl. His prospects of ever making a decent living now seemed even less than during the old regime, and he was anxious to leave China and seek his fortune elsewhere. He often discussed his problems with me, and I tried to help him by writing to friends in various parts of the world who might have been able to suggest an opening for him. His chief difficulty was to obtain an exit permit, and this was made no easier by his having a Chinese wife.

Some time later his cheerful demeanour suddenly changed, and he became silent and morose, and evidently reluctant to visit us. As I could think of no way in which we might have offended him, I asked his friend Mrs. Li if she knew what was wrong. After some hesitation, she told me that the police had ordered Wolfgang to keep a close watch on my activities and to report them. Evidently they had threatened him with dire penalties if he refused, but promised that if he complied with their instructions they would facilitate his eventual departure from China. Poor Wolfgang was terribly upset, for he felt himself indebted to us for our hospitality. The solution, however, was simple: I asked Mrs. Li to tell him that I would be delighted if he would undertake the task demanded of him, for it is far better to be spied upon by a friend than by an enemy. After that our relationship resumed its former cordiality. We never referred to the matter, so I have no idea of the content of his reports, but it must have been cogent enough to ensure his own freedom and not so damaging as to endanger mine. Unfortunately I lost touch with Wolfgang after I left China, but I heard that he eventually went to live in Israel.

Dr. Brown, another of our friends, was a distinguished American surgeon who, on retiring from practice in the United States, had decided to devote four years of his life to the service of mankind. For some reason he had chosen Yunnan for his philanthropy, though he had no previous connection with China. He was a man of extraordinary energy, and for three years he had worked with selfless dedication, operating, teaching and reorganising the Kunming hospital on modern lines. When the Provincial Government had defected to the Communists he had decided to stay on as he reckoned that his work was not complete. Since then, however, owing largely to the anti-American propaganda, his position had become increasingly precarious, and in the summer of 1950 he decided to leave. He also felt it his duty to go to Korea. When his application for an exit permit was rejected he resolved to escape, a plan which he divulged to only a few of his intimate friends.

In July I suffered from acute abdominal pains which Dr. Brown diagnosed as gallstones, and recommended an immediate operation; but, finding that my systolic blood pressure was only eighty, he decided to postpone it. When, a fortnight later, my blood pressure was still the same he let me into his secret and told me that as the plans for his escape had been carefully laid, he could not delay his departure any longer.

So I went into hospital and had my gall-bladder removed. The next morning he came to see me and, despite my vigorous protests, hauled me out of bed and marched me smartly up and down the corridor. He then said good-bye and told me that he would be leaving shortly. Twenty-four hours later the Chinese doctor who was looking after me burst into my room in a state of great agitation, and demanded to know where Dr. Brown was to be found. He told me that the only surgeon left in the hospital, a Chinese who had been trained by Brown, had just collapsed in the operating theatre with a strangulated hernia, and that unless he was operated on soon he would die. I knew nothing of Dr. Brown's plans, but I thought that, if he were still in Kunming, he might well be hiding in the house of Dr. Han; for, despite her Communist sympathies, they were close friends. My guess was right: a message reached Dr. Brown, who came to the hospital that night, performed the hernia operation successfully and then disappeared. Six months later I heard that he had been killed in Korea. About the same time Dr. Han was denounced for reactionary activities, though I do not believe that this had anything to do with her part in Dr. Brown's escape.

One day in September we heard that the staff of the French Consulate-General had been arrested. We never knew the precise nature of the charges against them, but shortly afterwards a public exhibition of "Imperialist Espionage" was opened. It displayed a heterogenous collection of junk, such as Very pistols and parts of what might have been clandestine radio sets, found in the possession of our French colleagues. In the cellar of our house there was a number of these compromising objects which had, I imagine, been put there during the war. Frank and I spent a long time cutting them with a hack-saw into small pieces, convenient for disposal during my rides in the mountains. In view of the fact that we were still in daily radio contact with Singapore, the operation might seem a little pointless; but as Chinese behaviour is not always strictly logical, I thought it worth the trouble.

At 11:00 one night, about a week later, soon after we had gone to bed, we heard a heavy banging on the door of our compound, and presently the night watchman came up to tell us that the police wanted me to go with them immediately. I sent him to fetch Mr. Chou while I dressed, and together we set off in one of the police jeeps, leaving Diana to wonder how long it might be before she saw me again. To my surprise we were taken, not to the local jail, but to the gate of the French Consulate-General. There I was ordered to take charge of a very large sum of money in U.S. dollars belonging to the French. At first I tried to decline, but soon it became very plain that I had no option in the matter. The money had first to be counted with meticulous care; the whole transaction was executed on the pavement outside the gate by the light of an oil lantern, and as most of the notes were of small denomination, it was nearly 3:00 a.m. before it was completed and Mr. Chou and I were allowed to return to our beds. Some time later we heard that the French Consular staff had been deported.

For the missionaries throughout the Province, life had become very difficult. Owing to the hostility of the local authorities, it was unwise for any Chinese to have dealings with them and thus, for the most part, their work came to a standstill. Moreover, their own position was far from secure, for they were liable at any moment to be arrested for fictitious misdeeds and even atrocities: some doctors, for example, faced charges of murdering patients who had died under their care, even several years before. Considering that most of the missionaries had dedicated their lives to their work in China, it is perhaps some measure of the hardships they suffered that, by the autumn of 1950, most of them had decided to leave the country. But it was far from easy to get the necessary exit permits. The authorities gave no reason for withholding them, which was doubtless the cause of most of the sinister rumours circulating at the time. One of these was a story that all foreign doctors were to be rounded up and sent to the battle front in Korea.

On October 6, 1950, our second son, John, was born. Diana believed in taking plenty of exercise during her pregnancy, and that very afternoon we had been for a strenuous walk in the hills together. Luckily, Dr. Han, though already in some trouble with the local authorities, was still free, for she had been looking after Diana, who had great faith in her. Labour began after supper, and John was born three hours later.

At the end of November we decided that it was high time for Diana to leave with the children. Among the many factors that prompted this decision were the increasing obduracy of the local authorities and the mounting international tension. The participation of large numbers of Chinese "volunteers" in the Korean conflict at that time seemed likely to lead to war with China. Diana was granted an exit permit in an unusually short time, and on January 5, 1951, she started on the long, uncertain journey to Hong Kong. Luckily she went with a group of missionaries who had also obtained their permits, and they did much to help her. Even so, it was a tough assignment with a boy of five and a baby of three months, and I was more than relieved when, five weeks later, I received a signal from Hong Kong telling me that they had arrived there safely. Diana's ordeal, however, was not quite over. When she arrived by air in London she was feeling very ill. The following day she discovered that she had mumps. She could not stay on at her hotel, and as her parents had recently died, she had nowhere to go. Luckily some kind friends set about telephoning to all the nursing homes in the London directory, and eventually found a compassionate matron who agreed to accommodate Diana and Nicky, so long as she could hide the nature of the disease. John was put in the care of a nurse.

In March 1951 I received the long-expected demand from the local police to hand over our radio equipment. Personally, I was not sorry; for during the past year I had grown increasingly aware of the ugly charges that could have been brought against us for transmitting messages abroad when it had been made abundantly clear that our consular status was not recognised; indeed, I was very relieved that the closure had not been effected in a much more drastic fashion. There was now little purpose in our remaining in Kunming, a point which I emphasised in my last signal to Singapore, and shortly afterwards I was instructed by the Foreign Office to close the Consulate and leave China as soon as possible. We had already destroyed our archives; as these had covered a period of fifty years, the operation had involved two days of intensive burning and evoked complaints from our neighbours of large amounts of smoke and charred paper drifting into their compounds.

For several months the chief topic of conversation among foreigners had been the problem of leaving China. It was interesting to notice that the degree of emotional stress displayed by people nearly always increased with their prospects of getting out. Those who had no immediate hope of leaving generally viewed the matter with philosophical detachment; when their obligation to stay had ended and they applied for exit permits they joined the ranks of the worriers; when at length they obtained their permits they could talk of nothing else, and became more and more apprehensive as the date of their departure approached. At first I was puzzled by this attitude and a bit impatient with it, but when I myself entered the latter stages and felt the same symptoms developing I became more sympathetic. Exit permits had been known to be cancelled at the last moment, and if this happened it was generally very difficult to get them renewed.

At the end of April Mrs. Hemingway, Frank and I were given permits to travel to Hong Kong, and we were instructed to fly to Chungking on May 10. A young Irish Catholic nun named Sister Maggie travelled with us. Bertie was to follow later. The documents were stamped with the date of our departure, and we were told that it was obligatory to complete the journey within one month. To my surprise I was told that I must take the radio equipment with me. It was packed in a single wooden case, weighing nearly two hundredweight, which had been sealed with flimsy strips of ricepaper. Apart from this, our baggage was not allowed to exceed fifteen pounds each, so that we had to leave most of our personal belongings behind. We were thoroughly searched before embarking on the plane.

It was necessary to be extremely careful in all our dealings with officials, for a tactless word or a display of irritation might have unpleasant consequences. For example, a missionary whom we met at a later stage of the journey got into serious trouble by cracking an innocent joke. He was travelling with his family from a remote part of Szechwan, and he had with him a metal cylinder containing pressurised insecticide. After explaining the purpose of this in fluent Chinese to an official examining his baggage, he was imprudent enough to add, "Well, anyway, it's not an atom bomb." For this pleasantry he was held for two months on a charge of attempting to ridicule the intelligence of the Chinese people. Eventually, after signing an abject apology he was allowed to proceed on his journey. A similar charge might be made if your baggage were found to contain a pair of those tiny, delightfully embroidered shoes worn by women with bound feet. If, on the other hand, you had secreted a porcelain vase you would probably have been accused of attempting to despoil the Chinese people of their art treasures.

Arriving at Chungking, we were again subjected to a thorough search. There was a tense scene when a woman examining my effects discovered, clipped in my passport, a certificate written in Chinese stating that I, the

British Consul-General in Kunming, had been inoculated against typhoid. She became very angry and abused me for my insolence in claiming this non-existent status. For a while I thought that I was going to be put on the next plane back to Kunming, where the authorities would deal appropriately with my offence. However, by expressing horror at the mistake made by the ignorant doctor who had written the certificate, by humbly apologis-ing for my inability to read Chinese script and by asking that the offensive document be destroyed forthwith, I managed to mollify the irate lady and escaped with a stern warning.

The next stage of our journey was to be made by river steamer down the Yangtze. At that time there were some 350 missionaries in Chungking await-ing onward transport by this means, most of them having come from remote areas in the west. They were despatched in batches as steamer accommoda-tion became available, but as others were arriving almost daily, their numbers remained fairly constant. We were allowed to stay in the house of the former Consul-General, who had already left, while Sister Maggie stayed with mis-sionary friends. On the afternoon of May 18, when we had been waiting for eight days, we received instructions to embark in a ship which was leaving in less than an hour. While Frank arranged transport for our monstrous box and looked after Mrs. Hemingway, I dashed off to fetch Sister Maggie, who was included in the summons. I had some difficulty in finding her, and by the time she had collected her meagre belongings, most of the hour had been spent. No taxis or rickshaws were available, so we started running hand in hand through the crowded streets to the river. At one point, while dashing zigzag through the traffic across a main thoroughfare, she tripped over the folds of her habit and fell flat on her face in the muddy street. Her comments, in a rich Irish brogue, were stronger than I would have expected from one of her calling. We reached the steamer with a few minutes to spare, and found that my other two companions were safely aboard.

We were lucky enough to secure comfortable accommodation: Frank and I had a two-berth cabin on the starboard side, and Mrs. Hemingway had a similar one backing on to ours on the port side; the two were sep-arated by a thin wooden bulkhead. That night shortly after we had gone to bed we were disturbed by the sound of an altercation. One voice was

that of Mrs. Hemingway (who spoke no Chinese), raised in indignation
to a high pitch: the other was male, Chinese and much calmer. We leapt
out of bed and dashed round the decks to find the cause of the trouble.
Apparently the man had entered the cabin when Mrs. Hemingway was
already in bed and had started to undress. But obviously his intentions
were entirely innocent: he had seen through the porthole that one of the
bunks in the cabin was empty, and all he wanted was to occupy it. Acutely
aware of the folly in our situation of quarrelling with any Chinese, I apol-
ogised for the misunderstanding and persuaded Mrs. Hemingway to move
to our cabin, while Frank and I slept on the deck outside.

Early the next morning the ship entered the Yangtze Gorges. The navigation by steamer of this famous defile was made possible by the research
and ingenuity of British pilots in the latter part of the nineteenth century.
It was a bold achievement, and even now that the river has been accurately
charted the handling of the vessels demands great skill, particularly at the
entrance to the upper gorge, where the water races through a narrow channel between whirlpools and half-submerged reefs. Beyond, the river flows
between steep and lofty slopes which reminded me of a Himalayan valley;
it was a strange feeling to be gliding through it on the deck of a ship the
size of a cross-Channel steamer. That evening we reached Ichang in the flat
country east of the mountains, where we were ordered to disembark.

Together with about fifty missionaries we were conducted by an armed
escort to an inn where we were told to wait until a ship arrived to take us
on to Hankow; no indication was given of how long that would be. We
were forbidden to leave the building on any pretext, and told that the inn-
keeper had been instructed to report to the police any attempt to do so.
Our quarters were squalid and grossly overcrowded. By a judicious use of
screens we managed at night to achieve a partial segregation of the sexes,
but otherwise there was no privacy. During the day the heat was stifling, and
the nights were little better. We were fed three times a day on well-cooked
rice and vegetables fried in rancid fat; the smell pervaded the whole establishment. Behind the inn was a wooden hut which contained a row of three
crude latrines; there the stench was appalling, and the place swarmed with
well-nourished flies.

The days passed in monotony. At first we whiled away the dragging hours exchanging accounts of our experiences—it was then that I heard the story of the ill-timed atom bomb jest; but it became increasingly difficult to avoid discussion of our immediate situation. The river could not be seen from the inn, but often we heard hooters which seemed to herald the arrival or departure of steamers; and sometimes the inn-keeper would raise false hopes by saying that one would be coming for us the next day. As we were paying handsomely for our board and lodging, we were uncomfortably aware that it was in his interest to keep us there as long as possible. Our chief concern was the time-limit set for our journey; for the popular belief was that if we failed to reach Hong Kong before it expired we would be turned back at the frontier. The missionaries said that this had happened to several of their colleagues. With nothing to do and so much time for reflection, we found plenty of other things to worry about. In those insanitary conditions there was every chance of falling seriously ill, and the fact that there had been an epidemic of typhus in Chungking when we were there was discouraging. We knew also that the international situation in the Far East was still tense, and we had heard rumours in Chungking that a Chinese attack on Hong Kong was imminent. Frank and I had our private anxiety: the paper seals on our infernal radio case had been broken; this would be quite enough for some bloody-minded official at the frontier to have us arrested. The missionaries spent much of their time in prayer, and I was struck, not for the first time, by their informal intimacy with their Maker. On one occasion, when there seemed to be some immediate prospect of our departure from Ichang, I heard them asking Him to see to it that we did not arrive in Hankow on a Sunday. I had no idea why they asked this, but I found the homely simplicity of the request comforting.

At last, on June 4, when we had been at the inn for sixteen days, we were summoned to embark in a vessel bound for Hankow. It was so over-crowded, mostly with Chinese, that we could only secure a few feet of deck space in one of the holds. At meal-times buckets of plain boiled rice were dumped at intervals on the decks, from which the passengers helped themselves. Personally, I was so delighted to be on the move again that I would happily have spent the twenty-four-hour voyage in the rigging.

From Hankow, after a long struggle to get places on a train, we travelled to Canton, and on the morning of June 9, the day on which our permits expired, we reached the Hong Kong frontier. There we stood for some hours in a long queue of emigrants, edging slowly towards the barbed wire barriers. Beyond it we could see two British policemen and a flag-staff flying the Union Jack. We had heard that this was the most critical stage of the journey, and certainly the examination of the people ahead of us seemed to be extremely thorough. Perhaps we were lucky, for when at length our turn came, we found our examiners less hostile than usual, and after some discussion, they were even prepared to overlook the destruction of the paper seals on our radio case. A few steps and we were safely out of Communist China. The hills of the New Territories looked very beautiful in the evening light as, relaxed at last, I watched them glide by the window of the train to Kowloon.

| 8 |

EVEREST FROM NEPAL

THE WAR HAD NOT LONG been over when hopes of renewing
the attempt to climb Everest began to revive. The old Everest
Committee was re-formed as the Himalayan Committee, and the
British Mission in Lhasa was asked to sound Tibetan reaction to
the proposal. But the invasion of Tibet by the Chinese Communist
armies in 1950 made it virtually certain that we would never again
be able to approach the mountain by our old route through Tibet.
Meanwhile, however, the Nepalese Government had begun to relax
their traditional policy of isolation, and from 1947 onwards several climbing and scientific expeditions were allowed to visit various parts of the Nepal Himalaya. In the autumn of 1950 Charles
Houston and Bill Tilman made a brief visit to Solu Khumbu, where
they spent a day exploring the glacier flowing southward from the
Lho La; but they did not have time to reach the ice-fall below
the Western Cwm of Everest. The following May, at the suggestion of Michael Ward and Bill Murray, the Himalayan Committee
applied to the Nepalese Government for permission for a British
expedition to investigate this approach to Everest. It was granted
six weeks later.

Everest expeditions were very far from my thoughts when, in
the middle of June 1951, I arrived in England from China. Diana
and the boys had settled into a house in Hampshire, and I longed

to join them there for a spell of domestic peace, untroubled by thoughts of the future, and with time to enjoy the summer countryside and the sweet reasonableness of England. A fortnight later a bomb was lobbed into this idyll: it came in the form of an invitation to lead the new expedition. It would mean leaving England again in August, and with only a few weeks to organise the venture, most of the intervening time would have to be spent busily preparing in London; both contingencies were most disagreeable, particularly as I was feeling far from fit. But the chance at last of looking into the mysterious Western Cwm was hard to resist, while the prospect of visiting Solu Khumbu, of seeing for myself the almost legendary home of the Sherpas was even more enthralling. So, with Diana's generous encouragement, I accepted the invitation.

I thought it highly improbable that we would find a practicable route up the southern side of Everest. I did not doubt that we would be able to climb the great ice-fall which Dan Bryant and I had seen in 1935, though I was a little concerned about the danger of ice avalanches falling from the immense precipices which towered above the narrow entrance of the Cwm. Nor was there any reason to suppose that the final ridge between the South Col and the summit would present any serious difficulty. The unknown factor was the section between the Cwm and the Col, a climb of nearly 5000 feet. The walls of the valley that we had seen from Lingtren in 1935 were tremendously steep and festooned with hanging glaciers, and the general configuration of the mountains suggested that those at its head would be equally formidable. Bill Tilman agreed with this opinion, and so did General Norton, who reckoned the chances against our finding a route to the South Col at forty to one.

The nucleus of the party was already in being. Bill Murray who had taken a prominent part in the development of winter climbing in Scotland and had led an expedition to Garhwal the previous year, had assumed charge until I appeared on the scene when, with spontaneous generosity, he handed over the leadership. Michael Ward, a doctor and one of the most experienced of the post-war generation of British climbers, had been chiefly responsible for the initiation of the project. Tom Bourdillon, the third member, was a young scientist engaged in rocket development; a man of exceptional strength and a first-rate rock-climber, he had a record of remarkable achievement in the Alps.

Hitherto the objective of the expedition had not been defined, and there was some talk of trying to reach the summit. I knew that this was out of the question. In the first place it would be stupid to mount a full-scale attempt, with the expensive organisation that this would entail, upon a route most of which had not even been seen. Secondly, even if we were lucky, we would have only four or five weeks to operate on the mountain before the onset of winter; from the point of view of acclimatisation alone this was totally inadequate. Thirdly, there was not nearly enough time to collect even the minimum amount of specialised equipment needed for climbing to extreme altitudes. I decided, therefore, to limit our objective to a reconnaissance of the approach to the Western Cwm and to reaching a point from which we could see if the South Col could be climbed from there. I thought that this purpose could best be achieved by a party of four, lightly equipped and supported by a few Sherpas recruited from Solu Khumbu.

Even so, we had a hectic scramble to get ready; it was already July, and our stores and equipment had to be packed for shipment by the end of the month; for the date of the next sailing to India after that would have been much too late. Things had changed since pre-war days when I used to boast that I could organise an expedition in a fortnight. Now, all essential materials, down for sleeping bags, windproof cloth, rope, were in short supply, and it was very difficult to obtain them at short notice. Moreover, everyone seemed to be away on holiday, and we were frustrated at every turn. Campbell and Peggy Secord very kindly allowed us to use their house in Carlton Mews as an office and a dumping ground for stores and equipment, and for weeks their lives were made almost intolerable by endless telephone calls from the Press, applicants to join the party, equipment firms, food cranks, money-lenders and inventors of all manner of strange gadgets. To cover the cost of the expedition the Committee made a contract with *The Times* for a series of articles and despatches; the first two of these I had to write immediately. The day before our stores and equipment were due at London Docks they were still piled in an unsorted heap in the Secords' garage, and there were many other urgent matters requiring attention. So I telephoned to the headquarters of the W.V.S. and explained the situation. Their response to my pitiful appeal was so prompt and effective that by the next morning everything was neatly packed and ready for shipment.

Bill and Michael travelled by sea to Bombay to accompany the baggage and arrange for its onward transport across India. Tom and I were to follow by air on August 18. Two days before we left I received a cable from the President of the New Zealand Alpine Club, saying that an expedition of four of his countrymen was climbing in the Garhwal Himalaya, and asking if two of them might join my party. He did not divulge their names. The correct answer was obvious: I had already turned down several applicants with very strong qualifications on the ground that I wanted to keep the party small; our slender resources of money and equipment were already stretched, and I had no idea where the two unknown climbers were or how to contact them. I was about to send a negative reply when, in a moment of nostalgic recollection, I recalled the cheerful countenance of Dan Bryant, and I changed my mind. I soon began to regret this, for apart from the complications resulting from the last-minute inclusion of two new members of the party, still in some remote Himalayan valley and with no permits to enter Nepal, I found it far from easy to explain my totally irrational action to my companions. They could not altogether hide their dismay, though they were too polite to express it. Eventually the two New Zealanders caught us up when we were half-way across Nepal. Then, for the first time, we learnt their names; they were Earle Riddiford and Edmund Hillary. My momentary caprice was to have far-reaching results.

We had decided to approach Solu Khumbu from Jogbani, the Indian railhead on the frontier of Nepal, almost due south of Everest. This route was selected because it appeared on the map to be the shortest, and because it had been followed by Houston and Tilman the previous autumn; they were the first Western travellers to do so. The choice, however, proved a bad mistake; for whereas they, marching in the dry season, had taken only a fortnight we, in the height of the monsoon, took nearly a month to complete the journey, only eighty miles in a straight line. It was, in fact, the most arduous trek I have ever done through the inhabited regions of the Himalaya. One of our chief difficulties was recruiting the twenty-five porters we needed to carry our baggage; for the local people had a strong dislike of travelling in the monsoon, and even when, with great reluctance, they agreed to come, they did not stay with us for the whole journey.

Tom and I reached Jogbani at midnight on August 24; Bill and Michael had arrived with the baggage two days before. The next day Angtarkay came from Darjeeling, in response to a letter from me telling him of our plans. It was wonderful to see him again after twelve years and to find that, apart from having cut off his pigtail, he had in no way changed from the shy, humorous, charming person I had known. Though he had become something of a business tycoon, he still went on expeditions as a sirdar (foreman): the previous year he had distinguished himself with the French on Annapurna. On August 26 we went by lorry to Dharan, thirty miles within the Nepalese border at the foot of the range.

The first four marches led us along an easy track over two ranges of foothills, 6000 feet high; from the second of these we descended into the valley of the Arun River. This was my first link with former days, for I had known it well as an infant stream, the Phung Chu, meandering gently across the Tibetan plateau, before its Stygian passage through the sunless gorges of the Everest massif transformed it into a mighty waterway. It took seven hours to ferry our baggage across the river in a dugout canoe; we then followed its western bank for two days through dense tropical forest. At less than 1000 feet above sea-level the heat was oppressive, and we were glad at length to climb out of the valley to the village of Dingla, where it was pleasantly cool. There we had to stay for four days collecting a fresh team of porters. On September 8 the New Zealanders arrived; having very little baggage with them, they had made a rapid march from Jogbani. Ed Hillary has described their astonishment when, instead of the spruce *pukka-sahibs* they had expected to meet, they found four scruffy tramps.

Beyond Dingla the worst of our troubles began. On leaving the Arun valley we were travelling north-westward, across the grain of the country, which meant that we had to traverse a series of ridges, 10,000 or 12,000 feet high, separated by deep, precipitous gorges. We could get little or no information about the way ahead, as the local people rarely left their own valleys; few of them had even heard of Solu Khumbu. At the outset we found that a bridge spanning one of the rivers had been swept away, which forced us to make a detour, involving several extra days' march, along tiny forest tracks which were very difficult to follow. Sometimes we had to cut our way through the undergrowth. This was infested with leeches; on a single twig a score of the creatures could be seen, stiff and erect, like a cluster of black sticks, ready to attach themselves to us as we brushed past. It rained incessantly, and for much of the time our surroundings were hidden in mist. It was terribly hard work for the porters, for the steep ground was often slimy with mud and they constantly slipped and lost their balance under the shifting weight of their sodden loads. It was not surprising that several times they refused to go any farther; luckily on each occasion we managed, after much cajoling, to persuade them to change their minds. It was hard to believe that the barren plateau of Tibet was less than sixty miles to the north. There, in a single day, we had been able to ride thirty miles in a direct line. Here it took us nearly a fortnight to cover that distance.

On the evening of September 20, when we had crossed the final pass of over 10,000 feet, the weather suddenly cleared; the monsoon had ended. After ten days of perpetual rain and mist the clear air and warm sunlight were delicious; the forest was no longer oppressive but light and green, and gay with clusters of rhododendron, still, strangely enough, in bloom; waterfalls, cascading down the huge precipices flanking the wide valleys of the Dudh Kosi, sparkled like threads of silver hanging from ice peaks, 12,000 feet above our heads.

We had reached Solu Khumbu, and our progress up the valley began to resemble a triumphal procession. I have never known such a welcome. At each village along the path all the Sherpa inhabitants, men, women and children, turned out to greet us, and we were invited, often dragged, into one of the houses for a session of *chang*-drinking. I met scores of friends from pre-war expeditions, and many others whom I did not recognise claimed acquaintance. After a while I found it increasingly difficult to recognise anyone, and I marched along in a happy alcoholic haze. On the 22nd we reached Namche, the main village of Khumbu, perched 2000 feet above the upper gorge of the Dudh Kosi.

Despite the fine weather and our eagerness to start our explorations, we had to stay there three nights to attend a series of parties arranged in our honour. A Sherpa party, as I already knew from experience, is a formidable affair. Its salient features are a banquet, accompanied and followed by the drinking of much *chang* and non-stop dancing throughout the night. Linked together in a great semi-circle, the dancers, men and women intermingled, perform an endless repetition of an involved, shuffling step in time to a rhythmic but rather tuneless dirge. The Sherpas are passionately fond of this dance and take it very seriously. Indeed, they normally perform it with a solemnity so at variance with their usual cheerful demeanour that a stranger might suppose them to be mourning some terrible calamity. Our participation, however, produced an atmosphere of wild hilarity. For hours on end, until we retired exhausted, our inept caperings were greeted with roars of hysterical laughter from the great gathering of villagers. Certainly the sight of Ed, tall and long-limbed, supported between two stocky Sherpa wenches, an expression of powerful concentration on his face, would have diverted a much more sophisticated audience. Eventually, about midnight, we were helped to our beds, while the Sherpas then settled down, with proper gravity, to dance—and drink—till dawn.

On the 25th, feeling somewhat jaded, we marched on to Thyangboche, a monastery built at 14,000 feet on an isolated spur high above the junction of the Dudh Kosi and the Imja Khola, the river draining the southern flanks of Everest. On the way we met my old friend Sen Tensing, the "Foreign Sportsman." He had heard the news of our approach while grazing his yaks in a valley three days' march away, and had hurried down to greet us, bringing gifts of *chang*, butter and curds. He came along with us, and for the rest of the day regaled me with memories of our many journeys together. When, in the evening, we reached the monastery it was shrouded in mist. It has close religious ties with the Rongbuk monastery on the opposite side of the sacred Chomolungma (Everest); though it would be difficult to imagine a greater contrast than the setting of the two places. We were welcomed by the monks, who had pitched a large, beautifully embroidered Tibetan tent for us in a nearby meadow.

During the past few days we had become accustomed to the startling beauty of the country, but this in no way lessened the dramatic effect of the scene when we awoke next morning. The sky was clear; the green meadow, starred with gentians, had been touched with frost, which sparkled in the early sunlight; it was surrounded by quiet woods of fir, tree-juniper, birch and rhododendron, silvered with moss, and though the deciduous trees were still green, there were already splashes of brilliant autumn colour in the undergrowth. To the south, the forested slopes fell steeply to the Dudh Kosi, the boom of the river now silenced by the depth of its gorge. To the north-east, twelve miles away across the valley of the Imja Khola, stood the Nuptse–Lhotse ridge, with the peak of Everest just showing behind it. Even this stupendous wall, nowhere less than 25,000 feet throughout its five-mile length, seemed dwarfed by the slender spires of fluted ice nearer at hand.

The pre-war expeditions had given me an intimate acquaintance with the country along the Tibetan side of the range, country which, but for our Everest passports, would have remained inaccessible. Certainly for much of the time we were confined to the ugly wilderness of the Rongbuk Valley or to our camps amid the harsh sterility of the East Rongbuk Glacier; but when the monsoon had put an end to serious business we could claim our reward of wider travel. Then, too, there was the summer of 1935, when a liberal interpretation of our reconnaissance brief had given us months of delicious freedom to wander over hundreds of miles of that medieval land, with its vivid desert colouring, its curious ice-capped hills and its sweeping horizons. The enjoyment of those wanderings had derived an added piquancy from a sense of isolation; for southward across the range, cutting us off as it were from our logical exit, were the forbidden valleys of Nepal. During those years the region had been our *terra incognita*, so close but for us so utterly remote, that its secrets grew always more intriguing the more familiar we became with our surroundings. It had then seemed certain that none of us would ever see the dramatic change of landscape we knew to be there. Now the impossible had happened, and the reality was even lovelier than the dream.

Three easy marches took us from Thyangboche to the head of the glacier we had seen sixteen years before, and which we now called the Khumbu Glacier. There, surrounded by familiar landmarks, we pitched our base camp. On September 30, while Michael, Tom and Earle crossed the glacier to reconnoitre the lower part of the ice-fall, Ed and I climbed one of the buttresses of Pumori. Our purpose was to study the ice-fall as a whole, and particularly to assess the danger of avalanches falling from the hanging glaciers on the precipices of Everest and Nuptse above it. I did not expect to see much more of the Western Cwm than I had in 1935; but I was wrong.

We reached a point just over 20,000 feet high, and from there we had an astounding view. The whole of the north-west face of Everest was visible, with every step of our old route from the North Col to the Great Couloir. Ed was thrilled to see this historic ground, and one after another, with no prompting from me, he identified all its salient features, naming them with a kind of reverence. He was as excited as a small boy opening his Christmas stocking, and I had some difficulty in diverting his attention to a much more dramatic aspect of the view; for there before us, emerging from a band of cloud, was the head of the Western Cwm, the west face of Lhotse and the slopes leading to the South Col.

What was more, we realised at once that there was a perfectly feasible route leading from the Cwm to the Col. This was a momentous discovery, for it was the main object of our quest.

The next task was to find a way up the wild labyrinth of walls, chasms and towers of the ice-fall. A careful study of the ice avalanches falling on to it from the gigantic precipices above satisfied us that this menace could be avoided by keeping well away from the sides. We managed to climb up the centre of the ice-fall; but the deep snow, which had fallen during the monsoon, not only made the work very laborious but was unstable and liable to avalanche. So, after a narrow escape near the top of the ice-fall, we decided to leave it for a fortnight to allow the dangerous snow to consolidate. We had intended to carry a camp through into the Cwm; but we abandoned this project largely because of a remarkable cataclysm which occurred during our absence. We found, on our return, that the cliffs and towers over a wide area along our route had been shattered as though by an earthquake. It had evidently been caused by a violent movement of the main mass of the glacier, which had left the tumbled ice blocks precariously poised above a maze of newly opened crevasses. Though in all my experience I had never seen anything remotely like this, it seemed obvious that the whole area was now so unstable that, until it had time to settle, a process which might take many weeks, it would be foolish to take laden porters up through it. The only way round the shattered area lay close under the left-hand retaining wall of the glacier, which was exposed to frequent bombardment by ice avalanches. It was disappointing not to be able to go to the head of the Cwm, though in fact there was little of importance to be learned by doing so.

Between our two spells on the ice-fall we spent the time exploring the unknown country in the immediate vicinity of Everest, Ed and I to the east, the others to the west. Our main objective was to find a way through the tangle of ranges to the Kangshung Glacier, which flows from the eastern flanks of Everest, so as to link up with the explorations of the 1921 expedition and our journeys in 1935. The Sherpas told us that there was a way over to Tibet from the head of the Imja Khola, though none of them claimed to know it; but we found that the upper valley was enclosed by an unbroken cirque of very high mountains, dominated by Lhotse. However, we managed to cross a difficult col to the south into the basin of the Hongu Khola, a region unknown to the Sherpas. From there we reached a saddle 20,300 feet high, leading into a vast valley system at the western foot of Makalu, which we later identified as that of the Barun, the largest tributary of the Arun.

All this time, which spanned the period of the full moon, the weather was fine. The nights were very cold and the mornings crisp and sparkling. Each afternoon cloud welled up from the valleys and hid the peaks; each evening at sunset it dissolved. It was then, in camp, that we saw our stupendous surroundings at their best, for each peak in turn was framed in shifting mist, its golden tracery of ice glowing in deep relief, no longer a mere part of the mountain mass, but floating in majestic isolation. Before the cloud had quite vanished the moon would climb above some lofty crest, and soon all the peaks were there again, frozen against the night sky.

When at the beginning of November we returned to Namche from the ice-fall we decided to travel back to India by way of Katmandu instead of Jogbani. The New Zealanders, anxious to get back as soon as possible, followed the most direct route, across the Tesi Lapcha Pass and through a deep gorge known to the Sherpas as Rolwaling. The rest of us, with the object of exploring the country to the north of that region, went up the Bhote Kosi, a large valley running northward to the Nangpa La. This pass, despite its height of 19,000 feet and the long glacier approach to it from both sides, was the only way by which the Sherpas could maintain close ties, trade and cultural, with Tibet. Its eastern portal is Cho Oyu, a mountain of nearly 27,000 feet; on its western side is an unnamed peak of 23,000 feet. This forms the northern bastion of a long chain of high mountains running southward along the line of the Bhote Kosi. Our immediate purpose was to discover whether this great mountain barrier was a subsidiary spur or whether it formed part of the main axis of the Himalaya. To do this we had to cross it.

On November 5 we reached the entrance of the Pangbuk Chu, the largest of the valleys running westward towards the barrier range. The next day Michael and I, with Angtarkay, Sen Tensing and four other Sherpas, started up this valley, while Bill and Tom continued up the Bhote Kosi to visit the Nangpa La and to look for alternative routes to the west. It was arranged that they would return four days later to follow us up the Pangbuk, if we ourselves were not back by then.

At noon we reached a sharp bend in the valley, and beyond this we entered a vast basin, bounded on the east by a chain of small peaks. Michael and I climbed one of them, reaching the summit, 18,600 feet, at 5:00 that evening. As we had hoped, it commanded a splendid view of the barrier range and of five glaciers flowing from it. Only one of these offered any chance of a route; it came from the direction of a lofty snow saddle, and only the upper part of this was visible. Far beyond it, in a direct line with the setting sun, we saw a sharp spire, whose great height suggested that it stood on the main axis of the Himalaya. Before dawn the next day Michael, Angtarkay and I set out to reconnoitre the saddle, having instructed the other Sherpas to carry the camp across the basin to the glacier. Climbing as fast as we could, it took us until 2:00 to reach the saddle, which was more than 20,000 feet high, and which we later named the Menlung La. The view westward was puzzling. Immediately below us was a wide glacier flowing southwards towards Nepal; straight across it, towering in lofty isolation, was a superb peak (later named Menlungtse), whose topmost spire we had seen the day before. At the head of the glacier there was a col, 1000 feet below us; beyond this, far away to the north across the Tibetan plateau, we saw the desolate mountains of the Lapche Kang range.

We had to climb some way down the far side of the saddle before we were sure that we could descend to the glacier. But where did it lead? Whether the unknown region was in Nepal or Tibet depended upon the answer to this question. We could see the glacier for several miles along its southerly course, heading directly towards a great wall of mountains, which stretched from east to west across its path. It was too late to solve the puzzle before nightfall. Reluctantly we turned back, and though we went very fast, it was dark before we regained the Pangbuk.

Early the next morning we set off again for the saddle; this time Sen Tensing came with us, and we carried a tent and food for seven days. Angtarkay and the other Sherpas waited for Bill and Tom to arrive so as to guide them over the Menlung La. The steps cut the previous day offset the weight of our loads, and again at 2:00 we reached the saddle. An hour and a half later, after descending an easy ice-fall, we reached the glacier beyond. There we sank to our knees in a powdery snow which, with our loads, made slow going.

At 4:00 we were astonished to see a line of tracks converging on the direction of our advance, and evidently coming from or going towards the col at the head of the glacier. My first thought was that it had been made by Bill and Tom, who had found another pass farther north; but, remembering our view of the barrier range, I realised that this was scarcely possible.

When we reached the tracks we saw that they were fresh, certainly not more than a few hours old. This could be clearly determined by the little balls of snow which had been dislodged and which had not melted into the surface, despite the warm sun which had been shining all day. The possibility that any of the local people had been up there was very remote, for neither the Tibetans nor the Sherpas ever visit the upper reaches of these glaciers by themselves, except when they lie on well-established routes, such as the Nangpa La.

Sen Tensing was the only one of us who had no doubts as to the origin of the mysterious tracks. With complete confidence he pronounced that they had been made by *Yeti* ("Abominable Snowmen"). He told us that two years before he had seen one of these creatures at a distance of twenty-five yards. He described it as being the height of an average man, tail-less, with a tall, pointed head and covered with reddish-brown hair except on its face, which was bare. I knew him too well to doubt his story, though I was still far from convinced by his explanation of the tracks. We followed these down the glacier. Gradually, as we descended, the depth of the snow diminished, until there was barely an inch covering the glacier ice. Hitherto the individual footprints had been rather shapeless, but here we found many specimens so sharply defined that they could hardly have been clearer had they been made in wax. We could tell, both by comparing one print against another and by their clean-cut outline, that there had been no distortion by melting; and this again provided ample evidence that they had been very recently made. The footprints, which were pointing down the glacier, were some twelve inches long and five inches wide. There was a big, rounded toe, projecting a bit to one side; the next toe was well separated from this, while three small toes were grouped closely together. We found several places where the creatures had leapt over small crevasses and where we could see clearly that they had dug their toes into the snow to prevent their feet from slipping back.

Several times before, both in the Himalaya and the Karakoram, I had come across unaccountable tracks in the snow, but I had never seen any so fresh and clearly defined as these. Hitherto I had been open-minded, perhaps a little sceptical, on the subject of the *Yeti*; but now I became convinced, particularly by the unmistakable evidence of the toes, of the existence of a large, ape-like creature, either quite unknown to science or at least not included in the known fauna of Central Asia. For, whatever creatures had made those tracks, they were neither bears nor human beings. Sen Tensing and I were both well acquainted with the tracks of both species of Himalayan bear; and people do not wander for miles over snow-covered glaciers with naked feet.

Shortly after five we started to descend an ice-fall. For a while we could still follow the tracks over this rough terrain, but it became increasingly difficult, as the snow gave place to bare ice. Night was falling when we reached a moraine at the side of the glacier, where we camped. It was a clear, still night, and when we had settled in our sleeping bags the silence was broken only by the occasional creaking caused by the movement of the glacier. I could not altogether suppress an eerie feeling at the thought that somewhere in that moonlit silence the strange creatures that had preceded us down the glacier were lurking. I was not surprised to find that Sen Tensing, lying beside me, was pondering similiar thoughts.

"You know, Sahib," he said, "the *Yeti* will be very frightened tonight."

"Why?" I asked.

"Well, no one has ever been here before; we will certainly have scared them."

I found this assurance comforting, particularly coming from such a well-informed source. But for the next few days I was very aware of the presence of the monsters, and often wondered if they were watching our movements, perhaps from one of the many caves we passed.

As soon as it was light we resumed our journey, postponing breakfast in the hope of finding some juniper wood to make a fire. Before long we reached a point where the valley took a sudden plunge, and from there a new prospect opened before us—vast amphitheatre formed by the junction of the barrier range and the lofty wall stretching from east to west in front of us. From this semi-circle of mountains several large glaciers descended towards us. These and the glacier we were on met in a large *concordia* below, and we could now see that they drained westward through a deep valley, still largely hidden by a buttress of Menlungtse.

A little later we found juniper in a hollow beside the glacier, where we settled down in the warm sun to a breakfast so large and leisured that it was past midday before we had finished. The next problem to be solved was whether this new west-bound valley drained to the north or the south of the main range. Upon this depended the answer to the question uppermost in our minds: were we now in Nepal or forbidden Tibet? So it was with some excitement that we approached the buttress. We expected to find a narrow canyon, but, rounding the corner, we entered a wide valley. The river flowing from the glaciers split into several streams and meandered over a flat expanse of gravel and meadow. Several miles farther on, the valley disappeared round a northerly bend under the precipices of a giant peak, now capped with cloud. We camped early that evening, tempted by a grassy plot beneath an overhanging cliff, where we built a big fire of juniper logs.

The next morning, leaving our camp standing, we went on to the bend of the valley; then, skirting the western flanks of Menlungtse, we climbed a rock pinnacle which commanded a splendid view to the north. Indeed, it was so extensive that it was some time before we could adjust our eyes to the great distances. Far below, we could see that our valley plunged into a deep, forested ravine which, several miles to the north-west, joined another much larger gorge. It appeared to be running northward, but presently we realised that this was not possible, for in that direction lay the Tibetan plateau, whose barren, rust-coloured hills we could see beyond. Suddenly I realised that we were looking into the valley of the Rongshar, one of the amazing rivers which, like the Arun, rise in Tibet and cut straight through the main axis of the Himalaya.

This discovery, for me quite as exciting as my first view up the Western Cwm, gave us the key to the problem of our whereabouts, and at once the geography of the region became clear. The ravine below us contained the Menlung Chu, a river whose lower end had been reached by the first Everest Reconnaissance Expedition in 1921. The great peak, which the previous day we had seen standing above the northerly bend of our valley, was Gauri Sankar, once believed to be the highest mountain in the world. Its summit was now clear. Our view also included the northern aspect of Menlungtse, and we saw that, like Nanda Devi, it was isolated in a glacier-basin. On every side its colossal granite walls were pale and smooth as polished marble. Each evening they glowed coral in the sunset.

The fact that our valley led to the Rongshar placed us in a teasing dilemma. For not only did it mean that we were now in Tibet but we knew also that there was a large monastery at the end of the Menlung Chu and that the point where the Rongshar entered its great defile was commanded by a *dzong*, or fort. It seemed highly improbable that we would be able to pass undetected through those narrow gorges. Even in the old days, to be caught in Tibet without a special permit was a serious matter; now, with the country in control of the Chinese, there was no knowing what our fate might be. Having so recently emerged from Communist China, I was specially sensitive on this point, and was not prepared to take the risk. It was most tantalising: I have always been fascinated by the great gorges of the Himalaya, and a passage through this fabulous defile which had never been penetrated by a Western traveller would have made a superb finish to our journey.

The unsatisfactory alternative of returning to Khumbu by the way we had come could only be avoided by finding a way across the mountain wall forming the southern rim of the Menlung basin. The next day, starting before dawn, we succeeded in reaching the lowest point in the crest of the wall, 19,500 feet high, and from there we looked down a 7000-foot drop into the Rolwaling. The precipice was so steep that most of it was invisible. Michael and I thought we should try to climb down it; Sen Tensing, most emphatically, did not.

When we returned to camp that evening we found that Bill and Tom and the Sherpas had arrived, having followed us across the Menlung La. They told us that our tracks on the glacier of three days before had almost disappeared, and of course they were quite unaware of the *Yeti* tracks. We explained the situation and our plan to attempt to cross the wall into the Rolwaling. But after supper Angtarkay asked me to reconsider my decision not to descend into the Rongshar. In the first place, he argued, the influence of the Communist regime in Tibet had not yet penetrated to those remote parts. Secondly, he said, as many Sherpas visit the Rongshar each year, our presence would not attract much notice; and anyway, if we were brought before the *dzongpen* (local governor residing at the fort) we had only to explain that we had strayed into Tibet by mistake and were anxious to get back to Nepal as soon as possible.

I was not convinced by these arguments. The Sherpas have never been able to understand our scruples about crossing forbidden frontiers, partly because for them these frontiers have no real significance, and partly because they were brought up in the tradition of an apparently omnipotent British Raj. I suspected, too, that the real reason for Angtarkay's plea was the Sherpas' reluctance to cross another high glacier pass, strengthened by Sen Tensing's alarming account of the precipice we had seen that day. However, I was by no means reluctant to be persuaded, and nor were the others; so when Angtarkay went on to suggest that, as the moon was nearly full, we could travel through the Rongshar by night to avoid being seen, we agreed to take the chance; though I must confess that I had grave misgivings.

It was a beautiful autumn morning, clear and crisp, as we walked on down the valley. The way was easy, and with only a few days' food left, our loads were light. From the northerly bend we raced down the steep scree of an ancient moraine, and in two hours reached an area of level ground forming a sort of lip of the basin, where its two rivers united before plunging into the ravine of the Menlung Chu. Here, at the upper edge of the forest, we halted for breakfast, basking in the sun and gazing up at the lovely pyramid of Menlungtse.

We found a path along the precipitous side of the ravine, and by the late afternoon we were nearing its junction with the Rongshar. On the way we met two Tibetan peasants. They were so astonished to see us that for a moment I thought that they were going to bolt back down the path. Luckily they were prevented by the friendly intervention of the Sherpas. As they were on their way up to some high pasture, we had no fear that they would report our arrival. A quarter of a mile from the junction we came in sight of the Chuphur monastery, 500 feet below us. We could see the people walking about in the courtyard and hear the deep clang of the ceremonial gong.

Scrambling some way above the path, we hid in the forest until nightfall. While we were eating our supper a party of women appeared gathering fuel, a couple of hundred feet below. They saw us, but, to our relief, they did not seem to be greatly concerned, and we hoped that the story of their encounter would not spread beyond their homes, at least until the following day. When it was nearly dark we climbed down to the path, half a mile below the monastery.

The moon had risen and was shining on the mountain-tops beyond the Rongshar. Though it would be some hours yet before it shone into the bottom of the valley, its reflected light was enough for us to see the path; indeed, we were glad to be in the shadow. The only serious risk of detection lay in passing through the village where the fort was situated. At night, in this narrow, rugged and forested valley, with no local knowledge, it was impossible to avoid this hazard, for if we left the path we would become hopelessly lost. Once beyond the village, we would be reasonably safe, for it was the last inhabited place on the Tibetan side of the frontier, which presumably lay somewhere in the middle of the gorge.

Though I have a vivid recollection of many details and impressions of that night, I have no clear memory of time. I think it was about 10:00 when we reached a relatively open section of the valley and saw near the path the dim outline of scattered houses. A dog barked, and that started the inevitable canine chorus that greets the visitor to every Tibetan village. But there were no lights visible, and we hoped that all the inhabitants were asleep in their smoke-filled rooms. Some twenty minutes later a massive building loomed in front of us. There was no mistaking the *dzong* with its high, slightly sloping walls.

Angtarkay had suggested that if we were challenged by a night watchman he should explain that we were a party of Sherpas returning to Nepal, and that he had a friend living at the other end of the village, with whom we proposed to spend the night. The story seemed a bit thin, but it was worth a try; for if we were detained there would be little chance of persuading our captors to let us proceed with our journey. In my experience Tibetan *dzongpens*, in common with most civil servants throughout the world, are rarely willing to accept unnecessary responsibility. The man in charge of the fort, however agreeable he might be as an individual, would feel bound to hold us while he referred the matter to higher authority in

Tingri. From Tingri the buck would be passed to Lhasa; and I could well imagine the zest with which the new Communist rulers in that city would welcome the capture of four British "spies."

I had pondered these matters all day, and I confess that in the last few hours, since reaching the Rongshar, I was in a state of some nervous tension, and even regretted that we had embarked upon this foolish venture. But suspense is always worse than the moment of crisis, and I was very glad to see the *dzong* so close. The next few minutes would decide the issue and, with any luck, in another half-hour we would be past the village, cloaked in the security of the forest beyond.

Though we were still in shadow, the moonlight had come down the western side of the valley to within a few hundred feet above us, and it was much lighter than before. The dogs, thank heaven, had stopped barking, and except for the boom of the river, echoing from some crags above, all was silent as we crept along under the walls of the *dzong*, trailing our ice-axes, the rubber soles of our climbing boots treading noiselessly on the earth street. Beyond the fort we saw no more houses, and presently the path narrowed through dense thickets and descended steeply towards the river. An hour later we rounded a sharp corner, and there, feeling profoundly relieved, we stopped for a short rest.

We were now in an S-bend; in the bright moonlight which flooded this east–west section of the valley it looked like a vast rectangular basin completely enclosed by gigantic cliffs. The wall at the far corner was split by a black fissure, the entrance to the gorge. The path climbed steeply towards this, and when we reached it we were several hundred feet above the river, which roared its thunderous protest at the sudden constriction of its bed. It was dark in the gorge; so dark that even when my eyes had become accustomed to the change, I could barely see the outline of the man ahead of me. We had no lamp, but the Sherpas have a remarkable ability to feel their way along an apparently invisible track, and we had only to follow closely behind them.

I felt as though I were living in a world of fantasy. I was tired, but, as in a dream, it required no effort of will to climb up and down the steep inclines. The events of the past thirty-six hours, since we had stood on the crest of the range overlooking the Rolwaling, seemed very remote. For some time I was aware that the gorge was filled with grey mist; then I chanced to look up and saw that, apparently straight above my head, the mist was edged by a curving silver band. It was a lovely sight, and I pointed it out to Tom, who was behind me. We paused for a moment, gazing up. The silver edge was strangely still. Suddenly I realised that the mist was an illusion: we were looking at the opposite wall of the gorge, bathed in moonlight; the silver band was the edge of the ice capping the precipice, how many thousand feet above I could not even guess.

Some time in the small hours of the morning the track led us to the bottom of the gorge, where there was a strip of level ground beside the river. The Sherpas stopped and suggested a meal. It was not an unreasonable request, for we had been going fairly continuously for the best part of a day and a night, and it was a long time since we had eaten. I agreed to make a short halt, but I was anxious to keep going until we were well beyond the frontier, wherever that might be. For although we had passed the *dzong*, apparently unobserved, I thought it would be tempting Providence to relax. A fire was lit and tea brewed. I lay down—and fell asleep.

I awoke in broad daylight. With much cursing I roused my companions, who obviously thought my ill-tempered urgency quite unreasonable. The path now kept close to the bottom of the gorge, so with little climbing to do we made rapid progress. The morning air was fresh and sweet and, presently, as I swung along the track, I began to feel calmer. Perhaps, after all, it was ridiculous to have any lingering fear of pursuit. Even if, by some unlucky chance, our presence in the Rongshar had been discovered and reported to the *dzongpen*, it was unlikely that he would have taken any action until this morning, and we had come a long way from the fort. An hour passed and then another. Surely we could not be far from the frontier now! How absurd to think of a frontier in this wild, fantastic canyon!

We were walking along a strip of open shore between two forested spurs, when suddenly there was an uproar behind us and we turned to see seven Tibetans charging down upon us, brandishing swords and uttering wild cries, their pigtails flying out behind them. It was a bizarre sight, but no less terrifying for that. I was relieved to see that the Sherpas stood their ground with apparent nonchalance, which suggested that they, at least, did not expect to be cut to pieces. When the strangers reached us, still brandishing their swords, they poured out a frenzied torrent of words. I had never known Angtarkay outdone in a shouting match, and he entered the fray with such fervour that it was a long time before I could induce him to tell me what it was all about. Not that I needed his explanation: the men had clearly been sent by the *dzongpen* to demand our immediate return to the fort.

It was useless to bemoan my stupidity in embarking on this crazy venture, useless to curse our folly in falling asleep at the last halt when we could so easily have escaped beyond the frontier by dawn; but I did both, and bitterly. I reflected ruefully that we had only 1200 rupees left and, though I would willingly have offered many times that sum to purchase our release, I doubted if it would have tempted a man in the *dzongpen*'s position; certainly not if Communist control had reached as far as the Rongshar.

When the verbal storm had spent some of its violence Angtarkay turned to me and suggested that the four of us should walk to the end of the shore and wait in the forest, leaving the Sherpas to discuss the matter with our captors. To my surprise we were allowed to do this, and I began to see a glimmer of hope. Twenty minutes later he appeared, wearing a broad grin.

"Everything is settled, but," he added apologetically, "I'm afraid it cost seven rupees to buy them off."

In extenuation of his extravagance, he explained that the men had demanded ten rupees; this, he had told them, was a ridiculously high figure, considering how easy it would be to explain to the *dzongpen* that they had been too late to catch us before we crossed the frontier. I was at last convinced that the revolutionary changes I had seen in China had not yet penetrated to this remote corner of Tibet.

It appeared that the women whom we had seen gathering firewood the previous evening had told their story. At first, the tale of bearded strangers had not been believed in official circles, but very early that morning it had received confirmation by the discovery of our boot-marks in the village street. The *dzongpen* had acted with significant despatch. His henchmen had displayed an extraordinary turn of speed and, considering the unknown nature of their quarry, no little courage. I felt sorry that they had not been more generously rewarded.

The Sherpas had also learned that the frontier, now two miles away, was marked by a bridge over the river. In another hour we were across it, lying stretched in the sun, the smoke of our breakfast fire curling up into the warm scented air. A fortnight later we reached Katmandu.

Returning to England early in December 1951, I was astonished by the amount of public interest aroused by our reconnaissance of Everest; it seemed much more widespread than it had been in the 1930s. I had felt distinctly diffident about writing such long and numerous articles for *The Times*, which included so much well-known history, and the publication of a Special Supplement repeating it all seemed to be grossly overdoing it. But the demand for information about Everest appeared to be quite insatiable. A public lecture I gave in one of the largest halls in Liverpool, for example, had to be repeated three times, and on the fourth occasion the hall was as full as on the first. I attributed this wave of interest, which had been similarly aroused by the climbing of Annapurna and the voyage of the Kon-Tiki, to the aftermath of the war creating a need for simple diversion from austerity. But perhaps the popular attitude towards these things had undergone a more lasting change. Formerly one was often asked to explain why men climbed mountains, crossed ice-caps or sailed alone round Cape Horn; now these questions are rarely heard. It is no longer necessary to invent spurious reasons for these useless activities, nor to evoke the "Spirit of Man" in justification. Can it be that an increasing fear of the encroachment of a universal suburbia has led to a wider sympathy with the desire to escape it?

We had hoped, of course, to follow up our reconnaissance of the Western Cwm by a full-scale attempt to climb Everest by the newly discovered route. We were disappointed when we returned to find that the Swiss had been granted permission by the Nepalese Government to send an expedition for that purpose in the spring of 1952. They suggested that we should unite with them in a combined effort under the joint leadership of

Dr. Wyss-Dunant and myself. After careful consideration, however, the Himalayan Committee decided to decline this generous offer. The main reason was our belief that neither joint leadership nor a team of mixed nationalities, however idealistic in theory, was likely to work smoothly under the physical and psychological stresses peculiar to an attempt on Everest. I fancy that the Swiss were relieved by this decision, for their own preparations were already well advanced. At their invitation, I paid two visits to Zürich to show them our photographs and give them all the information I could.

As it happened, from a nationalistic viewpoint, the postponement of the British attempt was fortunate; for there would have been far too little time to make adequate preparations for the spring of 1952. Not the least important of these was the selection of a strong party. Owing to the war, few of the younger generation of British climbers had experience of the Himalaya, and I knew only too well that proficiency in mountaineering technique was no guide to a man's performance at great altitudes. It was decided, therefore, that I should take a large party of likely candidates to climb in the Everest region, to provide them with training, acclimatisation and experience, and to furnish me with the data necessary to choose a team for an attempt in 1953. Another vital matter was oxygen. Largely because of the wartime development of lightweight alloys, it was now possible to devise oxygen apparatus for climbing far less cumbersome and more reliable than any produced for the earlier expeditions. Nothing had so far been done about this, and a 1952 attempt would not have been provided with oxygen. The project was now taken in hand by scientists in Farnborough and elsewhere, and the year's delay enabled them to produce excellent results.

The first objective of the 1952 expedition was Cho Oyu. But the only way we could find of climbing the mountain was up the north-west face, which could be approached only by crossing the Nangpa La; and our attempt was frustrated by my unwillingness to risk involvement with the Chinese by establishing a well-stocked base at its foot. Later, it appeared that I had been over-cautious, for during the next few years several attempts were made on the face, two of them successful, without interference from

Tibet. However, we spent an excellent season exploring the range west of the Bhote Kosi, which we had crossed in 1951, and climbing there and elsewhere. In all, we climbed eleven mountains between 21,000 and 23,000 feet, and a number of smaller peaks. Hillary and George Lowe also succeeded in making the very difficult crossing of the Nup La to the Rongbuk Glacier and back. In terms of training, the value of the expedition may be gauged by the fact that the five of its members who were chosen to go to Everest the following year, Evans, Bourdillon, Hillary, Lowe and Gregory, were those who climbed to and above the highest camp at 27,900 feet.

Early in June, while the rest of the party returned to Katmandu, Hillary, Lowe, Charles Evans and I set out with eight Sherpas on a long journey across the unexplored region east of Khumbu. To begin with we followed the route which Ed and I had discovered the previous year to the saddle beyond the Hongu basin. There we paused for two days to climb two peaks of 22,000 feet, which gave us superb views of the unknown south-eastern aspect of the Everest massif. Though it was already the middle of June, long after the normal time for the breaking of the monsoon, the weather was perfect; there was not even a light breeze, and one or two small clouds which formed high above the top of Everest were stationary. If only we had been blessed with such a season on one of our pre-war expeditions, I have little doubt that Everest would then have been climbed, with or without oxygen.

We then descended to a large glacier flowing southward under the western face of Makalu and, two days later, reached a gap at its head overlooking the Kangshung Glacier, thus establishing another link with the explorations of the 1921 Expedition. Then, on June 18, the monsoon broke with a heavy snowstorm, which forced us to retreat down the glacier to the Barun Valley.

Before starting on the journey we had been very concerned as to whether the Barun Valley was inhabited; for we guessed that it must be at least twenty miles long, and I had enough experience of Himalayan gorges to realise that, if it were not, we would be faced with a formidable task. Charles, however, had made a rapid reconnaissance to the end of the glacier, whence he had seen some stone shelters, which showed at least that the place was visited by the people beyond. When we came in sight of the valley below we were delighted to see, half a mile away, two men engaged in building a hut. The Sherpas were some way behind, so we stopped to wait for them, intending to creep up on the men together so as to get close enough to explain ourselves before they had time to take fright. But as soon as the Sherpas saw them, they rushed down the hill uttering wild cries. After a moment of stunned surprise, the men fled down the valley like a couple of deer and disappeared. Seeing a mob of strangers charging down upon them from a vast range of mountains they knew to be impassable, their panic was hardly surprising.

I was very angry with the Sherpas for their thoughtless behaviour, though I should not have expected them to resist so excellent a joke. It was important for our welfare during the next week that we should establish friendly relations with the people of the Barun, and to be regarded as a mass invasion of *Yeti* would scarcely help us to achieve this. Luckily, the two men, probably over-estimating our speed, must have waited in hiding, for when, a few hours later, we reached a shepherd encampment we found the people unalarmed, and we were able to make a more diplomatic approach. They were a tough-looking lot, which made us doubly glad not to have incurred their hostility. Though quite different racially from the Sherpas, they were evidently Buddhists and could speak some Tibetan dialect. We managed to persuade them to sell us a sheep and to provide us with a guide.

From the lovely, open pastures of the upper Barun, we descended into a mighty gorge, filled with dense forest, which became more and more tropical as we reached lower altitudes. Had it been trackless, it would have taken us many weeks to get through. As it was, without the shepherd to show us the way, we would have run into serious trouble, for the lower ten miles of the canyon had never been penetrated, even by the local people. To avoid it, our guide led us along a track which climbed steeply through the forest for 7000 feet to a plateau. There, in astonishing contrast to the vast ruggedness behind us, we entered a region of grassy hills, of small tarns fed by bubbling, mossy streams, of emerald meadows covered with multi-coloured carpets

Charles Evans

of primulas and huge cowslips, interspersed with rhododendron thickets of crimson and white. Beyond this Elysian plateau, the ground fell abruptly to the valley of the Arun, 10,000 feet below, and for the next three days we went down; down along narrow ridges between deep, cloud-filled valleys; down through steep forest dank and silent; down, at last, to the terraced fields and banana trees of scattered mountain villages where we revelled in the luxury of abundant food.

Charles and two of the Sherpas had left us to continue the eastward journey round the base of Kangchenjunga to Darjeeling, while the rest of us followed the Arun downstream. It was now nearly the end of June, and as I was anxious to return to England as soon as possible to set in motion the preparations for the next year's expedition to Everest, we travelled fast, starting at 4:30 each morning. On the evening of the third day of our journey along the Arun, when we were encamped on a stretch of wooded shore, the New Zealanders devised a plan to relieve the tedium of forced marches by floating down the river on air mattresses. I was not entirely happy about the idea, but they insisted that if they kept close inshore they could come to no harm. Though the current was swift enough to carry them a whole day's march in a few hours, the water was smooth, and it was a long time since we had seen rapids, which in any case could always be heard from a long way off. With characteristic zeal, they set about preparing their voyage. Placing two inflated mattresses side by side, they fixed them firmly together by lashing a number of staves across them. Then, having made a couple of paddles from pieces of drift-wood, they launched their craft for a trial trip along the shore. It was amply buoyant and stable; and, though not very manoeuvrable, they had some measure of control with their paddles.

It was still dark the next morning when the Sherpas and I resumed our march through the forest along the river bank, leaving Ed and George to complete their preparations and to wait until dawn. We had agreed upon a rendezvous for breakfast about six miles downstream. After a mile or so, we came to a little bay enclosed by a semi-circular cliff. It was then light enough to see that, on the far side of the bay, the cliff formed a promontory, 200 feet high, jutting far out into the river; so far indeed, that it diverted a large part of the current into the bay. The end of the promontory was sharp and vertical, like the prow of a great ship. Dashing against the point, the smooth surface of the water heaved up and fell back upon itself in a great "bow-wave." The water on the inside was swept round by the curve of the cliff into a powerful eddy which formed a huge whirlpool, with a spinning mass of flotsam, in the centre of the bay.

At once I realised that the New Zealanders were in grave danger, for it was evident that unless their raft was well over towards the opposite bank of the river (here about 500 yards wide) it would be dashed against the promontory or swept into the whirlpool. Dropping our loads, we ran round the top of the cliff and scrambled to the summit of the promontory, hoping to be in time to warn them to paddle towards the opposite bank. As we reached the top the raft came into view from round a bend, 300 or 400 yards away. We yelled and waved our arms; but they did not need our warning, for as soon as they saw the great rock jutting out into the middle of the river, they realised the danger and started paddling frantically across the stream. At first I hoped that they might manage to get far enough out to be carried round the promontory; but they were coming down the river fast, and I soon saw that they were making almost no lateral progress. A moment later the raft began to spin, and I realised with sickening horror that it was completely out of control and being swept directly towards the point of the promontory.

For a long and desperate moment I waited to see the raft smashed to pieces, 200 feet below me, against the very cliff I was standing on. Unable to do anything to avert the disaster, I could only wait and visualise the collision and the struggling form of my friends being hurled into the curling wave. Once in the water they would be sucked under immediately. The moment of impact came. But instead of disintegrating, the buoyant raft mounted the "bow-wave" and, like a bobsleigh sweeping round a steep corner, slid sideways into the relatively calm water of the bay, Ed and George, miraculously, still on it. The relief was short-lived; for the current in the whirlpool was so strong that they could do nothing to influence the circular course of the raft. Round it went, out into the main stream, to be hurled once more against the point of the cliff. Again and again the same thing happened. It was obvious that sooner or later the lashings holding the mattresses together must give way. Also there was serious danger of their being punctured by repeated collision with the mass of flotsam and tree-trunks whirling round the pool.

From where we stood, the cliff appeared to be vertical all round the bay and there was no vestige of shore along its base. Half-way round the bay, however, there was a shallow gully; at the bottom of this I thought it might be possible to obtain some purchase. We hurried back to the loads to get two climbing ropes and then raced to the head of the gully. While the Sherpas held one rope at the top, I slid down it with the other over my shoulder. The gully was not so steep as it had appeared, and when I reached the bottom I found a narrow ledge just above the level of the water. I uncoiled the second rope and waited for the raft to reach the nearest point on its circuit. Luckily the distance was not great, and I had no difficulty in throwing the end of the rope to George and hauling them in.

A week later we reached Jogbani. In our filthy, tattered mountain clothes and heavy climbing boots we were ill-clad for our two-day train journey across the hot Indian plains. But this did little to mar the pleasure of lounging in the comfort of a second-class compartment, eating enormous quantities of fruit. In the first twenty-four hours we consumed 160 bananas and countless mangoes, with the inevitable consequences.

On July 28, a week after I had returned to England, the Himalayan Committee met to hear my report on the training expedition and to consider plans for the organisation of the attempt on Everest the following spring. It was clear that the Committee assumed that I would lead the expedition. I had, however, given a good deal of thought to the matter, and felt it right to voice certain possible objections. Having been to Everest five times, I undoubtedly had a great deal more experience of the mountain and of climbing at extreme altitudes than anyone else; also, in the past year I had been closely connected, practically and emotionally, with the new aspect of the venture. On the other hand, long involvement with an unsolved problem can easily produce rigidity of outlook, a slow response to new ideas, and it is often the case that a man with fewer inhibitions is better equipped to tackle it than one with greater experience. I had more reason than most to take a realistic view of the big element of luck involved, and this was not conducive to bounding optimism. Was it not time, perhaps, to hand over to a younger man with a fresh outlook? Moreover, Everest had become the focus of greatly inflated publicity and of keen international competition, and there were many who regarded success in the coming attempt to be of high national importance. My well-known dislike of large expeditions and my abhorrence of a competitive element in mountaineering might well seem out of place in the present situation.

I asked the Committee to consider these points very carefully before deciding the question of leadership, and then left them while they did so. When I was recalled the Chairman informed me that they had reached the unanimous decision that I should be asked to lead. He was kind enough to add that I had the full confidence and backing of the Committee, who considered that my prestige alone, particularly among the Sherpas, made it most desirable that I should accept. I did so, and at the same time asked that Charles Evans should be appointed deputy leader. Incidentally, if the Committee had asked me to withdraw I would have recommended most strongly that Charles should be invited to take my place, for I had formed the highest opinion of his ability and temperament.

To take full advantage of the many technical advances made during the war in such things as cold-weather clothing, diet and oxygen, a great deal of research and experiment would be needed in addition to the normal work of preparation. For this reason, it was decided to appoint an organising secretary, preferably a mountaineer qualified to take part in the expedition itself. The first choice was John Hunt, whom I interviewed a few weeks later. We had a frank discussion, and John told me that he did not feel able to accept the position unless he were made deputy leader. While I understood his point of view as a high-ranking Army officer, I could not, of course, agree to his terms, since I had already nominated Charles Evans as my deputy. Also, it was clear to both of us, and admitted, that our approach to the enterprise, both practical and temperamental, was so fundamentally different that we would not easily work together. We parted, however, on friendly terms. The post of organising secretary was filled by Charles Wylie, and we started work at the Royal Geographical Society.

The next meeting of the Himalayan Committee was on September 11. I was surprised to find that the first item on the agenda was the "Deputy Leadership," and still more so when I was asked to go out of the room while this was discussed. An hour later I was recalled and told that John had been appointed "Co-leader" with me. Then, for the first time, it dawned on me that there must have been a great deal of backdoor diplomacy since the last meeting, of which I had been totally unaware. It seemed particularly strange to me that I should have been expected to accept the proposal, especially remembering the views expressed the previous winter on the subject of joint leadership by most of the Committee and by myself. In declining, I told the Committee that if they wished to reconsider their former decision regarding the leadership, they were, of course, free to do so. I then withdrew for a still longer period. I returned to be told that it had been decided to appoint John Hunt in my place.

The influences which caused the Committee's *volte-face* are still obscure. Assuming both the need and the desirability for a large heavily organised expedition, their ultimate decision was right. My taste for simplicity would certainly have influenced my conduct of the enterprise. Moreover, partly because of this disposition, I am neither an efficient organiser of complicated projects nor a good leader of cohorts. Even so, the chagrin I felt at my sudden dismissal was a cathartic experience which did nothing to increase my self-esteem. I had often deplored the exaggerated publicity accorded to Everest expeditions and the consequent distortion of values. Yet, when it came to the point, I was far from pleased to withdraw from this despised limelight; nor could I fool myself that it was only the manner of my rejection that I minded. I was further humbled by the loyalty of Tom Bourdillon, who was so incensed that, without telling me, he wrote to the Committee resigning from the expedition. Knowing how desperately keen he was to take part in the attempt on Everest, I was fully aware of the extent of his sacrifice. It took me a long time to persuade him to retract.

| 9 |

PATAGONIA AND
TIERRA DEL FUEGO

CROSSROADS AGAIN. THIS TIME IT seems we took the wrong turning; or maybe the germ of madness was in us and we would have met calamity on whatever path we had followed. As before the choice was diverse. At the suggestion of a high-ranking officer of the Colonial Service, I applied for the job of "H.M. Consul and Agent" in Tonga. A few years in the Friendly Islands was a charming prospect, particularly after our recent experiences in China. Unfortunately the incumbent of the post had just been granted a year's extension, and though I could have filled the time profitably, I decided instead to accept the wardenship of the Outward Bound Mountain School in Eskdale. I was far from happy about this, not because I doubted the value of the project, but because I could not see myself as a leader of youth: for though I like people individually and certainly have a capacity for enthusiasm, I felt I was too much of an introvert to impart it to large numbers of boys. However, I found that this could be safely left to a carefully chosen staff of instructors, and my chief function was to guide the design of the courses into imaginative channels. In this I believe I was reasonably successful until, at the end of 1954, the conduct of my private life made my position no longer tenable, and I was discharged.

Diana and I had started to form attachments more or less simultaneously, based, I suppose, upon the attractions of qualities that we had found lacking in each other. Both began as light-hearted flirtations, developed through a series of vicissitudes, and resulted eventually in our divorce. I was mostly to blame, which made it all the more remarkable that Diana never showed a sign of bitterness or animosity; and we were thus able to salvage from the wreck our continued friendship—and my affection. Her affair prospered, mine did not.

Tormented by self-reproach at having made such a monumental mess of things, I felt a strong urge to escape into obscurity; so, after a few half-hearted attempts to get another executive job, I settled down as a casual forestry labourer on an estate in Shropshire, with intermittent spells of writing to occupy my spare time. There is nothing like hard physical work in the deep, English countryside to restore serenity, and after a while I became so content with this way of life that I wanted nothing more. It did not occur to me to try to resume my former pursuits until I accepted an invitation to lead an expedition of students from the Imperial College of Science to the Karakoram in the summer of 1957. Though, after that, I happily resumed my casual labouring for another year, the enchantment of the untravelled world had once more cast its compulsive spell.

Even in the 1930s, when deeply involved with the limitless horizons of Central Asia, I had hoped some day to venture into another field. New Guinea, Alaska, Colombia all had strong attractions, but none so persistent as the mountainous regions of Patagonia and Tierra del Fuego. The appeal lay partly in their association with the voyages of Magellan and other circumnavigators; mostly in the haunting vision evoked by Darwin's account of those mysterious, storm-swept ranges, hidden in a perpetual shroud of mist, guarded by primeval forest amidst a vast labyrinth of fjords forming thousands of miles of uninhabited shore. My decision at last to go there was taken largely as a result of random talk with Geoff Bratt during a storm on the Siachen Glacier.

It is a curious anomaly that with so much available to modern youth, their rebellion should be so violent and intractable. Perhaps the real cause of their revolt lies in their intolerable dilemma of having no valid reason for complaint. Compared, say, with the Twenties and Thirties there is a vast range of opportunity open to students of today, whether to relieve the sufferings of humanity or to expand their own horizons. The course of Geoff's education was an example of this. The son of a cobbler in Tasmania and one of a large family, he had no private means; yet he was able not only to come to England to study for his Ph.D. in chemistry at the Imperial College, but also to take climbing holidays in the Alps, to join the Karakoram expedition financed from college funds and later to participate in two expeditions to South America before returning to Tasmania to settle down in a job. Moreover, the work of these expeditions had no relevance whatever to his subject. But Geoff, though a robust individualist, had enough humility to be gratefully surprised at the good things that came his way.

We met in London from time to time to discuss the expedition to Patagonia which we hoped to launch towards the end of 1958. With little idea of the potentialities of the region for exploration or scientific research, and with no knowledge of local conditions, it was hard even to begin to make a detailed plan. Our chief difficulty was to define some plausible objectives, for without these we could hardly expect to receive financial support; yet, until we could discover the kind of work likely to evoke support, our objectives could not be chosen. We made several visits to the Natural History Museum, casting about in the various departments for some glimmer of enthusiasm; but as Geoff was working for his final examinations and I was digging ditches and erecting fences in Shropshire, we made little progress towards a solution. Neither of us cared very much what we did so long as it gave us the chance to see something of Patagonia. For my part I regarded the trip primarily as a reconnaissance into a new field, for I had no doubt that once I understood the problems and possibilities of exploratory travel there, a swarm of exciting projects would soon be clamouring for attention, just as they had in the Himalaya twenty-five years before.

In June the Botany Department of the Museum offered to send Peter James with us to make a comprehensive collection of plants, lichens and mosses, and to furnish a grant to cover his share of the cost. This was the break-through we needed, for it provided a foundation upon which to build the expedition. Shortly afterwards John Mercer offered to join us. He had already been twice to the Andes of Patagonia and was anxious to return there to continue a line of study aimed at determining the dates of successive periods of glacial advance. As Geoff himself was keen to do some glaciological work, this fitted in very well. I was also put in touch with Peter Miles, an Anglo-Argentine farmer in Santa Fé Province, and an amateur naturalist, who agreed to come with us to make a collection of birds and insects for the British Museum and the Darwin Institute in Buenos Aires. Thus armed with a battery of scientific objectives, we were able to obtain further grants from the Mount Everest Foundation and the Percy Sladen Trust, which provided the money we needed. On November 1, 1958, we sailed for Buenos Aires in rather squalid third-class accommodation.

The name Patagonia, "land of big feet," refers to the whole of the mainland of South America south of latitude 40° S. The bulk of it lies in Argentina, east of the Andes, and consists of prairie, some of it flat, much of it hilly, nearly all of it dry, treeless and covered with coarse grass and open scrub. By contrast, most of the Chilean side is rugged, mountainous country, a land of wild tempest and torrential rain, of mighty glaciers and dense forest. The Pacific coast, immediately west of the Andes, is split by a vast network of fjords which bite deep into the mainland, forming an archipelago 1000 miles long, and which is curiously matched on the eastern side of the range by an intricate system of lakes. There are two extensive ice-caps, the only examples of their kind outside Polar regions; and many of the innumerable glaciers radiating from these flow through heavily forested valleys, the haunts of parrots and humming birds, right down to the sea or the lakes, where they launch massive icebergs.

In 1958 most of this strange mountain region was still unexplored, and though during the last forty years many sorties had been made into it from the eastern side, few had achieved more than a very limited objective, while only one party had penetrated inland from the hundreds of miles of uninhabited Pacific coastline. The main reasons for this were the prevailing weather conditions, said to be some of the roughest in the world; the fact that most parts of the range, even many on the eastern side, could only be

An unnamed peak above the northern ice-cap in Patagonia

approached by water; the difficulty of penetrating the forest zones; and the unusually broken nature of the glaciers in their lower reaches.

Geoff and I had chosen the section of the Andes west of Lago Argentino because it was the most easily accessible. This great lake is shaped like a squid with eight long tentacles, some of which penetrate deep into the heart of the range. With the help of a government launch which had been placed at our disposal, we established successive bases at the heads of these fjords, spending several weeks at each; and while Peter James and Peter Miles were busy with their collections (the former secured 4000 specimens of plants and lichens), Geoff, John and I climbed into the glacier regions beyond. Between each of these sorties we returned to rest and collect fresh supplies at the small town of Calafate on the shore of the main lake, which made a delightful change and also enabled us to meet some of the local sheep farmers. Thus, this first expedition provided a fairly gentle introduction to the mountains of Southern Patagonia; but though we were never exposed for long to the full fury of the weather, I saw enough of it to develop a healthy respect, particularly for the shattering windstorms, which were worse than any I had known before. In spite of this, the occasional glimpses we had into the unknown country on the Pacific side of the range kindled my timid ambition to embark on a long exploratory journey through this wild, lonely region.

Meanwhile, however, there was an intriguing little problem to be solved. Since the discovery of the great lakes of Southern Patagonia towards the end of the nineteenth century, evidence had accumulated of volcanic activity somewhere on the southern of the two great ice-caps. For example, in 1913 some travellers near Lago Viedma had reported that large quantities of volcanic ash had fallen around them; later, ash deposits were found on several of the glaciers farther north, while settlers near the shores of Lago San Martin claimed on several occasions to have seen great columns of smoke rising over the ice-cap, far to the west. In 1933 a party led by Dr. Reichert, the first man to reach the ice-cap, saw looming out of the mist, "a volcanic cone, 3000 metres high," with clouds of steam issuing from it. For some reason Reichert's report did not receive the credence it deserved, and in the subsequent speculation about the existence and whereabouts of the volcano it seems largely to have been ignored. His route to the ice-cap was followed twice, in 1957 and 1958, but no fresh evidence had emerged.

The man chiefly involved in the discussion was Dr. Lliboutry, a distin-guished French glaciologist, who, from a careful study of the evidence, had come to the conclusion that the main focus of the eruptions lay in the centre of the unexplored northern half of the southern ice-cap. He had also seen, on an air photograph of the Viedma Glacier, what he took to be an active crater in a large rock outcrop in the upper basin. He flew over it himself in 1952; what he saw convinced him that he was right, and the outcrop became known as "Vulcan Viedma." When, however, Geoff, John and I succeeded in reaching it in January 1959 we found it composed only of sedimentary and metamorphic rocks; but on our way there we discovered a great deal of pumice scattered over the surface of the Viedma Glacier.

I decided to devote my second expedition, in the southern summer of 1959–60, to a search for the mysterious volcano with a party recruited from Argentina and Chile. We reached the head of one of the western arms of Lago San Martin in an inflatable rubber boat, *Zodiac*, a replica of that used by Dr. Bombard for his voyage across the Atlantic, which I had brought from England. Some three weeks later, after back-packing our loads up a glacier in a series of relays, we reached the edge of the ice-cap with enough supplies to last us for a further month. There was no need, however, to hunt for our objective: not fifteen miles away across the plateau was a mountain with clouds of dark vapour pouring from a great black fissure in the ice below its summit and an occasional eruption of ash. The volcano was far to the south of the area I had originally intended to search, and but for its timely resumption of activity, we would certainly not have found it; for, in periods of quiescence, the fissure would be deeply buried by snow. Though the mountain bore no resemblance to a cone, we had no doubt that it was the one seen by Reichert.

Travelling on skis, we carried three weeks' supplies to a rock outcrop, or *nunatak*, near the base of the volcano. For the next fortnight we were subjected to a series of violent storms, with torrential rain and winds often reaching hurricane force. The weather had been bad throughout our journey from the lake, but then we had been largely protected from

238 ~ THAT UNTRAVELLED WORLD

the westerly gales sweeping across the Plateau. The *nunatak* gave us little shelter. Two pairs of skis were blown away and never seen again; one of our two tents was destroyed; our clothing and sleeping bags became and remained completely saturated. The culminating calamity occurred when we had been there ten days: both our stoves ceased to function. Luckily, with the amount of rain falling, we had no need to melt snow for water. We had hoped to climb the volcano to examine the crater, and also to travel to a range of peaks forming our northern horizon to see whether they, too, were volcanic in origin. But at length it became clear that we were in no condition to undertake either of these projects, and as soon as there was a lull we started back, leaving most of the supplies we had carried up with so much toil.

Although we had achieved our main object of locating the volcano, I was very disappointed that we had managed to cover so little fresh ground. The expedition had, however, provided some valuable lessons, and I felt that I now had enough experience of exposure to Patagonian weather to tackle a much more ambitious venture. After much thought, and with the feelings of a non-swimmer about to plunge into the deep end of a pool, I decided to attempt a journey from north to south over the entire length of the southern ice-cap. Landing on the uninhabited Pacific coast, our first hazard would be the finding of a way up some unknown valley to the northern end of the Plateau. Once there, the problems would be navigation and weather. Though the first half of the projected route lay entirely over virgin ground, there should be plenty of room to provide a safe margin for directional error, and I was not worried on that score. But I was certainly scared of the weather, for it was not difficult to visualise a number of ugly situations: becoming storm-bound, for example, and unable to move for several weeks at a critical stage of the journey; or, worse, having the tent blown away by a sudden hurricane gust while it was being pitched; for in my experience the snow on the ice-cap was nearly always too sodden for the construction of caves or shelters. We would, however, have the great advantage of travelling more or less in the direction of the prevailing wind.

Before returning to England in 1960 I went to Santiago, where I received the generous assurance of the Chilean Naval Authorities that they would arrange for one of their ships to take my party to our chosen point on the coast. I also discussed the project with Jack Ewer, who had been a member of my recent expedition and agreed to join me again. Jack, a Cornishman, worked at the University of Chile, had spent two years in the Antarctic and is quite the most stubbornly optimistic man I know. We invited two young Chilean mountaineers, also from the University, Edouardo Garcia and Cedomir Marangunic, to complete the party. Both had previous experience of Patagonian mountains, a vital qualification, and were most enthusiastic about my plan. Cedomir, a geologist, had professional as well as aesthetic reasons for wanting to make the journey.

Bitter experience had convinced me that lightweight tents used in the Himalaya were totally inadequate for Patagonian conditions; so, on Jack's advice, I decided to use a double-skinned Antarctic pyramid. It was a horrible thing to carry, but convenient for sledging, easily pitched and, so long as the correct drill was observed, unlikely to be blown away in the process; once pitched, with its skirts well buried by snow, it was capable of withstanding the most devastating wind. The question of a sledge was more difficult; none of the standard patterns was suitable, since it would have to be carried for several weeks, probably through bog and forest and broken ice, often in a high wind, before it could be used. After listening to a mass of conflicting advice—for I knew nothing of sledging myself—I had one made of fibreglass; it was shaped like a shallow punt and divided into four sections which egg-shelled into each other to make a tolerable load. Because of the problem of carrying through forest, I decided to take snowshoes instead of skis; a mistake as it turned out. All the food we required was presented free by various firms in London. This and the equipment was packed in two large crates and shipped in S.S. *Salaverry*, due to reach Punta Arenas, the most southerly port on the mainland of South America, on November 18, 1960. Meanwhile, arrangements had been made for a vessel of the Chilean Navy to pick us up on December 10, and take us to our base.

This careful planning was upset by a strike of tally clerks, which delayed *Salaverry*'s departure by several weeks, and when at last she sailed on October 14 it was clear that we could keep our rendezvous with the

Chilean Navy only by a narrow margin. Reaching Punta Arenas by air on November 30, I learned that the ship which was to have taken us to our base was out of commission and that instead we were to be transported by a frigate, *Covadonga*, under orders to sail for Valparaiso at noon on December 7. This news was disturbing enough, but when, five days later, I heard that *Salaverry* would not be arriving until the 8th it seemed highly probable that my expedition would have to be abandoned. Admiral Balaresque, commanding the 3rd Naval Zone in Punta Arenas, was most sympathetic, but he made it clear that the frigate could not wait for the arrival of our baggage, and that there would be no other transport available for several weeks, too late for my companions, who were tied to the period of their long vacation.

The Admiral suggested that if I could induce the commander of *Salaverry*, Captain Thomas, to put our baggage ashore on one of the islands of the archipelago, *Covadonga* could pick it up on her way north. But although Sven Robson, the British Consul, persuaded the Chilean Customs authorities to allow this unorthodox procedure, it seemed hardly likely that Captain Thomas would be willing to undertake an operation which would further delay his ship and might involve some risk in those treacherous and usu-

ally storm-swept waters. It was even more improbable that he would be able, while still at sea, to extract our two boxes from the 2000 tons of cargo in his holds. But then I did not know Captain Thomas.

The morning of the 6th was spent by the Admiral and his staff calculating *Salaverry*'s probable position and marking on their charts the various points along the rugged, uninhabited coastline where our baggage could be discharged. I became so absorbed in

Cedomir Marangunic

this occupation that I almost forgot my despair. Soon after lunch Cyril Jervis, a local radio amateur, made contact with *Salaverry*. She was then approaching a difficult passage known as the English Narrows in thick weather, and the Captain was brought from the bridge to speak to me. I explained my dilemma, and he replied without hesitation that he would do his damnedest to help us out. Three hours later he came back with the wonderful news that our crates had been located and would be put ashore at Puerto Eden, a meteorological station manned by three naval personnel near the southern exit to the English Narrows, the only inhabited locality within hundreds of miles. In fact, the crates were too big to be accommodated in the ship's boats and had first to be repacked into twenty-seven parcels. This wonderfully generous action by Captain Thomas, coupled with a chain of lucky chances, had saved the day. Blithely unaware of the crisis, my companions arrived from Santiago with a few hours to spare, and the next day we embarked on the frigate for the 600-mile voyage northward through the channels.

The first two days were cold and stormy: the mountain-tops were hidden in cloud, and though it was nearly mid-summer, fresh snow lay on the wooded slopes almost down to the shore. But the morning of the 9th, when we anchored off Puerto Eden to pick up our baggage, was clear and still; the green forest, splashed with patches of white magnolia, was bathed in warm sunlight and the smooth water of the channel mirrored the glacier-capped peaks of Wellington Island. We met some families of Alacaluf, a primitive tribe of canoe Indians so near extinction that there appear to be only a hundred or so left. In the soft light of evening we made the tortuous passage of the English Narrows, and by dawn the next day the frigate was steaming eastward up Baker Channel, one of the largest inlets of the Pacific coast. At 9:00 a.m. she dropped anchor off a small island at the entrance to a bay stretching southward for ten miles. Forty years before this bay had been almost filled by the end of a huge glacier flowing northward from the icecap; since then its front had retreated six miles, leaving a strip of sandy shore at the southern extremity of the inlet. We were landed there by the ship's launch, and the frigate resumed her voyage.

Left on that lonely shore, 150 miles of rugged mountain travel ahead, the way to the Plateau unknown and no ready means of retreat—it was a stimulating situation; and I was glad to find my enjoyment of it was as keen as ever. My companions were no less delighted, and we spent the fine afternoon happily sorting and repacking our baggage. It was the last time we were to see the sun for nearly three weeks. The next morning, December 11, in heavy rain, we began the sombre task of back-packing our equipment and eight weeks' food; 720 pounds in all, requiring three relays.

As we had expected, the shrinking glacier had left a wide corridor of bare ground which provided excellent going for several miles inland and postponed the difficult choice between the broken ice of the glacier and the dense forest. We passed a large lake, the breeding ground of thousands of duck and geese; and later we had charming encounters with the local deer. Obviously these creatures had never seen humans before, and were so completely fearless that they often came within two or three yards of us. Despite these distractions and the perennial thrill of being on virgin ground, the first few days of back-packing were purgatory. At fifty-three I probably suffered a great deal more than my young companions; for ageing muscles take longer to train, and my whole body ached as though it had been flogged with a truncheon. Gradually, however, the torment eased and I gained an increasing enjoyment in rhythmic movement.

After a week we were forced by steep ground to take to the glacier. Happily, we were then beyond the riven ice of its lower section; moreover, a deep mantle of winter snow still reached down to 2000 feet, covering the crevasses, and two days later we were able to start sledging. This was much sooner than we had dared to hope; but our delight was eclipsed by the discovery that the labour of hauling the sledge was infinitely harder than we had expected. This was partly due to the design of the sledge, which was quite unsuited to the soft, soggy condition of the snow, and partly because, until we became more practised, our efforts were hopelessly uncoordinated. Also, to move the thing at all we had to lean so far forward that we could not use our snowshoes, and our feet sank deep into the snow. Two relays were still required to shift our baggage, and after the first day's sledging we returned to camp thoroughly exhausted.

Then, when morale was at its lowest ebb, a small accident happened which might have had grave consequences. Having removed my wet boots and socks, I was sitting on my sleeping bag brewing our eagerly awaited tea, when the stove tilted and the entire pot of boiling water poured over my naked feet. The scalded flesh became very swollen, and an open sore developed on my left foot. In the circumstances it was most important to prevent sepsis, and it would have been unwise to walk in wet snow until it healed. Luckily, I was only incapacitated for a week. Meanwhile the others continued the work of relaying the loads, which now included me, and reconnoitring a steep ice-fall at the head of the glacier. Later in the summer this might have been a formidable obstacle; as it was, masses of snow choked all but the widest chasms, and they had little difficulty in finding a safe way through. Though I did little to help in the gruelling task of hauling the loads up, at least I was able to climb it under my own steam.

On December 28, my foot quite healed, we reached the edge of the Plateau. In spite of the time lost by my stupid accident, we were well satisfied by our performance so far, and our mood of buoyant optimism was further lightened by a twenty-four-hour spell of fine weather, the first since our landing eighteen days before. Northward, the wide trough of the Baker Channel was still in view; a gently undulating expanse of snow stretched away to our southern horizon, while to the west, barely eight miles away, a group of superb rock spires stood above the Plateau, their vertical sides sheathed in ice, their summits crowned by huge mushroom cornices.

The respite was all too brief, and for the next ten days thundering gales and blinding drift were our daily portion. During this time we marched entirely by compass. It was no longer possible to relay, for, with visibility rarely more than fifteen yards, the risk of losing our dumps or our tent would be too great. Also, we were travelling with the prevailing wind, which was generally so powerful that there were very few days when it would have been possible to move in the opposite direction. As we still had 550 pounds to haul, not including the weight of the sledge or the snow and ice that encrusted the loads, it was extremely hard work, and our advance was pathetically slow. At first we found that we could pull for only ten minutes at a time before stopping to ease our bursting lungs, but gradually our performance improved, and on the third day we were doing twenty minutes without a halt. The leading man had by far the most exacting job, for besides his share of the hauling he had to break trail in the soft snow and concentrate most of his attention on the compass; so we changed the lead after every three spells. We estimated the distance travelled—surprisingly accurately as it turned out—by the time spent actually pulling and the average number of paces per minute.

Punctually at 3:30 each morning we began to prepare breakfast, composed of a mixture of oats, sugar, powdered milk and boiling water, followed by tea. We always aimed at being ready to start at 7:30, but rarely managed it. Reluctance to get out of our cosy sleeping bags and into cold, wet clothes was part of the reason; but the real time-consumer was the job of digging away the ice and drift-snow from around the tent and extricating the buried sledge and harness; this often took more than three hours. When the wind was not too strong we made a half-hour halt for lunch—biscuits, butter and cheese; and we usually stopped sledging at 3:00. Pitching the tent and bedding down inside generally took an hour in reasonable conditions; a great deal more in bad. The next three hours were mostly occupied in melting snow, cooking and eating: tea was followed by a stew mostly made of dehydrated meat-bars, and this in turn by a repeat of the breakfast menu. We were ready to sleep at 7:30.

Though this may sound like a monotonous routine, we found it far from irksome. For one thing we had all been well aware of the conditions we were likely to meet, and I suspect that, like me, the others had harboured some misgivings. But now that we were actually there coping with the weather, we gradually gained confidence in our ability not only to survive the worst that it could do but also to travel securely; and with this confidence came a positive exultation in the violence of the elements. On the whole journey there were only three mornings when we used the force of the wind as an excuse to lie up for the day; each time it was worse on the following morning, and we set out as usual. Unlike the previous year, snowstorms were heavy and continuous, and rain correspondingly rare. This resulted in a far greater density of drift, which restricted visibility and was particularly tiresome when striking and pitching camp; but it had two big advantages: the crevassed areas remained well covered, and we could keep our clothes and sleeping bags comparatively dry.

In the evening of January 2 we sighted our first "land-fall": a rock wall looming out of the mist, half a mile from our camp. The wind dropped, and the next morning dawned in unwonted stillness. Cedomir and Jack went to collect rock samples from the wall, while Edouardo and I loaded the sledge, an easy job for once. The mist was clearing; the serrated crest of the wall emerged, first as a dim spectre, then so sharply defined that it looked as brittle as a stage backdrop. There was no sun, but a small expanse of pale-blue sky was edged with radiant gold and a million crystals of frosted snow danced in the reflected light. In that moment I seemed to hold the grail of peace in solitude. Two hours later it was blowing as hard as ever.

The next two marches took us through an archipelago of rock peaks, rising from the Plateau like lofty islands. Occasionally we saw their tops, encrusted with rime, looming out of the mist and swirling drift. They were all of the same granitic structure as the wall, and there was no sign of volcanic rocks on this part of the Plateau. For nearly four days we saw nothing at all and began to get a little worried about the accuracy of our navigation. Then on January 8 the mist lifted, revealing a dark shape far ahead which Jack and I recognised, at first doubtfully, then with increasing confidence, as our *nunatak* of the previous year. We were astonished and delighted to find that, after so much "blind" travel and with no chance of fixing our position since reaching the northern edge of the Plateau, this first major objective was almost exactly on our line of march.

It was just four weeks since we had started relaying from the coast. Although we had far more than half the total distance still to cover, we had plenty of time in hand, for nearly the whole of the rest of the way would be straightforward sledging and most of it over known ground. Moreover, with our load diminishing by ten pounds of food and fuel a day, we would be able to travel faster and with less effort. Our old depot on the *nunatak*, buried under eight feet of snow, was hard to find. Most of the food was rotten, and we only salvaged twenty meat-bars and a two-pound tin of butter. However, Jack and Cedomir were delighted with this addition; for both had voracious appetites, which were not satisfied by our daily ration of 4500 calories. The only concession that Edouardo and I had made to their greater need was to allow them to scrape out the evening stew-pot—largely because it saved us the trouble of washing up. The extra two pounds of butter disappeared in twenty-four hours.

We stayed five days in the neighbourhood of the volcano, collecting rock samples and hoping for a chance to climb it; but the weather was atrocious, and we did not even see the crater. On the second half of the journey, though we suffered some of the worst blizzards, there were days when the sun shone in a cloudless sky and the storm-washed air was clear and still; then, our sight restored, we could exult in the splendour of our surroundings. Conforming to the pattern of Patagonian weather, these fine spells came with astounding suddenness, in the midst, it seemed, of the most violent tempest, and often on a falling barometer. They ended equally abruptly and were usually brief; though one lasted forty hours.

This occurred when we reached the upper basin of the Upsala Glacier, one of the largest in the Andes, flowing from the southern extremity of the ice-cap into Lago Argentino, our ultimate goal. Still with several days' food in hand we seized the opportunity to climb some peaks near by. There is a special feature in the mountains of Southern Patagonia that I have seen elsewhere only in Ruwenzori. The incessant wind, heavily charged with moisture, forms immense deposits of rime, draping vertical precipices, building vast cornices on the *windward* side of the ridges and a fairy-land of weird shapes, minarets, giant mushrooms, jutting gargoyles, all with a floral pattern of ice crystals. Seen from a distance, it is beautiful; to be in the midst of it is fantastic.

We climbed one peak and reached the summit ridge of a second at 4:30 in the evening. The sky was still cloudless, and with nearly six hours of daylight in hand, we were in no great hurry as we sat on the ridge trying to decide which of several ice towers was the highest point of the mountain. Then, without a moment's warning, we were in dense cloud and rising wind. It was as though a blanket had been thrown over us; and we began to grope our way down, by no means sure that we could find the way in such conditions, particularly as our tracks soon vanished in the drift. Luckily we were rescued by a brief clearing at the critical section of the descent; and the storm, which later developed into a full blizzard, was held in leash until after dark. By that time we were safely back in our tent.

The storm heralded the re-establishment of the normal regime of wind and sleet, and we went down the Upsala Glacier thinking of the fleshpots, now so near. Rather sadly we abandoned the sledge when the ice became too rough to use it, and shouldered loads still uncomfortably heavy because of Cedomir's rock samples. For two days we made maddeningly slow progress through a chaotic tangle of crevasses; but we broke through on the evening of January 30 and pitched our last camp on ice in a heavy snowstorm.

Early the following afternoon we were walking along a path through gentle woodland, stopping often to lie on banks of moss and leaves, gazing up at the trees, listening entranced to the song of birds and tasting the nectar of earth-scented air. This sensuous orgy induced a kind of opiate trance which lasted several days. At 6:00 we reached Estancia La Cristina, and the transformation culminated when, replete with a delicious dinner, we were engulfed in the supreme luxury of clean-sheeted beds. Then the varied emotions of the past fifty-two days, the physical misery and the exultation, merged into a single unit of experience, its enduring reward an exquisite sense of intimacy with one of the wildest regions on earth.

Estancia La Cristina, at the head of the north-western arm of Lago Argentino, was one of the most isolated farms in South America. Having stayed there two years before I already knew the owners, Mr. and Mrs. Masters and their son Herbert. In 1900 the old couple had come to Patagonia from England, where he had been a seaman and she a cook. After working for some years on the Atlantic coast they had made the long trek to the lake by ox-waggon, and eventually, in 1905, settled in this remote, uninhabited valley, which had been discovered only three years before. There, quite beyond the reach of medical help, faced with years of hardship, loneliness and privation, with few resources but their courage and their devotion to each other, they began the task of building their home and their farm (named after their daughter, who died when still a girl). For the next seventeen years Mrs. Masters, raised in the security of a Victorian home, never left the place. Now, both aged eighty-four, they owned 12,000 sheep, which ranged over twenty square miles, a comfortable house with electric light generated by a home-made system of water-wheels and a car which they kept at Calafate near the far end of the lake and used only at Christmas-time for their annual trip to the coast. Beyond all this they had achieved the serenity which shone in their faces.

According to the Masters, the weather that summer had been the worst in their fifty-seven years' experience. In one important respect this was good news, for it meant that, with our improved technique, we were capable of dealing with exceptionally severe conditions, and this assurance gave me the courage to chase a life-long dream.

Anyone with a taste for travel is surely familiar with the wistful longing to get to some remote place—Samarkand, Lhasa, the gorge of the Ethiopian Nile—which has captured his imagination. For as long as I can remember one of the most powerful of my geographical lodestones had been the Cordillera Darwin, on an uninhabited peninsula running 150 miles westward from the main island of Tierra del Fuego into the heart of the Horn archipelago. There the great chain of the Andes makes its final southward thrust into this notorious region of storm. Almost completely surrounded by sea, lashed by the ferocious gales that rage around Cape Horn, guarded by a massive rampart of forest which, nurtured by incessant rain, has a strangely tropical appearance, the mountains had such a reputation for inaccessibility that no one had ventured into the interior of the range.

It was a thrilling prospect, but rather too intimidating to permit much optimism. For conditions in the Cordillera Darwin, six degrees further south, might well be worse than those we had met on the ice-cap, even allowing for the exceptionally bad weather that summer. Also the problems of travel would be much more difficult. Although our journey had been many times longer than any previously made on the glaciers of Patagonia, it had been possible only because, during the whole period of maximum exposure to the wind, we were never separated from our belongings, with the pyramid tent always assembled, ready to be pitched without delay. It was almost as though we had been travelling snail-wise with our house snugly upon our backs. But it was most improbable that, in Tierra del Fuego, we would be able to use a sledge at all owing to the steepness of the ground; so, with the constant need for relaying and depot laying, and having to dismantle the tent for back-packing, we would be far more vulnerable to the weather, particularly to those hurricanes which often struck with devastating suddenness.

The channels of the Fuegan archipelago were formerly inhabited by two tribes of canoe Indians, the Yagan and the Ona, now virtually extinct. When Ferdinand Magellan was making the first passage of the Straits which bear his name he saw a large number of fires burning along the southern shore. They had probably been lit as rallying signals by these primitive people, who were no doubt astonished and terrified by the sudden appearance of his ships. This was the origin of the name Tierra del Fuego—"Land of Fire." Magellan thought that it was part of a great southern continent stretching away to the Antarctic, and it was not until half a century later, when Drake, having passed through the Straits, was blown by the north-westerly gales round Cape Horn back into the Atlantic, that it was discovered to be an island.

Luckily Edouardo and Cedomir were keen to join me again, for they both fully understood the problems and hazards, and I could not have wished for stauncher companions. Cedomir, then twenty-four, was a Yugoslav by birth and had emigrated with his family at the age of sixteen and settled in Punta Arenas, where there is a large colony of his compatriots. Tall and lean, his chief facial characteristic was a massive, underhung jaw, a correct indication of his determination. He had remarkably shrewd judgment, and though almost always right in any dispute about the current situation, he was much too reticent and good humoured for this ever to be offensive. His slow smile made his huge jaw stick out more than ever; his gentle voice was seldom raised except to make himself heard in a gale, and I never saw him rattled. He had a great love for the country of his adoption. Edouardo was much more Latin, quicker in movement and temper; but he had a sensitive humour, and there were few circumstances when he found nothing to laugh at. I was quite happy to leave to them the choice of the fourth member of the party, Pancho Vivanco, to replace Jack Ewer, who, unfortunately for us, had decided on a domestic holiday for his next summer vacation.

After careful study of the available charts and some air photographs we decided to approach the range from the head of a long fjord running southward from an inlet known as Brookes Bay, on the north coast of the Peninsula. The fjord, which appeared to stretch far into the mountains, was uncharted and, so far as we knew, no one had been up it, except perhaps Yagan Canoe Indians, who used to inhabit those waters. The Chilean Navy undertook to transport us from Punta Arenas to Brookes Bay; but as even their smallest ship was unlikely to get far up the fjord, I brought another *Zodiac*. This had the additional advantage that we would be able to select our landing point with greater care, and move to another should the first prove unsatisfactory. I was persuaded also to take a small radio transmitter supplied by the Royal Navy; and it was arranged that we should communicate with a Chilean naval station on Dawson Island while we were at our base, and that they would listen for us at 5:30 each evening thereafter until our return. In fact, this plan proved a complete failure, for though we received their messages, they could not hear ours, probably because of the steep mountains surrounding the fjord.

We sailed from Punta Arenas in the Chilean naval patrol ship *Lientur* on January 18, 1962, and reached Brookes Bay early the following morning. It was calm, but mist hung low over the water, and steady rain fell as the vessel groped her way southward. Five miles in, the bay began to shoal rapidly, and soon we saw a line of small breakers, denoting a reef which seemed to stretch right across the inlet. This was obviously where we must part company with *Lientur*, and we chose to be landed on the eastern shore of the bay, in a little creek, at the mouth of a stream, which served as a rendezvous point where we would be picked up eight weeks later.

The creek was closely beset by dark, dripping forest. I doubt if at that moment any of us had much stomach for the task in hand. Certainly my feet felt distinctly chilly as I watched *Lientur*, our last contact with the comfortable world, disappear into the murk. So easy to plan this venture in warm security at home; so easy there to set pulses racing at the mere thought of the untrodden mountains of Tierra del Fuego, to delude oneself that a single glimpse of their lonely summits would repay weeks of toil and hardship! Here, in the unrelenting rain and blanketing mist, icy water already cascading down my spine and cringing thighs, the affair wore a very different aspect. However, despite the rain, we must seize the lucky chance of calm water to make the voyage up the uncharted fjord and find a site for our base at its head. So, without even pausing for the statutory brew of tea, we packed our equipment and eight weeks' supplies into the *Zodiac*, shoved the heavily laden craft out of the creek, started the 10-h.p. outboard motor and braced ourselves for a long, cold trip.

We had to go carefully through the reef, avoiding dense masses of seaweed marking the submerged rocks, but in the clear water beyond we opened the throttle and sped over the gently undulating surface at a steady four knots. Presently the rain stopped, the fog lifted and there, faithfully reproduced, was my dream-picture of this mystic land. The fjord here was three miles across; the western shore opened to a wide gulf; at its far end a vast glacier swept up from the water's edge, draped in long scarves of cloud; the highest of these had a silver gleam, hinting the presence of snow peaks above.

Beyond the gulf, the channel narrowed between precipitous shores. Hundreds of water-fowl rose at our approach, and some delighted dolphins plunged about us, often within a few feet of the *Zodiac*. Miraculously, the weather continued to clear: a patch of blue sky, the sun, then one by one the great peaks appeared, floating high above the mist still clinging to the sombre forest on either shore. By 2:30 we were approaching the head of the fjord and the last cloud had vanished. A sharp westward bend of the channel took us into a wide lagoon set in a semi-circular wall of glaciers and mountains, 7500 feet high. The smooth, blue water was sprinkled with blocks of floating ice calved from three massive glacier fronts; the forest on the shores between them shone emerald in the sunlight. Whatever I had expected to find in the Cordillera Darwin, it was certainly nothing so exquisitely lovely as this.

The wonderful luck that gave us such an afternoon for our landing at the head of this unknown fjord was repeated again and again throughout the whole expedition. It was as though some benign Providence was guiding our every move, dictating our every decision. We could not, it seemed, put a foot wrong. The next miracle was already there, immediately above our landing-place: a great rock ramp, left by the recent shrinking of a small glacier cascading down almost to the shore; 1000 feet high, set at an easy angle for climbing even with loads, it provided a natural stairway, the perfect means of penetrating the worst of the forest belt. Though by the next morning the weather was bad again, we had seen enough to dispense with a reconnaissance, and in two days we had carried all our equipment and six weeks' supplies to a beautiful meadow just above the forest line. From there we looked down over the tree-tops and a tumbling ice-fall to the lagoon, 1500 feet below, and across, to the tremendous cirque around it.

That year I found those first few days of back-packing much less painful than usual; no doubt this was partly due to my delight at finding such an incredibly easy route, but it was mainly because, for the first time in my life, I had put in several weeks of practice before leaving England. My training ground was on the Clee Hill, in Shropshire, and I carried seventy pounds of pig-nuts borrowed from a local farmer and contained in an ordinary sack. The ground was on Lord Boyne's estate, and though there were public footpaths leading to the top of the hill, being rather self-conscious, I preferred to avoid them and keep to the wooded slopes. Normally I escaped detection, but on one occasion I had an embarrassing encounter with a gamekeeper, who naturally demanded to know what I had in my sack. To explain to a Shropshire gamekeeper that one is carrying a load of pig-nuts up the Clee Hill and down again so as to become fit to go to Tierra del Fuego is not as easy as it may seem—or so I found. Realising that my tale was not really getting across, I switched my ground and said that, in any case, I had the permission of Lord Boyne's agent for my eccentric pursuit; which happened to be true. But this ploy was even less successful, no doubt because of the improbability of the claim, and the man became very angry.

From our camp in the meadow we found an easy pass leading direct to the head of the Marinelli Glacier, probably the largest in the whole range. Eight miles wide, this great ice-stream flows parallel to our fjord and reaches the north coast of the Peninsula, where its huge front juts far into the sea.

Six days after our landing we established an advanced base, with all our supplies, on the vast expanse of its upper basin, in the very heart of the range, a task which we had expected to take three times as long. Appropriately, the very morning we arrived there was fine, which gave us a clear view, invaluable for the formation of our immediate plans, of the scores of peaks and valleys surrounding us.

In area, the Cordillera Darwin is equivalent to the Mont Blanc, Pennine and Oberland ranges of the Alps combined, while the extent of its glaciers must be far greater than those of the entire Alpine chain. We had already chosen three main objectives, though this was more a matter of form than because we had expected to achieve any one of them. The first was obviously to climb the highest peak, Monte Darwin. The second was to make a crossing to the Beagle Channel on the southern shore of the Peninsula, which seemed to be the right way of dealing with an unexplored range and likely to give Cedomir the clearest idea of its geological structure. The third, my companions' choice, was a beautiful spire standing above Parry Fjord, and which now was visible across the basin to the east; later we named it Cerro Yagan.

So far we had not been able positively to identify Monte Darwin, though we knew that it must be one of a group of peaks around a high coombe to our south. But the entrance to this was blocked by an ice-fall, 2000 feet high and too difficult to attempt in bad weather; so we decided to make a long detour to the west to look for an easier line of approach. As we also hoped to find a route across the range in that direction, we took three weeks' food with us.

For the next eight days, carrying our loads in relays, we groped back and forth in heavy wind and mist, rarely able to see more than our immediate surroundings. Often I felt utterly bemused, not knowing which way to go; but Cedomir had an unerring topographical sense and was seldom at a loss. We had to be extremely careful in siting our dumps, which often became obscured by drift-snow, for our tracks never lasted more than an hour or so and were sometimes obliterated in a few minutes. We used two compasses, checking each reading, one against the other. Crevasses provided another major hazard, largely because long spells of heavy rain had rotted the snow bridges. Whenever possible we used skis.

On the evening of February 2, after a strenuous climb, we reached the crest of a ridge, 8000 feet high. At that very moment, for the first time in nine days, the sky cleared. We were standing at one end of a semi-circular wall, like a large atoll in a sea of cloud. In the central "lagoon" lay the coombe we had seen from the Marinelli Glacier, and we could now identify the highest peak, Monte Darwin, standing directly opposite, at the other end of the horse-shoe, its summit only 700 feet above us. We camped under the lee of a huge ice-bulge; but we were too close to the crest of the ridge, and it gave little protection from a powerful storm which struck early that night. A bag containing two days' rations, which had been accidentally left outside the tent, was blown away and lost.

The next day we descended 2300 feet into the coombe, where, in comparative calm, we pitched camp at the western foot of Monte Darwin and, reducing our daily ration by one-third, settled down to a ten-day siege. But we had underrated our guiding angel! The morning of the 5th was clear and still. The timing was perfect; for we had spent the previous day cutting steps up the lower slopes and making a thorough reconnaissance of the route, so we were able to reach the summit with a few minutes to spare before it was once more wrapped in cloud, and to return to camp before the onset of the next storm.

Two days later we left the coombe for our second project, the crossing of the range to the Beagle Channel. Glimpses of the southern side of the range had helped us to plan a route, though with so many uncertainties that, but for Cedomir's extraordinary skill, I very much doubt if we would have found a way. Also, for the next few days, conditions were less severe than usual, and we had several brief spells of clear weather. When these occurred, usually in the evening or early morning, our sombre monochrome world became suffused with colour, fragile as egg-shell porcelain.

On the evening of the 11th we descended below the cloud level on to a high spur running southward between two inlets of the Beagle Channel, 4000 feet below. The next morning we left our camp standing and went on, blissfully free of loads. A swift glissade down a wide snow gully and a scramble down a series of cliffs brought us to terraced meadows where the warm air was heavy with the scent of flowers. Even unladen, getting through the forest belt to the shore was something of a struggle, but it provided an agreeable contrast to the work of the past few weeks.

On the journey back to our base on the Marinelli Glacier the weather was very bad indeed, with frequent gales and exceptionally heavy snowfalls; so, in case of delay, we again reduced our daily ration. An intermediate food dump was buried under six feet of fresh snow, and although we located its position within a few yards, we had to dig and probe for two hours before finding the top of an upright ski. Our main depot near the base, which we reached on February 20, was similarly buried, and we certainly would not have found it but for the fact that we had brought the radio this far, hoping from this higher altitude to make contact with Dawson Island. We had left the twelve-foot aerial mast so firmly planted that it had withstood all the storms, and its top was still sticking out of a featureless expanse of snow.

We now had a week left before we must start back to keep our rendezvous in Brookes Bay. It might be enough time to tackle our final objective, Cerro Yagan, if our phenomenal luck held. It did. Late in the evening of the 21st, after a long haul across the Marinelli basin, we pitched our tent at the foot of the mountain, intending the next day to carry it as high as possible so as to seize any brief spell of clear weather for a dash to the summit. But at 3:00 I awoke to find the full moon riding in a cloudless sky. We made a hurried breakfast and started. For once it was freezing hard, and on crusted snow we climbed swiftly to meet the dawn, the peaks around us still like sheeted spectres.

A thousand feet up, we were faced with a series of enormous crevasses backed by vertical or overhanging walls. Each in turn looked impassable; but each time the lucky chance of a slender snow bridge and a crack in the wall beyond enabled us to climb the obstacle. The last, barely a hundred feet high, took an hour and a half to surmount, while I fretted, unable to believe that the weather would hold. Beyond was a steep ridge of hard ice; from its narrow crest we looked straight down 7000 feet to Parry Fjord, shining in the sunlight between dark green shores. The ridge was topped by a bulge of ice which seemed to girdle the apex of the peak like a gigantic mushroom. But a narrow corridor gave passage beneath it until we found a break; and at 12:30 we scrambled through to the top. The issue had remained in doubt until the last moment; and once again we were only just in time to beat the cloud.

That night we were struck by the worst storm of all. It mounted through the early hours in a shattering crescendo, and at 4:30 the tent collapsed over our heads. I thought that the indestructible Pyramid had at last met its match and that two of the poles had snapped; but we discovered later that one of its sides had been driven four feet into the hard-packed snow beneath, and that the tent itself was quite intact. By then it was light, and in the pandemonium of madly flapping canvas, we managed to find our boots and windproofs and pack most of our belongings. Then I crawled outside, stood up and was immediately blown flat, while my balaclava was whipped off my head and disappeared. Cedomir's pack, weighing fifty pounds, was blown into a crevasse 200 yards away; it lodged on a ledge twenty feet down and was later recovered. Again and again we were hurled to the ground when we tried to stand, and it took us two hours to salvage the tent and tie it in a rough bundle. Then we dragged everything down into a steep ice-fall where we found some shelter. From the cliffs and corries of Cerro Yagan above came a noise like the thunder of an avalanche while dense clouds of snow were hurled into space. Though the storm continued, by 9:00 it had lost its extreme violence, and we returned across the basin.

The next day we reached the meadows, now deep in flowers, and once again our starved senses feasted on the colour and the smells of the living world. I found it specially exciting going down to the sea; for one thing, the cry of gulls sounded so deliriously out of context. With nearly a week to spare, we cruised down the fjord in easy stages, while Cedomir examined its geology and I made a collection of *collembola* requested by the British Museum. We chose the most attractive little bays for our camp sites, fished for star-crabs (*sentoya*) in the deep pools at low tide and even dived into the icy water from sheer bravado; we ate enormous quantities of mussels and sea-urchins, our appetite for fresh food offsetting the lack of condiments; we lazed beside fires fed with unlimited fuel; we were utterly content.

| 10 |

BOUNDARIES, TORTOISES AND BEARS

THOUGH MOST OF US LAMENT the passing of youth, it is not always our happiest time. Middle age can bring a philosophical relaxation often denied by our earlier concern for success or esteem, and we find ourselves enjoying the gifts of the present, if not always as passionately, at least with far greater serenity. This in turn can secure release from shyness and self-doubt, banes of youth (and the cause of much of its arrogance), which in my case persisted rather ludicrously in later years. Certainly I found my fifties the most agreeable decade of my life so far.

Apart from the delight of human relationships, Patagonia continued to absorb most of my attention. Immediately after returning from the Cordillera Danvin, Cedomir and I made a long and stormy voyage in the *Zodiac* to explore the interior of the Munos Gamero Peninsula, which we reached by a narrow isthmus and a chain of freshwater lakes known only to the Alacaluf Indians. Cedomir maintains that this was the best of all our adventures together; and while I do not agree, I can see what he means. The next year, 1962–63, brought two more expeditions—one to Mount Burney, the other to the eastern part of the Cordillera Darwin from the Beagle Channel; and in 1963–64 we made the first crossing of the Northern Ice-cap,

Hielo Patagonico del Norte. There the terrain was more complicated than on the other ice-cap; also we had to carry a boat which we needed to cross rivers and lakes on the far side of the range before reaching habitation. But the use of skis made sledge-hauling far less exhausting, and the weather was much kinder: in the six weeks that the journey lasted we had fifteen fine days.

Life between these expeditions was varied; it included lecture tours in Sudan, Ethiopia, South America and the West Indies. But Patagonia seemed to offer limitless scope; for each venture suggested some new and tempting project, another corner to round, and it became increasingly difficult to choose between the clamouring alternatives. In 1964, however, the rhythm was broken by an invitation from the Chilean Government to act as their geographical adviser in a boundary dispute with Argentina which, after some twenty years of diplomatic wrangling, had been submitted to the Queen for arbitration. Though I certainly had some practical acquaintance with the subject, I had never regarded myself as a geographer, and was very doubtful of the value of my advice. However, these objections were brushed aside with flattering firmness, and I accepted the role, more because of my gratitude to the Chileans for their generous help with my expeditions than for any other reason. I did not realise how deeply involved I would become.

The dispute was a legacy of a much larger confrontation, involving the frontier over the entire length of Patagonia, which had developed towards the end of the nineteenth century. The treaty of 1881 between Chile and Argentina stated, simply, that their mutual frontier would follow the line of the high peaks which forms the watershed between the Atlantic and Pacific. But whereas the main chain of the Andes south of the Bolivian plateau is a single spine of lofty mountains, a simple water-parting, the Andes of Patagonia conform to no such conventional pattern. They are largely composed of a series of massifs separated from one another by large rivers which rise in the pampas far to the east; while several of the great lakes lying on the Atlantic side of the range also drain through it into the Pacific. For the most part, therefore, the high mountains have no connection with the Continental Divide.

Realisation of this awkward fact dawned gradually during the decade following the signing of the treaty; and at the same time the settlement of Patagonia by people of both nations and from Europe gave the matter increasing importance. Each side invoked part of the original clause to substantiate its claim: Argentina contending that the frontier should be drawn along the line of high peaks, Chile that it should be established along the watershed. The issue aroused violent national feelings; an arms race ensued, particularly in the development of naval strength, and by 1898 the two countries had reached the brink of war. At the last moment the disaster was averted by an agreement to submit the matter to arbitration by Queen Victoria. It was not, however, until 1901, after the Queen's death, that the British Arbitration Tribunal was appointed, and Sir Thomas Holditch was sent to South America, with a small staff of Sappers, to investigate the situation. His Report, containing a detailed recommendation for the course of the boundary, 1500 miles long, formed the basis of the Award of King Edward VII, which was delivered in November 1902.

Considering the immense distances involved, the short time and primitive means of transport at his disposal, and the prevailing ignorance of the region, Holditch's Report was a masterpiece of ingenuity and compromise; that his frontier, if not wholly pleasing, was at least generally acceptable to both sides is a tribute to his skill. There was, however, one notable mistake (and several minor ambiguities). The Award disposed of the sector south of the Rio Palena (latitude 43° S.—nearly 400 miles north of the Northern Icecap) in these words: "From Post 16 the boundary will cross the Rio Palena and follow the course of the Rio Encuentro to its source on the Hill of the Virgin; ascending that peak by the shortest route it will then follow the local water-parting to Post 17 on the northern shore of Lago General Paz." In fact, no part of the Rio Encuentro is in any way connected with the "Hill of the Virgin," since another much larger river intervenes.

The confusion arose as a result of the work of two explorers who, groping their way through the tangle of ranges forming that part of the Patagonian Andes, approached the area from different directions. In 1898 Dr. Steffen, a distinguished Chilean traveller, tracing the course of the Rio Palena, gave the name "Rio Encuentro" to a minor tributary joining the river to the south. In 1901 Gunnar Lange, a Norwegian employed by the Argentine Government, set out to explore the region north of Lago General Paz. Soon he discovered a river flowing northward, which he named "Rio Engaño," and attempted to sail down it in a boat. Eventually, however, his boat was wrecked, and he and his companions were forced to return. For his main point of reference throughout the journey he chose a peak on a minor ridge which he called "Cerro de la Virgen." With the natural curiosity of explorers, he pondered the problem of the ultimate destination of his river, and came to the conclusion that it was probably the same stream as Steffen's Rio Encuentro, indicating his theory with a dotted line on his map. In fact, he was wrong; for the Engaño, making a westerly sweep, joins the Rio Palena many miles downstream from the mouth of the Encuentro.

It is strange that Holditch should have selected a minor stream (which he had never seen) to carry this section of his boundary; particularly in view of his manifest preference for mountain ridges. But it is understandable that, in an unchartered, nameless wilderness it must have been tempting to use the two points—Steffen's Palena/Encuentro confluence and Lange's "Virgen"—which seemed to have positive identity. For the next few decades, however, the area attracted little attention, and even when the mistake was discovered, no one but a few academic geographers was greatly disturbed.

Meanwhile, however, farmers from Chile, pressing inland from the heavily forested mountains of the Pacific coast in search of highland pasture, established settlements not only in the Palena but in the Engaño and Encuentro valleys as well. Argentine farmers, on the other hand, with vast areas of pampas to exploit, had no reason to penetrate the difficult mountain ranges to their west. Though the Encuentro was accepted as the frontier, the significance of "Cerro de la Virgen," a relatively minor peak on the western side of the Engaño, was largely ignored. In any case it is doubtful if, in those early days, the *pobladores* (peasant settlers) had much regard for anything so sophisticated as an international boundary. The communities survived—by British standards "prospered" would be too strong a word—and were administered and taxed by Chilean officials. It was not until the 1940s that the trouble began. Then the Argentine Government, under the nationalistic President Perón, awoke to the situation and claimed jurisdiction over the territory occupied by Chilean settlers, principally in the Engafio valley. Strong diplomatic notes were exchanged; "incidents" occurred between the settlers and Argentine *gendarmerie*; gradually the affair assumed an importance out of all proportion to the value of the land in dispute, and roused bitter public resentment in both countries. Finally, it was agreed again to submit the matter to British arbitration.

Each side appointed eminent Queen's Counsel, specialists in International Law, and engaged a large team of experts to help with the assembly and drafting of its case. In January 1965 the Chilean Government sent me by air to Santiago in unwonted first-class luxury. Expecting to get some mountaineering, I brought climbing boots, which I wore to save baggage weight, and carried an ice-axe which was stowed away among the mink coats. After attending several conferences at the Ministry of Foreign Affairs I travelled to the village of Palena in the delightful company of Commander Ayala, an officer of the Chilean Boundary Commission, Señor Barros, a diplomat who later assumed charge of the Mission in London, and Professor Gimpel. Together we spent two strenuous weeks touring the disputed area and much of the surrounding territory on horseback, meeting the settlers and climbing mountains to see the view, while the Professor explained his views on the geomorphology of the region. My chief contribution was to instruct my companions in the art of glissading, which they described delightedly as "ski sin (without) ski." It was attractive country of forested valleys and bare-topped mountains, with a few small glaciers in the more sheltered coombes; some of it wild and desolate, much of it soft and friendly; altogether a far milder land than I had known further south.

It had been agreed, pending the decision of the Court of Arbitration, that the representatives of both sides would be free to tour the disputed area unmolested; so as a rule we were accompanied only by the local people who supplied our horses; but for our visit to the upper valley of the Engaño we were escorted by an officer of the *caribeneros* and two of his men carrying tommy guns. One morning, as we were making our way through a stretch of dense, almost trackless forest, a troop of a dozen Argentine *gendarmerie*, similarly armed, suddenly emerged from the undergrowth to bar our way. A violent argument ensued, with some ostentatious fingering of triggers, about whether the Upper Engaño was in fact in the disputed area. I was reminded of some critical encounters with Chinese soldiery in Central Asia, and it was pleasant to be a mere spectator with no responsibility in the matter. All the same, with our fire-power outmatched by six to one, I was glad that my irate colleagues did not press their point too far. Later we climbed a peak, south of the "Virgen," which commanded a view over the whole basin of the Upper Engaño.

Meanwhile, and during the rest of that year, both teams were hard at work in London preparing their *Memorials*—written statements of their cases—for presentation to the Arbitration Tribunal headed by Lord McNair. The authority of the 1902 Award was not in question; and both sides sought to interpret its intent to their advantage. Basically the whole argument revolved around a single sentence which, founded upon the error in Lange's map, was largely meaningless. There were, of course, other relevant matters to be dealt with, such as the historical background, the reaction of officials and states-men of both countries after the discovery of the mistake, the nationality and wishes of the settlers, and the topographical nature of other sections of the boundary which might explain Holditch's overall intentions. Nevertheless, I was amazed at the minuteness of detail scrutinised and by the length of the statements: the *Memorial* of each side was contained in three large vol-umes, as big as London telephone directories. In addition, massive folders were compiled of geological, geomorphological, hydrographic and cadas-tral maps, topographical profiles and the sketch-maps of the early explorers. When these documents had been studied by the opposing sides each set about the compilation of its *Counter Memorial*, designed to refute the state-ments of the other.

In February 1966 the field Mission, composed of two members of the Tribunal and their aides, arrived in Palena to inspect the disputed area, while the teams of "experts" from both sides, their numbers now greatly augmented, assembled there to ensure that no relevant point was missed by the visitors. The Mission was housed in a bungalow specially built for the occasion, and their comfort cherished by a *maitre d'hôtel* and staff who would not have disgraced the Savoy; shell-fish and other delicacies were flown in from Puerto Montt and lobsters from Juan Fernandes Island. For three weeks the sleepy little village throbbed with excitement and activity, while between the contending parties there was an air of watchful cordiality, and the Mission maintained an admirable balance between detachment and jocular bon-homie. We toured the area in a small fleet of helicopters and light aircraft. On the only occasion when a visit was made on horseback, to the settlements in the Encuentro valley, every farmstead, even the poorest of shacks, was found to be flying a Chilean flag. But though the demonstration obviously angered our opponents and embarrassed my colleagues—for it was contrary to their explicit instructions—it was carefully ignored by all.

Not surprisingly, a cardinal factor in the dispute was the identification of the Rio Encuentro; but this was not quite so simple as it might appear. Three miles above its mouth, unknown to Steffen or Holditch, the river is divided into two branches: one rising in a range of high mountains far to the east; the other, known locally as the Arroyo Lopez, in a low saddle more or less in a line between the mouth of the Encuentro and the "Cerro de la Virgen." Now while there is no firm rule for distinguishing the mainstream of a river from its tributary, I had always assumed the chief points to be considered were length, volume of water and the area drained. As the eastern branch was greatly the superior in all three measurements, it seemed obvious that it should be awarded the palm; indeed, the whole Chilean case rested on this. But Professor Eric Brown of London University, the Geographical Adviser for Argentina, took a different view, which chanced to favour his side. He maintained that the eastern branch, for all its vaunted size, was a mere stripling, in age no more than a few score millennia; while the Arroyo Lopez flowed through a far older valley, carved by a noble river since diverted by glacial action into another course. He argued that this orphan stream, though only a brook in its upper reaches, was entitled to the headship of the Encuentro family by reason of its ancient lineage and its occupation of the ancestral home.

In the late summer of 1966 the Tribunal met in London, first at Lancaster House then at the Royal Geographical Society, for the final hearing of the case. A week and a half was allowed for the statement of the Argentine case, a similar period for the Chilean, and the whole debate lasted six weeks. It was fascinating listening to legal giants delivering their verbal bombardments for hour after hour with histrionic panache and a faultless flow of language, employing with passionate emphasis topographical terms whose very meaning they had learned only a short while ago. I was surprised by the depth of my own emotional involvement with the issue; and I was alternately crushed to despair by the devasting oratory of the opposition pouring scorn on our cherished contentions and elated by the rapier counter-thrusts of Counsel for Chile.

Judgment was delivered in the Queen's Award on December 15, 1966. Broadly speaking, the new boundary followed the eastern branch of the Encuentro to a point near its source, when a line was drawn to the summit of the "Virgen," dividing the upper basin of the Engaño from the lower. This meant that, while Argentina retained the larger part of the uninhabited territory claimed by Chile, Chile held all the land occupied by the settlers. Both countries seemed to be delighted with the verdict; surely an occurrence rare in international arbitration. A friend of mine living in Buenos Aires told me that the people there were so pleased with the result that they were almost prepared to forgive England for denying Argentina her rightful victory in the World Cup earlier that year.

There can be few places where humming birds can be seen drawing nectar from cactus flowers in a heavy snowstorm. I watched this unusual spectacle during a Saturday climb to 16,000 feet on Cotapaxi with Mr. Corley Smith, the British Ambassador, when on a brief visit to Ecuador, part of a lecture tour in 1963. I was astonished and delighted to find how accurate were the impressions I had formed, forty years before, from reading Whymper's *Travels*, the book which had originally set me dreaming of mountains. Encouraged by my kind host, I paid a second visit in March 1965, after inspecting the disputed area; and I persuaded Philip Hugh-Jones to join me in Quito, the most attractive of all South American capitals, to share some wider travel. Philip, a lung specialist eminent enough to get his fare paid to most parts of the world in return for a few lectures, hankered after the head-hunting tribes of the Amazon; but I managed to divert his buoyant enthusiasm to the Galapagos Islands.

Lying across the Equator, 700 miles from the coast of Ecuador, to which they now belong, the Galapagos were first sighted by Spanish sailors in the sixteenth century. They became known as *Las Islas Encantades*—The Enchanted Isles—a misleading title, for they were then regarded as thoroughly repulsive, and described by one early visitor as the nearest approach on earth to his concept of Hell. "Bewitched" would better convey the meaning of the term, which was based on their disconcerting habit of vanishing from their position on the charts and reappearing elsewhere. Some bewildered mariners were convinced that they were floating; and it was not until much later it was realised that the wildly erratic currents in the area and the prevalence of mist had resulted in gross errors of navigation. Until the nineteenth century they were quite uninhabited; now four of the two dozen islands have permanent settlements where the people are engaged in fishing and farming isolated pockets of soil.

In the course of her famous voyage, H.M.S. *Beagle* visited the Galapagos, and Darwin's world-shaping conclusions were very largely founded upon his observations of the inter-island variations in the habits and development of the animals there—in fact, a localised evolution. Considering that the vessel stayed in the archipelago only five weeks, and that much of the time was spent becalmed between the various islands, the amount and accuracy of the data he amassed is astounding. The centenary of the publication of *The Origin of the Species* was marked by a spate of biological investigation on Pacific islands. One result was the establishment in 1960 of The Charles Darwin Research Station at Academy Bay on Isla Santa Cruz under the auspices of U.N.E.S.C.O. and various wildlife organisations, to foster scientific study in the Galapagos and the conservation of the indigenous flora and fauna, much of it unique. For there is grave danger that some of the species may become extinct. Those strange creatures the giant tortoises, for example, were once there in vastly greater numbers than they are today. For centuries they were slaughtered in thousands by visiting seamen in search of food, and later by the settlers, until at length only those in the more inaccessible places survived. Still more devastating was the introduction of domestic animals and rats, which strayed into the wilderness, multiplied and played havoc with the native fauna.

Except in the very small inhabited areas, it is difficult to penetrate the interior of the larger islands. The coastal belts are mostly composed of vast

fields of jagged lava, utterly barren, while the slopes of the volcanic mountains are covered with dense vegetation, much of it thorn scrub. But the
main problem is the lack of water; for although a good deal of rain falls on
the high ground, the rock is so porous that it disappears immediately, so that
pools are extremely rare and streams non-existent. Because of these difficulties, very little of the interior of Albemarle, the largest island—100 miles
long—and of Narborough has yet been visited; thus not even an approx-
imate estimate can yet be made of the numbers of tortoises still surviving.

One of my objects in visiting the Galapagos was to explore Vulcan Alcedo,
the central of five volcanoes which, ranged in a long line, occupy almost the
whole area of Albemarle. Another was to climb to the crater of Narborough,
the westernmost island; it had been reached three times before and was,
apparently, a remarkable place. As Roger Perry, Director of the Research
Station, was both anxious to get some information about the fauna on Alcedo
and keen to visit Narborough himself, he kindly arranged the *Beagle*'s tight
schedule to fit in with these plans. The vessel—named, of course, after her
famous predecessor—was formerly a Cornish fishing lugger, and had been
sent to the Galapagos the previous year to serve the needs of the Station and
its visiting scientists. She had a crew of three and was commanded by Carl
Angermeyer, one of four brothers who had come from Germany after the
war to settle in the Islands.

On the morning after our arrival at Academy Bay I left the station
before dawn and after two hours' fast walking along a rough track reached
a small two-storied cottage set deep in the forest. It was the home of Mrs.
Horneman, a German lady, sixty-five years old, partly crippled by a spinal
injury, who lived there alone. A small herd of cows, some coffee bushes,
fruit trees and vegetables supplied her needs and a small surplus, which
was sent to Academy Bay to be exchanged for fish, flour and sugar. A grove
of avocados, planted thirty years before, had regenerated in such profusion
that she now made a practice of cutting down the trees as the fruit was
required. Her elderly Norwegian husband, with whom she had started the
"farm" in the early Thirties, was then living in Norway receiving treatment
for a prolonged illness. Her daughter, also in Norway, worked as a guide in

Hammerfest, while her son was studying electronics at the University of California. She spoke English, French, Spanish and Norwegian almost as fluently as her native German.

I arrived at 7:30. After a huge breakfast I became totally absorbed in conversation with my hostess, which continued almost uninterrupted until 5:00 when, with the greatest reluctance, I had to depart so as to return to the coast before dark. We covered a wide range of subjects: the account of her flight from Nazi Germany, which had earned the strictures of her friends, and of her rugged pioneering life on the island, so incompatible with her frail appearance, was fascinating. No less so were her philosophical views, expressed with gentle humour and disarming humility; for she had a deep fund of wisdom and penetrating judgment of people and affairs. Later, I paid several more visits to the "Wilderness," as she called her "farm"; they were all as delightful as the first, and each time I left with feelings both of elation and regret.

We left Academy Bay at dawn on March 10, 1965. Hundreds of turtles were floating lazily on the smooth surface of the water. With a favourable current, *Beagle*, making ten knots, passed the steep cliffs of Nameless and Duncan Islands, and by mid-afternoon was cruising close along the east coast of Albemarle, while we scanned the shore for a possible landing-place and a promising route through the rugged desert beyond. We had allowed only five days for the job, and Carl was frankly sceptical of our ability even to reach Alcedo and return in the time. He had taken part in the first ascent of Narborough, and had spent four gruelling, thirsty days climbing over glass-sharp lava, which cut his boots to ribbons, to climb the 4900 feet to the top.

He put us ashore in a sandy cove, nestling between two promontories of black lava and backed by a low cliff of pumice. In common with all Galapagos shores, it abounded with life: sea-lions, marine iguanas, scarlet crabs, flightless cormorants, blue-footed boobies, pelicans and—strange visitors in tropical waters—penguins. We spent the evening swimming in the sea, pleasantly cooled by the Humboldt Current; and slept on the beach, waking in the night to find sea-lions lying close beside us. To help us with carrying, Roger had sent with us an Amazon Indian named

Calapucho. Exiled from his native land because of some unfortunate incident which had incurred the wrath of a neighbouring tribe, he had found his way to the Galapagos, where, after a spell of work in a salt mine, he was employed at the Station as a handyman. He had a sensitive pride, and was apt to take offence at any breach of formal etiquette, a matter I am inclined to overlook when camping in the wilderness. His devotion to Roger was rather touching.

It was not yet light when we left the cove the next morning, Calapucho carrying five gallons of water, Philip and I lightly laden with food and sleeping bags, and made our way westward over a gently sloping corridor of pumice, smooth, firm and agreeably soft, between two lava flows. We were yet to appreciate our luck, for such terrain is probably unique in the Galapagos. For an hour we walked through the lunar landscape of the coastal belt, past occasional cactus, like pieces of Henry Moore sculpture in the twilight. By sunrise we were in open woodland, 1000 feet up, where we met a herd of wild donkeys, the first of hundreds that we saw during the next few days. Presumably their forebears had strayed from the small settlement at the southern extremity of the island, fifty miles away, across the lava fields to find this paradise of unmolested idleness. Fat and sleek, they clearly had plenty to eat, but at first we were puzzled to know how they managed for water. Soon we were to bless them for their tracks through the dense bush, which otherwise would have been almost impenetrable.

Crossing a line of low hills, we reached the foot of the final slope of the volcano at 10:00; there we made our base and sent Calapucho back to the shore. It was a pleasant spot, surrounded by trees (*pablo santos*) and tall grass, very green and lush, a remarkable contrast to the complete desert of the coastal belt only a few miles away. From there we spent three strenuous days exploring the volcano and, thanks to the tracks of our friends the donkeys, we managed to cover a lot of ground. We kept mainly along the rim of the crater, which is fifteen miles round, though we made two descents to its floor, a flat expanse of plate-lava, partly covered by forest. I lost my watch—a Rolex Oyster given to me for the Everest Expedition in 1951; it must have been torn off my wrist while struggling through dense bush.

We found plenty of giant tortoises; on the crater rim alone we counted nearly eighty. As our view of the ground on either side of us was usually restricted by the undergrowth to a few yards, we probably passed close to many times that number without seeing them. Considering, too, that we covered only a minute fraction of the total area, it seemed safe to assume that there must be some thousands in the upper part of the mountain. In fact, later investigation has shown it to be the largest surviving colony so far to be found in the Galapagos. It is to be hoped that there are similar communities flourishing in other parts of the Islands unvisited by dogs, goats, pigs, humans and other hostile intruders. (Evidently donkeys do not fall into this category.) We also discovered, under the southern wall of the crater, a boiling lake, from which a geyser erupted every few minutes, shooting jets of water fifty feet high. It overflowed into another lake where we swam. It was only slightly sulphurous, and it gave us the answer to the problem of where the donkeys found their water.

We returned to the shore in time to be picked up by the *Beagle*. Roger was on board with Alan Cox, a geophysicist from California, who was making a tour of the Galapagos to collect samples of lava. One purpose of his work was to determine the age of the Islands, which has an important bearing on the fascinating mystery of how they came to be inhabited by their present fauna, particularly the tortoise and the land iguana. It seems to be fairly certain that they erupted from the ocean in recent geological times and that they were never connected with the mainland of America. Professor Howell Thomas has suggested that the creatures drifted over on rafts of pumice; another theory is that they came on masses of vegetation swept out to sea by rivers in spate—Darwin himself subscribed to this view. One difficulty about both these theories is that the Humboldt Current, which could account for this strange migration, sweeps up from the coast of Peru; and while the Galapagos animals have some distant relatives in Central America and the West Indies, they have none in Peru. The debate is likely to exercise the ingenuity of scientists for a long while yet.

We anchored for the night off James Island, close to a lagoon inhabited by flamingoes, and on the 16th made the long voyage round the north coast of Albemarle, wild, rugged and utterly desolate: the lava flows, curving down from breached craters like great black glaciers, looked as if they had been created yesterday, though in fact they were probably not less than 50,000 years old. Trailing a line, we caught some large, brightly coloured fish; also, unfortunately, a blue-footed booby and a pelican which had dived for the lure. Later, a pelican came aboard and took up his stance beside the helmsman, swaying to the motion of the ship, which made the poor bird seasick. In spite of this, he remained our guest for twenty-four hours, and when eventually we put him ashore he looked distinctly hurt. That evening we reached Punta Espinosa, the only good anchorage on Narborough, and a wonderful place for marine birds and animals.

There is a great deal of speculation as to whether or not there are tortoises on Narborough. The only one ever to have been seen there, a unique sub-species, was captured and killed by a scientific expedition in 1906; though in 1964 "unmistakable tortoise tracks" were alleged to have been found by another party of biologists. It would be remarkable if Narborough, the only large island of the Galapagos almost completely free from imported animals, were also the only one devoid of tortoises. It has been suggested that one or more of the volcanic eruptions which have occurred during the last few decades may have destroyed them all. This seems unlikely in view of the large numbers of land iguanas there and the big area of undamaged forest. It was partly in the hope of finding tortoises that we decided to climb the volcano from the south, the side where there is the greatest amount of vegetation.

The next day Roger, Philip, Calapucho and I landed at the south-west point of the Island, while the *Beagle* went on with Alan Cox to complete the circuit. Near our camp was a shallow lagoon, where scores of sea-lion pups were frisking, and we added greatly to their enjoyment by joining them. At first their parents, worried by their strange new playmates, were inclined to be menacing; but soon they decided that we meant no harm and resumed their interrupted siestas. Again that night some of them slept beside us on the shore.

The previous day I had ricked my back when my foot slipped on the wet rocks while lifting a heavy load; and that evening it was so painful that

I could hardly walk. So, on the doctor's advice, when the others set off next morning I stayed behind and spent a miserable day lying flat on my back in the sweltering heat radiated from the surrounding rocks. That evening Calapucho returned, very exhausted, bringing a note from Philip to say that they had found the going horrible, but had reached the foot of the volcano.

The day's rest had done my back no good—indeed, it seemed worse than before—and I decided to apply the opposite treatment. So the following morning I struggled across the lava fields and climbed a small volcanic cone farther along the coast. The experiment was successful and, my back much improved, Calapucho and I set out at dawn the next day to look for tortoises in a large patch of forest I had seen to the north. Expecting to return that afternoon, we took with us only a packet of biscuits and a flask of water. But we made such rapid progress that by 11:00 we were at the foot of the mountain, and I decided to abandon the hunt and press on to the crater. My companion had no hesitation in saying what he thought of the idea, so while he returned to the coast, I went on alone.

I had been climbing for two hours when the mountain was enveloped by mist and heavy rain. All about me were jet-black crags and ropes of lava, coiled like the intestines of some monstrous animal, split here and there by cavernous fumaroles, encrusted with yellow sulphur, belching steam. At 2:30 I was on the crater rim; the ground plunged sheer before my feet. There was nothing to be seen for the mist and still pouring rain, so I waited. Clad only in a cotton shirt and trousers, I was soon very cold. I sat in the steam of a fumarole, but the stench of sulphur was overpowering. On a ledge a short way below lay several dead trees, evidently killed by a local eruption of lava, and I had half a box of matches dry in a plastic bag; so by making a pile of wood shavings in a little recess I managed to light a fire, though not until all but two of the matches were spent. Soon the blaze was strong enough to withstand the rain, and I spent the remaining hours of daylight collecting a great pile of wood to feed it through the night.

When darkness fell the sky cleared and the moon, just past its first quarter, was already high. In absolute stillness the walls of the crater, twelve miles round, stood black above a pool of silvered mist which stayed till dawn and then disappeared. The bottom of the crater, more than 2000 feet below, was partly covered by a lake, an unusual feature in an active volcano. Apparently it varies in size, and sometimes disappears. Being alone and without food, I resisted the strong desire to climb down into the vast cauldron and, after watching a superb sunrise, I started back.

When I reached the foot of the volcano the sun was high and the rock oven-hot. My mouth was parched, and the prospect of the weary scramble back over the lava fields was not attractive. Two hours later, struggling through the undergrowth of the forest, I was delighted to hear a shout which I thought was Calapucho coming to find me. The first assumption was correct, the second was not; and our meeting was less cordial than I might have wished. When I came upon him from behind a thicket he gaped at me for a moment in obvious disgust and said, "*Ah! Qué lástima*" (what a pity). He explained that he had been hoping to meet "*el Señor Director.*" However, he was magnanimous enough to give me a drink of water from his flask; and in silence we returned together to the shore, where I lost no time in plunging into the sea. The others arrived an hour later. They had succeeded in climbing down to the bottom of the crater. The water in the lake was sulphurous but drinkable, and they spent their second night there amid fantastic surroundings. They were surprised to find a large number of Galapagos pintails, a species of duck unique to the Islands.

The month that Philip and I spent in the Galapagos was all too short; but he had to get back to keep his lecture dates in Peru and Argentina, the ostensible reason for his travels, and I to meet some Ecuadorian mountaineers to climb Chimborazo. Though Roger was kind enough to press me to return to the islands, the opportunity did not occur until three years later. Luckily, however, he was still there, and in January 1968 I went with Andrew, the son of Peter Mott, who had been with me in the Karakoram in 1939.

We had two objectives: one, at Roger's request, to explore Vulcan Wolf, at the northern end of Albemarle, looking for tortoises and iguanas; the other, to make a more serious search for the mysterious Narborough tortoise. I had seen enough to realise that only a tiny proportion of the forested areas on Narborough had been visited, which seemed a sufficient reason why the creatures had not been found. But these areas are widely scattered, and separated by very rugged terrain; so that, without a helicopter, it would be extremely difficult to travel from one to another carrying sufficient water to survive for long. Another problem was that there were very few points along the coast where it was possible to land. My plan was to place large plastic sheets at various points along the crater rim to catch rain water—at certain seasons rain is reasonably frequent, and even a gentle drizzle would soon provide several gallons. With these reservoirs established, one could make a series of radial sorties down from the crater rim and cover the maximum area with the minimum lateral movement. To carry up sufficient water from the lake would be immensely laborious, and in any case the few people who had visited the lake all reported that drinking the water had given them violent diarrhoea.

We had intended to go to Narborough first, but at the last moment Roger asked us to reverse the order, for he was keen to join us for that trip, but was unable to leave the station until mid-February. Through no fault of his, the change of plan was to have most unfortunate results.

The *Beagle* had come to grief the previous year and, pending the arrival of a new ship, the Station chartered local craft. Andrew, Calapucho and I were sent to Albemarle in a small fishing boat belonging to Bernard Schreyer and his wife, whose delightful company more than compensated for its comparative discomfort and restricted quarters. They, too, had come from Germany after the war when they were newly married; and they gave us a fascinating account of their early struggles to make a living, first by farming, then by fishing, in their strange new home. They had two children, a girl and a boy, born in the Galapagos and now at the university in Quito. They also told us, at first reluctantly, then openly, but always simply and without rancour, terrible stories of their own childhood in Hamburg during the Allied bombing, and their later adventures hiding in the woods, half starved, from the ravages of the early Russian occupation. It was strange to listen to these tales of violence and suffering in our peaceful surroundings.

The following day we were put ashore in a rocky inlet on the north-east coast of Albemarle, and the boat returned to Academy Bay. Our first and most exacting task was to carry in relays a supply of water across the fields of broken lava and as high as possible on Vulcan Wolf. On the second day,

when we were half-way up the mountain, we saw a small fishing boat coming down the coast, close inshore. The crew must have seen our base, for
they ran into the inlet, where they stayed for fifteen minutes before resum-
ing their voyage. When we returned that afternoon we found that the base
had been rifled. Poor Andrew suffered the heaviest loss: his two cameras,
worth several hundred pounds, were gone, and with them his fond hope
of making a photographic record of his experiences. Among other things
stolen were his binoculars, our only compass—very important for finding
our way in mist—and some food and clothing, including my only pair of
trousers (I was wearing shorts at the time) and all the plastic sheets I had
brought to implement my plan for collecting rain water on Narborough.
Luckily our water supply, which had been put in a deep cleft for protection
from the sun, was intact.

It was incredibly bad luck that the boat should have come to that point
on an uninhabited coast, 250 miles long, on that day; for on the following
morning most of the things stolen would have been removed inland with the
last relay. Andrew bore his loss and his disappointment with admirable philosophy; and as there was nothing we could do about it, we continued with
our plans, though we left Calapucho at our base to guard it from further
marauders. In fact, he saw no other boat throughout his stay.

We spent a strenuous fortnight and covered as much ground as we
had hoped, including a two-day tour of the crater rim, where we found
great numbers of iguanas, and a descent into the crater which was quite
as impressive as that on Narborough, but without a lake. With no donkey
tracks to help us, we had great difficulty in penetrating the dense forest on
the flanks of the mountain, and though we found some tortoise colonies,
we did not see many of the creatures. Also my bare legs suffered a good
deal of laceration. By the time we returned to the coast to meet Roger
and the Schreyers our boots, brand new at the start, were full of holes and
stripped of much of their soles.

Roger had returned to Narborough several times in the past three years.
He suggested that, because of the anchorage there, we should climb the
mountain direct from Punta Espinosa, which we reached on February 15,
and as the moon was full and he knew the way we should climb at night.

We started at 4:30 that evening, carrying ten days' food and two litres of water each. Even after dark the heat reflected from the rock was oppressive: I poured with sweat, my mouth was soon unpleasantly parched and I had to exercise great self-control to ration myself to a few sips from my flask every two hours. Roger and Andrew displayed a stoic nonchalance which put me to shame. The going was very rough: for much of the time it seemed as if we were walking on cucumber frames, and our feet were constantly breaking through fragile lava bubbles. But the moonlight and the weird landscape made it a dreamlike experience, not wholly devoid of pleasure. By dawn we were near the crater rim, and we spent the rest of the day walking southward along its crest. On the 17th we climbed down to the bottom of the crater. The water of the lake tasted like Epsom salts— but it was bliss.

Andrew was anxious to make a collection of insects in the crater for the British Museum. As our plan for the tortoise hunt had been frustrated by the loss of my plastic sheets, Roger and I were happy to stay awhile in this remarkable place. Besides, our boots were in a delicate state and would not have withstood much more punishment. Roger had an idea that if we boiled all our drinking water its purgative effect would be less severe. The theory seemed to have been based more on faith than upon scientific reasoning; nevertheless, it worked and, apart from the effects of our initial indulgence, we suffered little discomfort. We remained in the crater for a week.

While Andrew was busy with his bugs, Roger and I made a careful count of Galapagos pintails. The task was facilitated by the fact that the ducks congregated in the numerous shallow lagoons where they found their food, so that we could count them in groups. However, there was a number of islands far out from the shore which also contained duck-inhabited lagoons; so, to complete the count, I swam to each in turn. As the jagged lava was hard on the feet, I carried my boots on my head. Now a peculiarity of duck the whole world over is their intense curiosity, and Galapagos pintails are no exception. The unusual sight of my booted head swimming through the water attracted all the birds from the neighbouring lagoons, and before long I had a flotilla of some hundreds following me, their leader not more than a couple of feet from my face. Roger, watching with binoculars from the distant shore, could see only my boots and my escort. In all we counted 1929 pintails; apparently far more than had been seen elsewhere in the entire archipelago. As there were some islands that I did not visit, and some reed beds where the ducks were hidden, we were satisfied that the total number on the lake exceeded 2000.

Less than four months later there was a major eruption in the crater of Narborough. So far little is known of the effects, but it seems that some of the immense walls of the amphitheatre collapsed. Animals, we are told, usually have premonition of such disasters, so I hope that the pintails escaped before the catastrophe.

Centenaries are much in vogue these days; they are celebrated on the smallest pretext. The reason, I fancy, lies in our nostalgic longing to recapture, even vicariously, the simplicity of bygone years, now so hard to find amid the complexities of the modern world. The Matterhorn was first climbed on July 14, 1865, and the centenary of such an event was not likely to be overlooked. The epic tale of triumph and disaster was retold in countless journals; the B.B.C. went to immense trouble and expense to televise an ascent of the original route. To mark the great occasion the Swiss and Italian tourist bureaux organised a massive gathering in Zermatt and Breuil and invited—fares and expenses paid—mountaineers from all over the world to attend.

As President of the Alpine Club—the oldest of all mountaineering associations—I could hardly decline the invitation; particularly as the proceedings were opened by a dinner given by our Club. But I would gladly have done so; for though I like the anonymous crowds of London streets which I find cosy, I am not at ease in convivial assemblies. I recognise this as a defect, which may have some psychological tie-up with my scholastic failures.

In fact, I enjoyed every minute of the Matterhorn Celebrations: our hosts were charming, there was a pleasant atmosphere of informality, we could do what we pleased and go where we wished, and it was delightful to meet so many people whom I had known hitherto only by name. One of these was Bob Bates, an American whose adventures in Alaska and on K2 I had long admired. We met on the first day and, finding a wide vista of common ground, we spent most of the week together. With him and others I climbed my first Alpine peak in thirty-seven years, a noteworthy achievement for one holding my current office.

One of the functions organised was a mass ascent of the Matterhorn on July 16. Bob and I felt ourselves morally obliged to join in; though for my part, I anticipated the event with such dread as to mar my enjoyment of the previous few days. It seemed no way to treat a mountain, while the risk of being hit by a rock dislodged by the hoards above was greater than I am wont to take. Happily, on the night of the 15th, when we were all assembled in the Belvedere, the hut at the foot of the Hornli Ridge, there was a violent storm and the project was abandoned. The hut was crowded far beyond capacity by climbers and press reporters; but Bob and I managed to fight our way to two vacant seats at the supper table. I introduced myself to my neighbour, whereupon, to my astonishment, he banged the table and shouted, "Shipton! I have been wanting to meet you for years. It was your maps that helped me to escape from prison." It was Heinrich Harrer, author of *Seven Years in Tibet*; he had arrived in Zermatt that day. Whether or not his claim was true, it was gratifying to meet such appreciation of one's work.

As a direct result of meeting Bob in Zermatt, I went to Alaska the following summer to join an expedition run by Ad Carter to climb in the Mount McKinley group. In April, on my way back from Palena, Bob had arranged for me to give a few lectures in the Eastern States which provided more than enough money to cover my summer expenses. On June 22 I left Copenhagen at 5:00 p.m., and after an eight-hour flight over the Arctic, arrived at Anchorage at 2:30 the same afternoon, where I was met by my colleagues. A few hours later we had to attend a reception given by the Alaska Mountaineering Club; the programme included a talk by me. Already a little punch-drunk, I gave a performance of slapstick buffoonery, quite out of character, which brought down the house. The party broke up at 11:00 p.m. when Ad, fearful lest we should miss a chance of fine weather, herded us into his station waggon and we drove through the daylight night to Talkeetna, a replica of the standard Western film set, whence we were to fly to our base. Luckily the weather that day was too bad for even Don Sheldon to operate, and I was able at last to get some sleep.

Don runs an air service which will take you anywhere within range of his small planes, while his wife, herself the daughter of another famous bush-pilot of a former decade, maintains radio contact with her husband and his far-flung clientele, while nursing the baby and performing her household chores. His business is mainly with miners working remote claims in the tundra along the foothills of the Alaska Range, but he has an increasing number of clients among sportsmen fishing for salmon in rivers difficult of access and climbers unable or unwilling to undertake the many weeks of back-packing otherwise necessary to reach their chosen peaks.

Alaska is as large as Western Europe, and has a population the size of Harrow. Life there is an amazing mixture of rugged pioneering and sophisticated American technology, of hardship and luxury. I had an example of this before going to sleep that morning. Don wanted to fetch a radio set from a log cabin two miles away across the river. The quickest way of doing this was to fly; so he flew, and I went with him. The cabin, whose owner, an old timer, had died the previous week, was primitive to the point of squalor, furnished with a weird collection of battered old junk. Yet it boasted no fewer than three electric washing machines.

The delay caused by bad weather meant that it took me all of two days to travel from London to a high glacier coombe, hitherto unvisited, in the western part of the Alaska Range. The flight from Talkeetna was most impressive; first over the tundra with the vast bulk of Mount McKinley clear before us, then a giddy zigzag through glacier-gorges and the final lift to a smooth ski-landing in the coombe—and silence. To have got there by other means would have taken at least a month. Our first objective was Mount Russell, and a few days later we had carried a high camp to the foot of its south ridge. From there we made one abortive attempt to reach the top. Then we were hit by a powerful storm which lasted two weeks. Ten feet of snow fell and two of our tents were destroyed, which made it impossible to continue. Luckily we were still able to make radio contact with Don, who, when the weather eventually cleared, came to fetch us out.

Despite the rough handling we received from the weather, I thoroughly enjoyed my brief acquaintance with the Alaska Range: its savage beauty more than satisfied my high expectations, and I was in delightful and stimulating company. It was my only experience of airborne operations on a mountain. As a method of approach it leaves much to be desired for those more interested in mountain travel than in climbing peaks; but it should be remembered that most of this great range is otherwise inaccessible to anyone whose time is limited to normal holidays, and it would be a pity to deny such a vast field of mountaineering to such a large majority of climbers. Also, the scope for these airborne landings is strictly limited; they are forbidden within the bounds of the McKinley National Park, which includes by far the main part (though by no means the whole) of the Range, while even outside the confines of the Park comparatively few of the peaks can have summer ski-landing grounds close enough to be of much use. So in regard to the Alaska Range at least, the purist need not be too concerned on this score, nor grudge the inhabitants of Anchorage (or London) the opportunity of making a first ascent there over the week-end.

From Talkeetna I travelled with Bob and his wife, Gail, to the northern side of the Range, where we spent a wonderful week wandering among the foothills, watching moose, caribou and Dall sheep and enjoying magnificent views of the great peaks. Then I returned south hoping to meet my old friend Cedomir, who two years before had come to work at the Institute of Polar Studies at Ohio University. For the second summer he was in charge of a small scientific party investigating the effects of the ice movement of an enormous landslide which had fallen upon the Sherman Glacier, near Cordova, during the 1964 Alaska earthquake. Having heard that I was coming to Alaska, he had sent me a pressing invitation to visit his camp.

In Anchorage, which I reached by train late in the evening of July 24, I was met by several members of the Mountaineering Club, including Gary Hansen, a young British architect who had come to Anchorage four years before and was working there as a private consultant. He kindly put me up in his one-roomed flat, which also served as an office. The next morning, Monday, he took me to buy a ticket on the noon flight to Cordova and then to the Survey offices to get some maps of the locality. Neither of us knew how to reach the Sherman Glacier, and as our study of the map suggested that it might be a difficult operation, Gary at once offered to come with me. On the way back to the airline office to get him a ticket we met another member of the Club, Frank Nosek, a lawyer practising in Anchorage, and at that moment dressed as such. Gary briefly explained our plans. It was then 11:00. We had time without undue haste to collect our gear and catch the plane; but Frank only just managed to scramble aboard as they were shutting the door. He had gone to his office, told his secretary to cancel all his engagements for the week and hastened home to change and collect his climbing equipment. As his wife was out—buying his lunch, no doubt—he left it to his secretary to inform her of his departure. I was deeply impressed by the apparent elasticity of city life in Alaska.

Cordova airport is some twelve miles along the Copper River Highway, east of Cordova, in the general direction of the Sherman Glacier. When we arrived there we debated whether to start walking towards the glacier or whether to take the airport bus back to the town in the hope of getting some information about the best route. As we had agreed to spend no more than four days on the whole operation, time was a matter of some importance. However, the fact that it was raining, and the desirability of supplementing the somewhat scanty provisions we had grabbed from Gary's flat, induced us to adopt the latter course. The driver of the airport bus took a keen interest in our plans and offered to bring us back along the Highway that evening.

Cordova, whose main industry is fishing, reminded me very much of one of the small towns of Northern Patagonia on the Pacific coast; indeed, the whole region, with its steep, forested mountains, its rain and its network of fjords and lakes, bears a striking resemblance. After an excellent lunch of salmon we made contact with Tom Parker, a local bush-pilot who had been engaged to drop mail to Cedomir's party from time to time. He did not know where their camp was situated, but offered, for $40, to take us in a float plane to a small lake near the snout of the Sherman Glacier as soon as the cloud ceiling rose to 500 feet. As this phenomenon seemed unlikely to occur for several days, we decided to approach the glacier on foot. From the map it seemed best to make for the Sheridan Glacier, which lay only about five miles north-east of the airport, and then to cross its lower reaches to the flats below the Sherman. Parker, however, told us that this route would be extremely difficult owing to the broken nature of the ice which he had seen from the air. The alternative was to go ten miles farther east to a valley known as Salmon Creek running northward to a low col, and thence down another river running north-west to the flats. Beyond the fact that the country was forested, which we could see from the map, and that there was a path running three miles up Salmon Creek from the road to a forester's cabin, we could get no further information about either valley. The bus driver had undertaken to go that evening to salvage a vehicle stuck in the mud, most conveniently for us, twelve miles beyond the airport on the Copper River Highway; so at 6:30 p.m. he dropped us at the path leading into Salmon Creek.

The rain stopped and we had a pleasant walk of an hour and a half through the forest to the cabin, delightfully sited on the shore of a small lake. We dumped our loads and went on to reconnoitre. Almost immediately the path petered out in dense undergrowth. Clambering over the debris of a big snow avalanche, we found to my dismay that the forest beyond was apparently trackless. It was too late, however, to change our plan, and we decided at least to spend the next day attempting to reach the head of Salmon Creek, though I had little hope of reaching our objective. It was so warm and comfortable in the cabin that we overslept, and it was 8:00 before we started the next morning. It was raining again and the undergrowth was so wet that in less than half an hour our clothes were soaked through. Not far beyond the avalanche we discovered an old trail which must have been used by miners several decades ago. Though completely overgrown, it was blazed by axemarks on tree-trunks, and the side-streams were spanned by stout log bridges. It led us far up towards the head of the valley before it disappeared; even so, our progress was slow and laborious, and it was 1:00 before we found ourselves in an open glade at the top of the col, where, cold and very wet, we ate some lunch. We had come barely three miles from the cabin.

According to the map, the valley on the other side was nearly as long as Salmon Creek; there was no reason to suppose that the forest there was any less dense, and we certainly could not expect to find another trail. Though we still had nine hours' daylight, it seemed very probable that it would take us more than that to make our way down the valley, and we might well have to return by the same route. I felt very guilty for having brought my companions on this futile bush-whacking expedition in search of a Chilean geologist unknown to either of them; and I suggested that we should abandon it forthwith. However, they claimed to be enjoying themselves and voted to go on. Their staunchness was rewarded, for, in fact, our troubles were nearly over. A steep descent through thick undergrowth led us to a glade in the floor of the valley. Here we came upon a bear's lair so recently vacated that some droppings there were still warm; indeed, the sound of our approach may well have disturbed the creature. The forest in this valley proved to be much more open, and we were able to walk rapidly through a series of glades, for the most part following fresh bear tracks, probably made by the same animal. He may have been a grizzly, though it is more likely that he belonged to the less-aggressive species of black bear. In any case we were not keen to meet him at close quarters. Gary began to chant, "Go away bear," which sounded rather ridiculous; but I realised that the creature was as likely to respond to this appeal as to any other, so I joined in the plaintive chorus, which we maintained for the next two hours.

The rain stopped, the clouds lifted from the valley and at last we could see and enjoy our lovely surroundings. From the lower end of the valley we came out on to flat ground covered with tangled scrub and intersected by a network of rivers. Luckily these were fairly shallow, and we could wade along them to avoid further bush-whacking. At 5:30 p.m. we reached the lake on the wide gravel flats below the Sherman Glacier, where we built a large drift-wood fire, dried our sodden clothes, cooked supper and spent a pleasant evening watching the peaks emerge from the clouds. At 2:30 the next morning I brewed some tea and roused my companions, and we set off an hour later, leaving our camp standing. We hoped to breakfast with Cedomir, and I was determined not to be late.

The landslide, which had resulted from the collapse of a peak above one of the tributaries of the Sherman, had covered the glacier with rubble over an area of three square miles. It looked exactly like ordinary surface moraine, so evenly spread that I could hardly believe that it had been deposited there in one mighty fall little more than two years before. By 7:30 we stood whistling forlornly in the midst of this wilderness three miles up the glacier, opposite the tributary from which the debris had issued. There was no sign of a camp, and our hopes of breakfast began to fade. Eventually, however, we heard an answering whistle, and shortly afterwards we spotted a hut in the middle of the glacier and two figures approaching. One of them turned out to be Cedomir, who greeted me with a warm South American embrace. It transpired that they had heard our whistles some time before, but had thought that they came from a third member of their party who had left early that morning to make observations from a neighbouring hill and who, they concluded, had met with an accident. He, too, had heard the whistles and had been very puzzled. They had tried to sort the matter out on their walkie-talkies but had failed to establish contact.

The hut, which had been constructed in one day from timber they had brought with them by helicopter a week before, was well stocked and comfortable, though it already showed signs of being tilted by the ice movement. The party's only worry was that their radio transmitter would not function because of a dud battery. We promised to arrange for another to be sent up. We spent a pleasant day eating and talking while it snowed gently outside. Cedomir was delighted to have news from Chile, and we discussed plans for a winter expedition to Patagonia. He and his friends explained the nature of their work. Among other interesting discoveries they had collected ample evidence that the landslide had travelled across the glacier on a pocket of air, trapped and compressed by the fall; it had hardly disturbed the winter snow beneath. This accounted for the remarkably even distribution of the debris over the whole area. In the evening we returned to our camp, and the next day we made our way across the Sheridan Glacier and so back to Cordova. It had been exciting to catch even a glimpse of a tiny corner of this wonderful coastal range, most of it still untrodden.

My visit to Alaska left me with a vivid impression of its vast mountaineering potential, and of a dynamic group of young climbers revelling in their splendid heritage and eager to share it with a stranger.

| II |

THE SPRINGS OF ENCHANTMENT

WHILE I WAS WRITING THIS book friends often advised me to include plenty of personal anecdotes illustrating my private life, to descend from the peaks now and then to declare my beliefs and tastes, my loves and hates; in short, to reveal myself. This, they say, is the very essence of readable autobiography; for without the personal touch any life story must be cold and colourless. If I have failed to provide this leaven it was not through any reluctance to air my views or divulge my secret feelings but because of the difficulty of finding suitable context in the condensed style of narrative I have felt bound to adopt. Maybe it would have been better to cover less ground at a more leisurely, reflective pace. Perhaps even now it is not too late to put down a few random thoughts which, though certainly neither novel nor profound, might fill some of the gaps.

In that categorical manner of his which always delighted me, Noel Humphreys used to say that people never change. Certainly I am inclined to wonder if I am much altered from that pathetic little schoolboy portrayed in Chapter One. I still have the same fondness for argument—discussion I prefer to call it—and for sentimental tunes; I still have the same dread of reading aloud, and the same wish to be liked which too often results in moral cowardice. My interest in the analysis of motivations, my own and other people's— in short my taste for gossip—stems from a morbid curiosity which can be traced from childhood. Then also, as now, I used to wonder at the emergence, from the womb of the universe, of life, of thought and, above all, of the individual observer, the *self*, the only known witness to the whole amazing cosmic performance.

The agnostic standpoint seized upon with relief in my late adolescence has remained, though it is no longer prompted by terror of reading the lesson in church and of eternal confinement in a red-hot dungeon. I find the enigma of life more fascinating than appalling; but to my obtuse intelligence the materialist view that it results from a chance convolution of atoms is no easier to believe than the Christian doctrine, or this than the Hindu. I envy faith in others; it must be comforting, but it is not an attribute that I have greatly admired. For one thing it is often based upon wishful thinking, which I dread; for another, it is apt to lead to intolerance: whether religious or ideological, it seems to have been the cause of far more human suffering than, for example, greed.

Kurt Hahn once told me that for ten years he had sought a definition of "integrity," and had at last found one that satisfied him: "The triumph over self-swindle." I asked him if, in his view, I could rob a bank and still retain my integrity; to which he replied, "Yes, but I wouldn't advise it." I doubt if the definition would receive general acceptance, but I found it pleasing; for the quality I like most in people is the habit of straight-thinking, of avoiding protective affectation. In the words of one of C. P. Snow's characters, "Give me the man who knows something of himself and is appalled." To my mind this is the essence of humility; with it, most faults are tolerable, without it, the noblest virtues become tarnished. But to admire a quality is not to claim it—a coward may admire courage, a cheat honesty—and I am all too aware of my own deficiencies in this respect.

Among other eccentricities, I enjoy cooking, dancing, shopping in supermarkets, the English climate and the smell of the London Underground; returning from a spell abroad, the telephone gives me much delight. All these, people seem to find either odd or incongruous; but I am not aware of any major abnormality.

There is nothing unusual in the feeling for wild country which has been the chief and most constant influence shaping the course of my life; though

I have been exceptionally fortunate in being able to follow its inspiration. Those dreams in early childhood of chasing the moon over the wooded spurs of the Nilgiri Hills were symptomatic; the emotions they engendered have been repeated again and again through the years in a sense of fusion with the surrounding wilderness. Indeed, though it took me a long time to realise it, this has been the true motive for most of my wanderings.

Mountaineering provided a convenient means of getting into wild places and a simple objective; many other forms of activity might have been equally satisfying. For a while I was fascinated by the sheer technique of moving safely and easily over difficult ground; but even then I regarded the art as a means to an end, and neither reached nor aspired to more than a modest standard of climbing proficiency. After Mount Kenya I became less and less concerned with the mastery of technical difficulty, or even the ascent of individual peaks, but more and more absorbed in the problems and delights of movement over wide areas of mountain country. It was not that I lost any of my enjoyment in climbing peaks, but simply that I found the other still more rewarding. Whatever success I may have achieved as a mountain explorer was not due to exceptional toughness, stamina or physical skill: I am quite certain that I have never had more than an average capacity to tolerate fatigue, cold or hardship. Nor, despite my love of simplicity, am I the ascetic I may appear. I would, however, lay claim to an imaginative approach both in the choice of objectives and method of travel.

I used to suppose that my metamorphosis from climber to mountain explorer was simply the result of my good fortune in travelling so much in unknown ranges; that anyone, even the most ardent technician, placed in a similar situation would have reacted as I had. I was quite wrong, of course, as I discovered when I propounded my theory to Tom Bourdillon, a brilliant rock-climber and a dedicated mountaineer. He disagreed. We were sitting above Namche on the evening before starting for our reconnaissance of the Western Cwm. To test his sincerity (always a superfluous exercise in his case) I asked him whether, supposing I could offer him the choice, he would elect to spend the next month exploring the southern side of the Everest massif or climbing on the vast rock precipice which we could see across the valley of the Dudh Kosi. In that gentle, apologetic manner of his, he replied simply, "I'm sorry, Eric; I'd choose the rocks." I have since discovered that he was by no means alone in this; and have often wondered whether, had I possessed a measure of Tom's superb climbing skill, my attitude would have been very different. Perhaps I owe as much to my limitations as a mountaineer as to my ineptitude as a student.

There is today a wide gulf between the classical mountaineer and the practitioner of modern techniques. Many famous climbers, still in their prime, would be quite incapable of tackling the more difficult routes in the Alps, or even of using modern methods and equipment effectively. This is largely because, until comparatively recently, the development of these techniques was virtually confined to the Alps, while those who climbed widely in other ranges, where the new methods were still hardly applicable, had no need to employ them to break fresh ground.

British climbers took very little part in the achievements of the great era in the Alps between the two wars, when totally new standards were set by Continental mountaineers. Soon after the last war, however, some of the new generation, led by Tom Bourdillon, Arthur Dolphin and others, began to tackle the great new routes of the Thirties. Tom, at least, was inspired with a kind of missionary zeal "to put British climbing back on the map." They were followed by scores of young men trained on British rock. With a speed that I would not have thought possible thirty years ago, they adapted themselves to the Alpine environment, the ice, the unstable rock, the hazards of weather and avalanche, and the enormously greater scale of the climbs; they soon mastered the techniques of artificial climbing and learned the art of survival in bivouacs in the most rigorous and terrifying conditions, inseparable with these modern routes. Their performance won the respect of their Continental colleagues. Even more significant is the initiative they have shown in applying their methods and hard training to the more distant mountains of the world.

Young climbers of today are often criticised for being competitive and for running unjustifiable risks. But it is well to remember that my generation was the target of similar strictures. It can hardly be denied that there has always been an element of competition in mountaineering. Even in the

Golden Age in the Alps when, with so many unclimbed peaks and so few climbers in the field there was surely less excuse for it than now, it reared its ugly head, and the colourful record of acrimonious dispute in the archives of the Alpine Club is evidence enough that it has been with us ever since. Can even the most humble claim never to have harboured any feeling of rivalry; would any of us, for example, be as pleased to accomplish a second ascent as a first? No man can be blamed for wishing to excel in his craft, to measure his skill against the standards of the day; and it is hardly surprising that the desire is more marked in the young. It is when competition becomes the principal or, worse, the only motive for climbing that it poisons the springs of our enjoyment. By enjoyment in this context I mean the philosophical contentment to be found in close contact with and mastery over the environment of our choosing. I believe that young climbers today are at least as sensible of this kind of pleasure as we were, and that they prize it as highly. If their manner of seeking it may sometimes seem a little austere, I for one am hardly in a position to disparage it on that score.

The question of justifiable risk is very largely a subjective matter depending upon the temperament, the experience, the skill and the endurance of the individual concerned. Walter Bonatti and Joe Brown, for example, operate in realms totally beyond my experience, and I would be most reluctant to comment, still less to pass judgment, upon this aspect of their achievement. Obviously some risk is involved in any mountaineering venture. For a party climbing one of the classic routes in the Alps it is of one kind; for a small expedition in uninhabited regions, cut off from all outside help for a period of many weeks or months, when the smallest mishap could have ugly consequences, it is of a different order. Not so long ago, Polar explorers were often called upon to face hazards which today seem quite appalling. By what yardstick are we to judge the risks they ran? Are we to dismiss them as irresponsible fools? When Shackleton was stranded with a large, unwieldy party on the pack-ice of the Weddell Sea, with no means of communication with the outside world, their plight must have seemed hopeless. But Shackleton was a brilliant improviser, a superb leader in disaster. In his whole career he never lost a man. Again, consider the situation in which

Nansen deliberately placed himself when he and Johansen left the Fram to make their way over the shifting ice of the Arctic Sea towards the Pole, with no hope of finding their ship again because of the erratic drift, faced with months, possibly years, of frightful privation and a thousand unforeseeable hazards, with nothing but two canoes with which eventually to return from the edge of the pack. But Nansen was a master of the art of survival; he was well endowed not only with resourcefulness but also with that profound, imperturbable patience, a vital quality in any survival situation and, incidentally, an essential part of the equipment of anyone attempting these modern climbs.

Far from advocating foolhardiness, it is my belief that to take unreasonable risks deliberately is usually a sign of irresponsibility and arrogance, while to do so unawares shows lack of experience and judgment; and that a narrow escape should be deemed a failure of competence and not a matter for pride. I have been guilty of these lapses more often than I care to remember. Again, motive is a cardinal factor. If the dominant reason for climbing is to achieve fame or beat a rival, if there is no pleasure without success, the temptation to ignore danger may well be irresistible; but if the motive is a real feeling for mountains and a love of climbing as a means of giving expression to that feeling reasonable prudence is likely to prevail.

Personally, I welcome wholeheartedly the advance of modern techniques because it has widened the bounds of mountain adventure. There was a time, long ago, when I was oppressed by the thought that soon there would be no new peaks to climb and no new routes to explore. But the more I travelled in the remoter ranges of the world—Karakoram, Kuen Lun, Alaska, Southern Andes—the more I realised how vast is the field of fresh endeavour even for the traditional mountaineer. With the application of these new climbing and survival techniques, the horizon is truly boundless.

There are many ways of finding those moments of delight which come from a sense of complete harmony with wild surroundings. Some of us seek them through the mastery of difficult terrain or stormy seas, by quickening our awareness in contest with the elements. Others, more sensitive perhaps, can discover the same magic in quieter pursuits. Certainly it is not only to be found in unknown lands: my journey over the Karakoram trade route made as deep an impact on me as any through unexplored ranges; a sunrise seen from the top of Stromboli or a distant glimpse of the Cuillins can be as stirring as the view from a nameless peak in the Tien Shan.

The springs of enchantment lie within ourselves: they arise from our sense of wonder, that most precious of gifts, the birthright of every child. Lose it and life becomes flat and colourless; keep it and

> *. . . all experience is an arch wherethro'*
> *Gleams that untravell'd world, whose margin fades*
> *For ever and for ever when I move.*

INDEX

ABOUT THE AUTHOR

ERIC SHIPTON (1907–1977) was one of the great mountain explorers of the twentieth century. Together with frequent partner H.W. Tilman, Shipton explored new regions in the Himalaya, discovering the way to the Nanda Devi sanctuary, now a World Heritage Site. With Frank Smythe, he reached the summit of Kamet in 1931, then the highest summit to be reached. He participated in five Everest expeditions and was responsible for the inclusion of Edmund Hillary and Tenzing Norgay on the successful 1953 attempt. Shipton wrote half a dozen other books in addition to *That Untravelled World*; *Nanda Devi*, *Blank on the Map*, *Upon That Mountain*, *Mountains of Tartary*, *Mount Everest Reconnaissance Expedition 1951*, and *Land of Tempest* are included in the omnibus *Eric Shipton: The Six Mountain-Travel Books* (also published by Mountaineers Books).

KATIE IVES is the editor in chief of *Alpinist Magazine* and a graduate of the University of Iowa Writers' Workshop. Her writing and translations have appeared in various publications, including *The American Alpine Journal*, *Mountain Gazette*, *Circumference*, *91st Meridian*, *Outside Magazine*, *Patagonia Field Reports*, and *The Rumpus*. She served as a jury member for the 2011 Banff Mountain Book Festival competition, and her short story, "Transgressions," appeared in the 2013 anthology *Rock, Paper, Fire: The Best of Mountain and Wilderness Writing*. In 2014 Austria's *Climax Magazine* named her "Journalist of the Year." She lives in Vermont.

THE LEGENDS AND LORE SERIES honors the lives and adventures of mountaineers and is made possible in part through the generosity of donors. Mountaineers Books, a nonprofit publisher, further contributes to this investment through book sales from more than 600 titles on outdoor recreation, sustainable lifestyle, and conservation.

We would like to thank the following for their charitable support of Legends and Lore:

FOUNDERS CIRCLE
- Anonymous
- Tina Bullitt
- Tom and Kathy Hornbein*
- Dianne Roberts and Jim Whittaker
- Doug and Maggie Walker

SUPPORTERS
- Byron Capps
- Roger Johnson
- Joshua Randow
- Jolene Unsoeld

*With special appreciation to Tom Hornbein, who donates to the series all royalties earned through the sale of his book, *Everest: The West Ridge*.

You can help us preserve and promote mountaineering literature by making a donation to the Legends and Lore series. For more information, benefits of sponsorship, or how you can support future work, please contact us at mbooks@mountaineersbooks.org or visit us online at www.mountaineers books.org.

MOUNTAINEERS
BOOKS

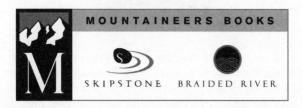

MOUNTAINEERS BOOKS is a leading publisher of mountaineering literature and guides—including our flagship title, *Mountaineering: The Freedom of the Hills*—as well as adventure narratives, natural history, and general outdoor recreation. Through our two imprints, Skipstone and Braided River, we also publish titles on sustainability and conservation. We are committed to supporting the environmental and educational goals of our organization by providing expert information on human-powered adventure, sustainable practices at home and on the trail, and preservation of wilderness.

The Mountaineers, founded in 1906, is a 501(c)(3) nonprofit outdoor activity and conservation organization whose mission is "to explore, study, preserve, and enjoy the natural beauty of the outdoors." One of the largest such organizations in the United States, it sponsors classes and year-round outdoor activities throughout the Pacific Northwest, including climbing, hiking, backcountry skiing, snowshoeing, bicycling, camping, paddling, and more. The Mountaineers also supports its mission through its publishing division, Mountaineers Books, and promotes environmental education and citizen engagement. For more information, visit The Mountaineers Program Center, 7700 Sand Point Way NE, Seattle, WA 98115-3996; phone 206-521-6001; www.mountaineers.org; or email info@mountaineers.org.

Our publications are made possible through the generosity of donors and through sales of more than 600 titles on outdoor recreation, sustainable lifestyle, and conservation. To donate, purchase books, or learn more, visit us online:

**MOUNTAINEERS
BOOKS**

1001 SW Klickitat Way, Suite 201
Seattle, WA 98134
800-553-4453
mbooks@mountaineersbooks.org
www.mountaineersbooks.org

The Legends and Lore series was created by Mountaineers Books in order to ensure that mountain literature will continue to be widely available to readers everywhere. From mountaineering classics to biographies of well-known climbers, and from renowned high-alpine adventures to lesser-known accomplishments, the series strives to bring mountaineering knowledge, history, and events to modern audiences in print and digital form.

Distinctive stories in the Legends and Lore series include:

My Father, Frank: The Forgotten Alpinist
Tony Smythe
This biography of Frank Smythe, written by his son, is "[t]imely, well-researched and written with the authority of a committed climber." –Doug Scott

Reinhold Messner: My Life at the Limit
Reinhold Messner in conversation with Thomas Hüetlin
A more thoughtful and conversational Messner emerges in this interview-format memoir of the world's premiere mountaineer.

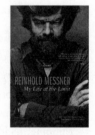

Everest 1953: The Epic Story of the First Ascent
Mick Conefrey
"An exciting, moving account . . . a fascinating piece of documentary writing as readable and as poignant as *Into Thin Air* or *Touching the Void*."–*Spectator* (London)

**Through a Land of Extremes:
The Littledales of Central Asia**
Elizabeth and Nicholas Clinch
The life and times of a largely forgotten Victorian couple who just happened to make some of the most amazing expeditions of their day, including nearly reaching the forbidden city of Lhasa.

**Brotherhood of the Rope:
The Biography of Charles Houston**
Bernadette McDonald
Charlie Houston was an authentic American hero, famous not only for his role in the 1953 attempt on K2 but also for his pioneering research on the effects of high altitude.

MOUNTAINEERS
BOOKS